# OPEN WATER SWIMMING

Steven Munatones

**Human Kinetics**

**Library of Congress Cataloging-in-Publication Data**

Munatones, Steven.
  Open water swimming / Steven Munatones.
    p. cm.
  Includes bibliographical references and index.
  ISBN-13: 978-0-7360-9284-5 (soft cover)
  ISBN-10: 0-7360-9284-6 (soft cover)
  1. Long distance swimming.  I. Title.
  GV838.53.L65M86 2011
  797.2'1--dc22

                                    2011009479

ISBN-10: 0-7360-9284-6 (print)
ISBN-13: 978-0-7360-9284-5 (print)

The Web addresses cited in this text were current as of April 2011, unless otherwise noted.

**Acquisitions Editor:** Tom Heine; **Developmental Editor:** Anne Hall; **Assistant Editor:** Tyler Wolpert; **Copyeditor:** Patsy Fortney; **Indexer:** Alisha Jeddeloh; **Permission Manager:** Martha Gullo; **Graphic Designer:** Joe Buck; **Graphic Artist:** Tara Welsch; **Cover Designer:** Keith Blomberg; **Photographer (cover):** Great Swim, Dave Tyrell; **Visual Production Assistant**: Joyce Brumfield; **Photo Production Manager:** Jason Allen; **Art Manager:** Kelly Hendren; **Associate Art Manager:** Alan L. Wilborn; **Illustrations:** © Human Kinetics; **Printer:** United Graphics

Human Kinetics books are available at special discounts for bulk purchase. Special editions or book excerpts can also be created to specification. For details, contact the Special Sales Manager at Human Kinetics.

Printed in the United States of America        10   9   8   7   6   5   4   3   2   1

The paper in this book is certified under a sustainable forestry program.

**Human Kinetics**
Website: www.HumanKinetics.com

*United States:* Human Kinetics
P.O. Box 5076
Champaign, IL 61825-5076
800-747-4457
e-mail: humank@hkusa.com

*Canada:* Human Kinetics
475 Devonshire Road Unit 100
Windsor, ON N8Y 2L5
800-465-7301 (in Canada only)
e-mail: info@hkcanada.com

*Europe:* Human Kinetics
107 Bradford Road
Stanningley
Leeds LS28 6AT, United Kingdom
+44 (0) 113 255 5665
e-mail: hk@hkeurope.com

*Australia:* Human Kinetics
57A Price Avenue
Lower Mitcham, South Australia 5062
08 8372 0999
e-mail: info@hkaustralia.com

*New Zealand:* Human Kinetics
P.O. Box 80
Torrens Park, South Australia 5062
0800 222 062
e-mail: info@hknewzealand.com

E5130

To my wife, parents and children, Sabrina, Skyler, Sydney, and Sofia, whose support is forever appreciated.

# CONTENTS

# FOREWORD

If you are reading this, you have probably already heard open water swimming's call. For me, it started at an early age while growing up in Hawaii, swimming at the beach and surfing and bodysurfing with friends after school. As I progressed from surf grom to swim club kid, the ever-changing conditions of open water proved an irresistible respite from the constant metronome of the pool. Open water swimming meant freedom—freedom to pit myself against the elements, freedom to work with the elements. Currents served as salvation or misfortune, offering an adventure and raw challenge that no pool workout could ever replicate. With no clocks on deck on which to base my performance, the open water demanded a heightened sense of awareness. Effort and a keen sense of adaptability reigned paramount—along with, of course, a little bit of strategy, technique, and luck too. Open water swimming resonated with my inner adventurous athlete.

No one understands the unique allure of open water swimming better than Steven Munatones. Through my travels as an open water competitor, I have crossed paths with Steven many times—from swimming the Waikiki Roughwater Swim as a child, to competing at the World Championships. Steven has shown more passion for the sport than anyone I have ever met. His unparalleled experiences and breadth of open water knowledge as a swimmer, coach, race organizer, Olympic commentator, and writer undoubtedly make him the go-to source for all things open water. He is open water swimming's best ambassador.

This book covers all aspects of open water swimming from finishing the swim leg of a triathlon to solo channel swims. It includes training and racing tips that will help both beginner swimmers and world-class open water swimmers. The wealth of knowledge put into this book makes it the best source for anyone braving the open water. I only wish I had access to it when I was starting my career.

The information comes from a person who lives and breathes the sport. Steven has always selflessly shared his passion and knowledge with others, but he is also always wanting to learn more. Without a doubt, this book is just one more step in Steven's desire to promote the sport and help others understand why open water is so compelling.

As he often says, "Expect the unexpected," and enjoy swimming without lines.

**John Flanagan**
**Professional triathlete and world-class open water swimmer**

# INTRODUCTION

Welcome to *Open Water Swimming*, a comprehensive book to help you navigate the world of open water swimming. This book provides a wealth of information and recommendations based on firsthand observations of elite athletes in training and competition, solid scientific research, and the personal experiences of a world champion who has swum in dozens of countries on five continents over the last 40 years.

*Open Water Swimming* divides the sport into three categories: short-distance swims under 5K, middle-distance swims up to 25K, and marathon swims over 25K. Each distance requires a unique type of preparation, both in the pool and in open water, to optimize performance. Pool training sets, freestyle swimming techniques, and specialized open water training for the three categories are explained in detail, so you will know what is required to perform at your best in every condition.

The sport of open water swimming—despite its inherent challenges and risks—is attracting a growing number of athletes from every background and of all ages and ability levels. Since the addition of triathlon to the 2000 Sydney Olympics and the inclusion of the 10K marathon swim in the 2008 Beijing Olympics, the sport has continued on an upward trajectory in terms of the number of athletes involved and events offered. The community of marathon swimmers is growing as quickly as the number of races under 5K. Although the largest demographic group in the sport is currently men between the ages of 30 and 49, women over the age of 40 comprise the fastest-growing segment of open water swimmers.

Open water venues include oceans, lakes, rivers, canals, bays, dams, reservoirs, and rowing basins with water temperature varying from 35 to 85°F (1.7 to 29.4°C) where you will inevitably encounter the unexpected. The conditions can range from glassy and calm to rough and windy, creating challenges for newcomers and professionals alike. *Open Water Swimming* offers tips, tactics, and techniques to overcome the natural elements you will face as an open water swimmer.

*Open Water Swimming* also describes the training tools and equipment needed for success at each distance. The range of equipment can be overwhelming for newcomers: short-distance triathletes use wetsuits, middle-distance swimmers take gels and drinks during a race, and marathon swimmers use feeding sticks and lanolin on their solo swims. *Open Water Swimming* offers convenient checklists to help you prepare for solo swims and races.

Based on sophisticated underwater analytical tests conducted on Olympic gold medalists and world champions—both in the pool and in open water—*Open

*Water Swimming* describes the optimal freestyle swimming styles and techniques that will help you swim faster and more efficiently at each distance.

The book also describes how to properly prepare logistically, physically, and mentally for open water swims one day, one month, and one year in advance. As your body acclimates to certain conditions as a result of a focused training regimen, you will gain the ability and confidence to reach your full potential.

*Open Water Swimming* explains basic and the most sophisticated open water racing tactics, for both newcomers and professionals. You will read about the best practices of professional open water swimmers from how to recognize the shape of a pack to how and where to quickly down a gel pack. You will learn how to make tactical moves in all kinds of racing situations, no matter what your speed, experience, or level of competition.

You can read the book from cover to cover or simply flip through it at your leisure.

Use the sample training plans for the three categories of the sport as is or as references so you can design a customized training program based on your own goals.

Whether you are an open water swimmer who does solo swims, a triathlete who races to win, or a newcomer initially exploring the waterways of the world, you will appreciate the sport more when you understand its unique duality: the simplicity of swimming from point A to point B and the complexity of doing so quickly, safely and efficiently.

The ultimate goal of *Open Water Swimming* is to help you swim faster and with greater efficiency. Enjoy the challenge.

Norma Connolly, Cayman Free Press

# THE OPEN WATER SWIMMER

People throughout history have feared swimming in natural bodies of water. The open water has been considered mysterious, a place where safety is not guaranteed. Oceans are filled with the unknown, and shorelines create natural boundaries. For millennia, people have believed that the depths of the oceans are best observed from the deck of a ship rather than being a resource to be enjoyed.

Safety and comfort were two important reasons to stay firmly rooted to solid ground. Terrestrial or aquatic—there was no question. The wisdom of the ages was not questioned.

But the fear of the open water has been largely transformed over the last century. Many people now embrace it as a place to explore and test their physical and psychological limits.

Whereas the open water was once the province of only sailors and fisherman, it now offers a strong allure to swimmers of all ages, abilities, and backgrounds. The fear of the unknown has been replaced by its challenge. Channels and lakes, once traversed only by boats, are now regularly crossed by swimmers without trepidation. Rivers and bays once primarily used for commercial shipping are now popular venues for fitness and competition. Previously, the open water was something to avoid; it is now fully embraced by those who accept its challenges.

Adventure, a sense of accomplishment, and the thrill of competition are a few of the many reasons millions of people are heading to the open water. Contemporary athletes' desire to accept the challenge of the open water is no longer questioned, but rather encouraged, supported, and celebrated.

The world of open water swimming is vast and growing rapidly, but what exactly is open water swimming? Who enjoys this sport?

Open water swimming is defined as swimming for pleasure, fitness, or competition in natural or man-made bodies of water including oceans, lakes, bays, rivers, reservoirs, rowing basins, seas, ponds, coves, lagoons, canals, channels, dams, estuaries, fjords, and gulfs. With over 70 percent of the world covered by water, scenic and safe venues for open water swimming are limited only by swimmers' creativity and willingness to swim beyond the shores.

Open water swimming can be in saltwater or freshwater, calm or rough conditions, warm or cold temperatures, and still or with currents, depending on the time of day, the season, and the location. Today, over 3,600 open water events are held in at least 84 countries—and this number does not include triathlons, solo swims, lifeguard competitions, polar bear swims, and other multisport events involving the open water.

**Types of Open Water Swimming**

| | |
|---|---|
| Rough water swimming | Swims in the ocean or any body of water with surface chop |
| Long-distance swimming | Swims up to 10K (6.2 mi) in distance |
| Marathon swimming | Nonstop swims at of least 10K |
| Ultramarathon swimming | Nonstop swims over 25K (15.5 mi) |
| Free swimming | Noncompetitive swims of any distance in natural bodies of water |
| Wild swimming | Noncompetitive swims of any distance in natural bodies of water |
| Night swimming | Swims done after the sun goes down and before it rises |
| Expedition swimming | Noncompetitive swims done with partners as part of guided tours |
| Swim trekking | Noncompetitive swims done with equipment and partners |
| Open water orienteering | Swims that require navigation between randomly placed buoys in the natural bodies of water |
| Cold water swimming | Swims of any distance done in cold water |
| Winter swimming | Swims of any distance done in winter, generally in cold water |
| Ice swimming | Swims of any distance done in near-freezing water |

# GOVERNING BODIES IN THE WORLD OF OPEN WATER SWIMMING

Because of the history and nature of the sport, there is no global organization that governs the entire spectrum of open water swimming. Instead, the sport is managed and promoted by a plethora of domestic and international entities, organizations, governing bodies, and individuals, including the Fédération Internationale de Natation (FINA) and its 202 member countries.

## International Governing Bodies and Associations

| | |
|---|---|
| FINA | International Olympic Committee (IOC)-recognized aquatic governing body with 202 member federations |
| UANA/ASUA | Unión Americana de Natación governing body for the Americas |
| AASF | Asian Amateur Swimming Federation for the Asian continent |
| ASC | African Swimming Confederation for the African continent |
| OSA | Oceania Swimming Association for the Oceania region |
| LEN | Ligue Européenne de Natation for the European continent |
| CS&PF | Channel Swimming & Piloting Federation for the English Channel |
| CSA | Channel Swimming Association for the English Channel |
| BLDSA | British Long Distance Swimming Association for Great Britain |
| ILDSA | Irish Long Distance Swimming Association for Ireland |
| GSSA | Gibraltar Strait Swimming Association for the Strait of Gibraltar |
| CLDSA | Cape Long Distance Swimming Association for Cape Town, South Africa |
| SSO | Solo Swims of Ontario in Canada |
| JIOWSA | Japan International Open Water Swimming Association for Japan |
| RLSA | River and Lake Swimming Association in Great Britain |

| | |
|---|---|
| OSS | Outdoor Swimming Society in Great Britain |
| IMSHOF | International Marathon Swimming Hall of Fame |
| VOWSA | Vancouver Open Water Swim Association in Canada |
| IOWSA | International Open Water Swimming Association |
| SOWSA | Stage Open Water Swimming Association |
| WOWSA | World Open Water Swimming Association |
| TCSA | Tsugaru Channel Swimming Association |
| IISA | International Ice Swimming Association |
| IWSA | International Winter Swimming Association |

## U.S. Governing Bodies and Associations

| | |
|---|---|
| USA Swimming | With 59 Local Swimming Committees |
| U.S. Masters Swimming | With 52 Local Masters Swimming Committees |
| CCSF | Catalina Channel Swimming Federation |
| NYC Swim | For swims around Manhattan Island in New York City |
| SBCSA | Santa Barbara Channel Swimming Association in California |
| ASA | American Swimming Association in Austin, Texas |
| NEMSA | New England Marathon Swimming Association in Boston |
| NEKOWSA | Northeast Kingdom Open Water Swimming Association |
| FISA | Farallon Islands Swimming Association |
| LTSA | Lake Tahoe Swimming Association |
| GLOWS | Great Lakes Open Water Swim Series |

Besides the domestic governing bodies in the United States, there are triathlon sanctioning bodies, lifesaving associations, independent race organizations, and municipalities with full autonomy over their own events. Because so many organizations have oversight in the open water world, the sport's rules and regulations vary from country to country, from venue to venue, and from race to race, which can be confusing.

On the other hand, these open water swimming organizations offer events with four key benefits:

1. Athletic competitions in scenic and natural environments

2. The challenge and enjoyment of swimming from start to finish in an open body of water

3. The enjoyment of group swimming with many swimmers in the open water compared with standing up on a starting block alone in a pool

4. Camaraderie with like-minded athletes in a sport that combines collegiality and competition

# RULES OF OPEN WATER SWIMMING

The watershed event in open water swimming history occurred in 1875 when Captain Matthew Webb became the first person to swim across the 21-mile (33.8K) English Channel. His effort, and the way he crossed, set in place the widely accepted rules of open water swimming.

His legacy was followed at the 1896 Athens Olympics, the 1900 Paris Olympics, and the 1904 St. Louis Olympics, where the swimming events were conducted in open bodies of water. In the case of competitive swimming, no flotation devices or artificial aids were allowed and no touching of other people or objects for assistance was permitted. In the case of channel swimming, swimmers were required to "clear the water" under their own power.

In 1927, the Channel Swimming Association was established to organize, regulate, and authenticate swims in the English Channel based on Captain Webb's precedent. The 2010 Channel Swimming Association Ltd. Handbook posted on their website states the following:

> No person in an attempt to swim the Channel shall use or be assisted by an artificial aid of any kind, but is permitted to grease the body before a swim, use goggles, wear one cap and one costume. A "Standard Swim Costume" (for both sexes) shall be of a material not offering Thermal Protection or Buoyancy and shall be Sleeveless and Legless. "Sleeveless" shall mean the Costume must not extend beyond the end of the shoulder onto the Upper Arm; "Legless" shall mean the Costume must not extend onto the Upper Leg below the level of the Crotch.

With the advent of triathlons and the acceptance of wetsuits in the open water, millions of new enthusiasts have joined the sport. Although traditionalists have strictly adhered to the original rules of the Channel Swimming Association, the evolution of swimwear technology led to a schism in the open water world. The latest swimwear provides buoyancy, reduces hydrodynamic drag, maximizes water repellency (i.e., does not absorb water), and incorporates muscle compression panels. Compression panels reduce vibrations of the chest, thighs, and gluteal muscles and reduce the accumulation of lactic acid in the blood. Reducing muscle vibrations increases the energy available to propel the swimmer through the water, and reduced lactic acid levels lead to faster performance. Wetsuits and new swimsuit technology have led to evolving rule interpretations that continue to be debated. Differences in the uses of swimwear have led to the creation of different divisions and separate awards for athletes who use wetsuits and those who do not.

But, Commander Gerald Forsberg, longtime president of the Channel Swimming Association, observed in 1957, "Despite the march of time and progress, the basic essentials remain precisely the same. Whatever the era, a Channel swim is, and always will be, a battle of one small lone swimmer against the sometimes-savage vastness of the open sea" (Long Distance Swimming).

## CATEGORIES OF OPEN WATER SWIMMING

For ease of explanation, the sport can be generally divided into three categories: short-distance (up to 5K, or 3.1 mi), middle-distance (up to 25K, or 15.5 mi), and marathon-distance (over 25K) events. In an age of specialization, each distance can be further broken down, each with its own subset of enthusiasts, equipment, training methodologies, and racing strategies.

Solo swims, stage swims, circumnavigations, charity swims, relays, sanctioned races, competitive swim series, cold water swims, mass participation events, eco-swims, expedition swims, Paralympics, and Special Olympics races represent the variety of genres of the open water world.

Solo swimmers are supported by escort teams that include kayakers, paddlers, and motorized boats. These swims tend to be marathon distances and are conducted under English Channel rules (e.g., no wetsuits or touching a person during the swim). Exceptions are made depending on the circumstances, the organizer's creativity, and the goals of the swimmer. These swims use modern technologies including global positioning system (GPS) units and micro-weather forecasting. Additionally, the swimmer's progress and results, as well as photographs and videos, are often reported and shared in real time via e-mail, text messages, tweets, blogs, and photo- and video-sharing websites over online social networks.

Stage swims are conducted over a specific number of consecutive days; the swimmers start at the location where they exited the day before. Circumnavigations are swims around islands that dot shorelines from coast to coast, ranging from Alaska (8.2 mi [13.2K] Pennock Island Challenge) and California (3.2 mi [5K] Alcatraz Island Swim) to Florida (12 mi [19.3K] Swim Around Key West) and New York (28.5 mi [46K] Manhattan Island Marathon Swim).

Charity swims can be competitions, relays, solo swims, or stage swims of any distance. Financial contributions are solicited and received from people around the world, sometimes via specialty online charitable donation aggregators.

Open water relays include any number of swimmers, although two to six is generally the norm. Relays held under English Channel rules, first established

StrelSwimming.com

Martin Strel of Slovenia swam 3,273 miles (5,267K) down the length of the Amazon River over 66 days in 2007.

in 1964 by the Channel Swimming Association, require people to swim for one hour each in the same order from start to finish and without substitutions. Other competitive relay events (e.g., Maui Channel Swim in Hawaii) have different time periods that can be shorter as time passes (e.g., 30 minutes for the first leg and 10 minutes for subsequent legs). In the extreme, freestyle relays give swimmers complete flexibility to decide for themselves their rotations, their substitution patterns, and the length of time they swim during each leg. Environmentally oriented relays, called carbon-neutral relays, require swimmers to complete their swims without the benefit of a motorized escort boat. In these events, swimmers rotate between swimming and powering themselves with paddles in an outrigger canoe or other non-motorized watercraft.

Eco-swims have different goals and characteristics:

- Focus on protecting, conserving, or calling attention to the environment or ecology
- Focus on improving or protecting the welfare of marine life or the local area
- Are conducted in an ecologically sustainable or environmentally friendly manner
- Are held in areas that are under environmental protection
- Raise money or provide direct financial benefits for conservation, marine life, or environmental protection, research, or education
- Lobby governments or local officials for access to, protection of, or a clean-up of a waterway

Many open water events also have fun short-distance parent–child relays to introduce children to the sport in a relaxed atmosphere. On the competitive side, 5K (3.1 mi) team pursuit races have been introduced in which same-sex or mixed-gender teams of athletes start, swim, and finish together in a peloton, separated from the other teams in a staggered start. A team's finish time is taken when the last swimmer crosses the finish line.

Groups of swimmers are also increasingly coming together to see how far they can swim as a team. In 2010, the Ventura Deep Six became the longest open water relay swum under traditional English Channel rules when they swam 202 miles (325K) along the Southern California coastline in the Pacific Ocean. The longest continuous open water relay swum with wetsuits consisted of 220 swimmers, each completing one leg in Camlough Lake in Northern Ireland. They collectively covered 426.5 miles (686.4K) nonstop in 10 days.

Sanctioned races are officially and legally overseen by recognized governing bodies, each with certain standards regarding safety, awards, timing requirements, and course measurement. The most visible of these sanctioned races is the Olympic 10K Marathon Swim.

Competitive swim series offer prizes for the overall series winners. These events include amateur races of the same distance (e.g., New Zealand Ocean Swim) and professional marathon swims ranging from 9 to 54 miles (14.5 to 87K) (e.g., FINA Open Water Swimming Grand Prix). The world's fastest open water swimmers participate in the highly competitive FINA 10K Marathon Swimming World Cup, the proving ground for athletes who qualify for the Olympic 10K Marathon Swim.

Cold water swims, often marketed as polar bear swims, are celebrated in the winter months and during winter holidays; swimmers jump in water often less than 50 °F (10 °C) with occasional snow on the ground. The most serious cold water swimmers participate in competitive ice swimming events in bodies of water less than 41 °F (5 °C), sometimes carved out of frozen rivers or lakes and part of the International Winter Swimming Association and the International Ice Swimming Association.

Many athletes with physical and intellectual disabilities participate in competitive open water races and do solo swims on their own, but there are also exclusive events for Paralympic and Special Olympics athletes.

## FACT

The 2008 Olympic 10K Marathon Swim was held in a rowing basin outside Beijing. The 2012 open water race will be held in a man-made lake in Hyde Park in the center of London, and the 2016 race will be held in Copacabana Beach in Rio de Janeiro, Brazil.

Great North Swim, Dave Tyrell

**Start of the Great North Swim in Lake Windermere, England.**

Mass participation swims are open water's signature events, drawing thousands of swimmers to scenic locations around the world. In the United States, hundreds of events take place during the summer: the La Jolla Rough Water Swim in California, started in 1916, annually attracts its maximum field of 2,300, and the Great Chesapeake Bay Swim in Maryland reaches its maximum number of 600 entrants in less than an hour via online registration. In Asia, the largest open water swim is the Sun Moon Lake Swimming Carnival, in which over 25,000 people swim 3.3K (2 mi) across Taiwan's largest lake. Africa's largest open water swim, the Midmar Mile in South Africa, attracts up to 19,000 swimmers. In Europe, the Great North Swim attracts 20,000 swimmers to England's Lake Windermere, and nearly 10,000 swimmers participate in Sweden's Vansbrosimningen event. In the Middle East, 6,000 swimmers participate in the annual 4K (2.5 mi) swim in the Sea of Galilee, and nearly 5,000 swim 7.1K (4.4 mi) across the Istanbul Strait in Turkey's Bosphorus Cross Continental Swim. In Australia, thousands enter the 19.7K (12.2 mi) Rottnest Channel Swim, the Lorne Pier to Pub swim, the Cole Classic, and many other events along the sun-drenched Australian coasts.

## TOOLS, TIMES, AND TYPES OF STROKES FOR OPEN WATER SWIMMING

The world of open water swimming is so broad that the tools, training times, and types of swimming strokes vary according to the athlete's specific goals.

## TOOLS

The equipment of open water swimmers has stayed consistent over time (i.e., goggles, swim caps and swimwear), but their training tools and navigational equipment continue to become more sophisticated. The biggest question facing open water swimmers is the great divide between wearing or not wearing a wetsuit. The advantages that wetsuits offer in terms of buoyancy and warmth are so significant that for purists there is no question that wetsuits are taboo. For triathletes and some newcomers, there is similarly no question that wetsuits are essential. Beyond wetsuits, open water swimmers use a range of equipment from earplugs and underwater video analytical tools to GPS units and feeding sticks. Chapter 4 explains in detail the types of equipment that open water swimmers use.

## TRAINING TIMES

You can train at any time depending on your work or study schedule and personal preference. Many swimmers prefer training in broad daylight, whereas others enjoy swimming at sunrise or sunset. A very small minority enjoy swimming at night, especially under the moonlight on a cloudless night.

Because most triathlons and open water swims start early in the day, many people prefer swimming in the morning so their body clocks get accustomed to competing at that time. Morning hours in the world's waterways also generally lack boat traffic, water skiers, and windsurfers, who tend to arrive later in the day. In locations where there is surf, morning training sessions are also good because surfers tend to be out and can help in emergencies and provide advice on water conditions. However, because morning conditions tend to be flatter than afternoon or evening conditions, experienced swimmers also occasionally practice during the late afternoon to get accustomed to rougher conditions.

Most swimmers who are initially apprehensive about swimming at night do so in preparation for marathon swims that start or end at night. Although you may never have any reason or motivation to swim at night, many swimmers are enthralled with the bioluminescence (an ocean phenomenon in which marine life generates light that reflects off the water's surface) that only becomes visible during the night in saltwater. It is not found in freshwater.

## TYPES OF SWIMMING STROKES

Humans have swum since prehistoric times, but two groups swam particularly well in the open water while attired in their military gear: Japanese samurai and knights in the Middle Ages. Later, native people in the Americas, West Africa, and the South Pacific used early forms of the modern-day freestyle, which became the dominant swimming stroke during the early 20th century.

Chapter 5 explains in detail how you can build a faster, more streamlined, and more efficient freestyle.

But even today, some people prefer the breaststroke that Captain Matthew Webb used when he swam across the English Channel in 1875 (table 1.1 lists the record times of main strokes used in crossing the English and Catalina channels). Breaststroke open water swims are held in the Netherlands, Taiwan, Japan, and many other locations throughout the world. Very few marathon swimmers prefer other swim strokes.

**Table 1.1   Swimming Stroke Records**

| Stroke | English Channel | Catalina Channel |
|---|---|---|
| Butterfly | Julie Bradshaw (UK), 14:18 | Vicki Keith (Canada), 14:53 |
| Backstroke | Tina Neill (USA), 13:22 | Tina Neill (USA), 10:37 |
| Breaststroke | Frederick Jacques (France), 13:31 | Jason Lassen (USA), 15:59 |
| Freestyle | Petar Stoychev (Bulgaria), 6:57 | Penny Dean (USA), 7:15 |

http://www.channelswimming.net and http://www.swimcatalina.org

# COMMON CHARACTERISTICS OF OPEN WATER SWIMMERS

The allure of the open water has attracted athletes from all walks of life and nearly every age group. Enthusiasts include triathletes, solo channel swimmers, people motivated to raise money for charities, lifeguards, competitive teenage swimmers, adult fitness swimmers, professional marathon swimmers, and weekend warriors.

Open water swimmers' athletic backgrounds are not as important as their willingness to swim without lanes, lines, and walls in a dynamic environment. Initially nervous, many open water swimmers soon thrive on the aquatic wilderness they encounter. They possess a strong sense of adventure, yet they understand that it is natural to feel disoriented and challenged in the rolling swells and turbulence of the open water among both seen and unseen marine life.

People in the open water swimming community tend to be adaptable, energetic, and optimistic. This is likely because the sport demands flexibility, above-average health, and a positive outlook.

Most open water athletes aggressively accept challenges and love to experience the thrill of competitions or solo challenges in settings in which their normal sensory systems are impaired. Many love to evaluate the variables of open water swimming (e.g., wind, waves, currents) in their attempt to swim as quickly, efficiently, and straight as possible while others like to let their minds wander.

Marathon swimmers tend to conduct pre-swim planning at a higher, different level because of the length of their swims and the risks they face in an environment that can change from hour to hour. Other swimmers simply like to get in the open water for exercise and forget the worries and stresses of the terrestrial world.

## CHAMPIONS, PIONEERS, RECORD HOLDERS, AND ENDURERS

The best and most celebrated open water swimmers are often described as falling within the following types: champions, pioneers, record holders, and endurers. Each type of swimmer has added to the annals of open water swimming history.

Champions are swimmers who are fastest in head-to-head competitions against other great open water swimmers of their era. Abdel Latif Abou-Heif of Egypt in the 1950s, John Kinsella of Indiana in the 1970s, Paul Asmuth of Florida in the 1980s, Shelley Taylor-Smith of Australia in the 1990s, and 2008 Olympic 10K Marathon Swim gold medalists Larisa Ilchenko of Russia and Maarten van der Weijden of the Netherlands are examples of these champions.

The pioneers include swimmers who have done unprecedented swims of historical proportions that pushed the boundaries of human capabilities and expectations. Lynne Cox's 2.7-mile (4.3K) swim across the 39.2 °F (4 °C) waters in the Bering Strait from Alaska to Russia, Lewis Pugh's 20-minute swim in the 29 °F (–1.7 °C) waters across the North Pole and the 32 °F (0 °C) waters of Antarctica, and Jon Erikson's triple crossing of the English Channel are examples of the exploits of these pioneers. Some pioneers also endeavor to have a social theme and tie a special message to their swims. These have ranged from promoting peace between nations to calling attention to climate change.

The record holders include swimmers who break established records of acknowledged distances or at certain races. Dr. Penny Dean of California, Philip Rush of New Zealand, and Petar Stoychev of Bulgaria are accomplished swimmers

Terje Eggum

Lewis Pugh diving into the sea of the Antarctic Peninsula in 2005.

who set the bar by breaking English Channel records. Although there is always some luck in swimming under optimal conditions (with favorable currents, minimal wind, comfortable water temperatures, and no jellyfish), there is no doubt that these record holders are among the fastest to ever swim in the open water.

The endurers include swimmers who chose to swim the longest and farthest in terms of absolute distance or time (or both). These swimmers include Diana Nyad of the United States, who swam 102 miles (164K) from the Bahamas to Florida; David Meca of Spain, who took over 24 hours to swim 50 miles (80K) from the Spanish coast to an island in the Mediterranean Sea; and Skip Storch of the United States, who swam three times around Manhattan Island in 32 hours and 52 minutes. The drive of these athletes to push past mental and physical barriers during these lengthy and difficult swims is legendary.

Champions, pioneers, record holders, and endurers have earned great respect from others in the open water community, but many swimmers can justifiably see themselves as examples of these types of swimmers.

Champions include teenage and adult swimmers who strive to win their age-group divisions in local races. Pioneers include relay teams and individuals who swim unprecedented courses or distances in their local areas to share social messages or support charitable organizations. Record holders include swimmers who set records in lakes, dams, channels, and ocean courses, either for themselves or in their age groups. Endurers include those who simply get in the water and strive to achieve what they may have initially thought was impossible, no matter the distance, time, or conditions.

## CHALLENGES AND INTANGIBLES

A swimmer's visibility and navigational abilities in the open water can be severely impaired by waves, surface chop, the sun's glare, rain, haze, or fog. The inability to see turn buoys, landmarks, and the finish area leads many open water swimmers to follow the swimmer ahead of them hoping that person is swimming in the right direction.

This innate trust in one's fellow athlete leads to the creation of intangible bonds and camaraderie among swimmers of all ages, abilities, and backgrounds. Before a competitive race or solo swim, swimmers tend to be quiet and introspective. This is in stark contrast to their outlooks and personalities after the finish. The common bonds created in the open water lead many to colorfully share their experiences with their competitors, including those who they did not know or speak with before the swim.

Even when swimmers take their own navigational lines in a race, they often want to learn about how their competitors swam the event, making mental notes of any perceived or actual navigational advantages for the next time they swim. Their quest for improvement is ongoing because the dynamic nature of the open water constantly presents different conditions for each swim.

## FACING OBSTACLES

Open water swimmers understand the multitude of obstacles they may face: cold water, long distances, waves, oncoming currents, surface chop, fog, jellyfish, seaweed, sea nettles, sharks, alligators, reefs, flotsam, jetsam, and pollution. Although the sport cherishes its champions and awards the fastest swimmers, most open water athletes do not swim to win, but rather, to compete well or simply to finish, enabling them to achieve a certain level of self-satisfaction.

UCLA basketball coaching legend John Wooden, in his famous Pyramid of Success (http://www.coachwooden.com/index2.html), defined success as "peace of mind which is a direct result of self satisfaction in knowing you made the effort to do the best of which you are capable." This definition is tailor-made for open water swimmers, many of whom have trepidations during their swims and are satisfied simply to finish.

## HOW FAR AND HOW COLD?

When making plans for upcoming open water swims, most athletes ask two questions: "How far is the swim?" and, "What is the temperature of the water?"

Because the water temperatures (50 to 88 °F, or 10 to 31 °C) and distances (1 to 54 mi, or 1.6 to 87K) vary so widely in open water competitions, the answers to these two questions lead to subsequent decisions about the amount and type of training necessary.

The 54.6-mile (88K) Hernandarias-to-Paraná race in Argentina is the world's longest professional marathon race. The 50-mile (80.5K) Indian National Open Water Swimming Competition in the Bhagirathi River in West Bengal, India, is the world's longest amateur race. The annual 28.5-mile (46K) Manhattan Island Marathon Swim is the longest race in America, although a 60-mile (96.6K) professional race was once held in Lake Michigan in 1963.

Some swimmers wear wetsuits if the water is cold, which is a relative issue based on the swimmer's experience and residence. Athletes may wear wetsuits in USA Triathlon–sanctioned races up to and including a water temperature of 78 °F (25.6 °C). For purists, there is no reason or excuse to wear a wetsuit. The hardiest athletes feel challenged, and often proud, to never wear a wetsuit, no matter how cold the water is. But many open water swims around the world offer the option of using wetsuits.

This flexibility in permitting the use of wetsuits has helped the sport grow beyond its traditional roots. Previously, the sport rules dictated that no swimwear that aids in buoyancy or helps contain body heat was allowed. Many races have relaxed this restriction. Some newcomers to the sport start by wearing wetsuits and then make a transition to swimming without wetsuits. Others feel more comfortable wearing wetsuits all the time.

If the distance of your open water swim is longer than you have ever swum before, then you must properly plan your physical and mental training. Chapters 2, 6, 7, and 8 provide information on how you can acclimate your body to tolerate long distances under extreme water temperatures. There are no easy shortcuts. To swim far, plan accordingly and train hard. To swim in very cold or very warm water, acclimate your body to withstand temperatures that can vary between uncomfortable and impossible.

## Choosing a Course

If you are inexperienced, consider the configuration of the open water course. Point-to-point courses along seashores are different from out-and-back courses in a lake, swims across a channel, and races down a river. These various conditions are enticing in different ways to different athletes.

For example, if you dislike swimming in ocean waves, then shy away from point-to-point sea courses, in which you must swim parallel to shore and beyond the shore break. If you enjoy navigating around turn buoys in a bay or a lake more than catching currents across a river, then participate in lake swims instead of river swims. The beauty of open water swimming is that there are venues for every taste.

## Importance of the Buddy System

The buddy system is highly advisable for all open water swimmers, experienced or not. A sense of calm and comfort comes when swimming with a friend. It is certainly safer than swimming alone. The buddy system, especially when you are paired with a more experienced or faster swimmer, is a great way to improve. Almost without exception, experienced swimmers relish the opportunity to share information on swimming techniques and provide navigational tips to those who are less experienced.

Alternatively, a friend or family member can escort you in a kayak, paddle board, canoe, stand-up paddle board, or small inflatable raft. Your escort can serve as your eyes in the water once you get past the waves or shoreline. If you cannot find someone to be with you in the water, ask someone to walk alongside the shoreline while you swim parallel to shore. Enjoy and appreciate the benefits and feeling of safety while someone looks out for you.

### FACT

According to the Channel Swimming & Piloting Federation (http://www.channelswimming.net), "During solo swims, a swimmer may be accompanied in the water by one person only and not accompanied at all until after the first three hours. This accompaniment will be for a maximum of one hour and cannot be repeated until at least two hours have elapsed after the cessation of the accompaniment. The second swimmer may swim alongside, but not in front of, the solo aspirant and must not impede the solo swimmer."

In the world of solo marathon swimming, pace swimmers are sometimes allowed. Pace swimmers join competitors in the water under certain conditions. Their role is to boost the psychological outlook of the swimmer by sharing the experience of a difficult swim. Pace swimmers can be teammates, family or friends.

## SWIMMER DEMOGRAPHICS

In an analysis of 3,659 swimmers ages 8 to 79 who participated in six short-distance open water races (RCP Tiburon Mile in California, Waikiki Roughwater Swim in Hawaii, Flowers Sea Swim in the Cayman Islands, Sandycove Island Challenge in Ireland, New Zealand Ocean Swim Series in Auckland, and the Vibes & Scribes Lee Swim in Ireland) in 2009, 65 percent were male and 35 percent were female, with an average age of 36.5 years. Men between the ages of 30 and 49 comprised 32 percent of all participants and are consistently the largest single group across all open water swims. This 30- to 49-year-old male group looks to remain the largest demographic group in open water swimming for the foreseeable future, but the fastest-growing group is women over the age of 40. Women between the ages of 30 and 39 comprise the greatest percentage of women, while women over the age of 40 consistently outnumber women under the age of 30.

Data among the marathon-distance swimming community is interesting. The ages of the 811 successful English Channel swimmers (as of 2010) range from 12 to 70 with a median age of 31, but 65 percent of the swimmers crossed when they were between 20 and 39 years old.

The vast majority of swimmers focus on local short-distance swims under 3 miles (5K). Eighty-eight percent of the 900 established open water events in the United States are short-distance swims. Only 4 percent of the events are middle-distance swims, and 8 percent are marathon-distance swims, which indicates that at least a percentage of the open water swimming community relishes solo challenges that require years of focused training. Other than distance, perhaps the greatest differentiator among these types of swims is the amount of physical contact that occurs. In general, the shorter the race, the greater the amount of physical contact swimmers may experience—or initiate—with their competitors.

## GEOGRAPHIC LOCATION OF OPEN WATER EVENTS

With few exceptions, open water swims draw a high percentage of participants from the local surrounding area; however, the Great Chesapeake Bay Swim in Maryland annually attracts competitors from 36 states. The sport has grown to the point that, now, 42 states and 84 countries have swims that attract a minimum of 200 competitors. In the United States, open water swims are geographically dispersed from coast to coast with 56 percent of the events located west of the Mississippi River. California (134) and Hawaii (55) have the greatest concentrations of events; the largest mass participation events occur year after year in these two states.

## GROWTH OF OPEN WATER SWIMMING

Open water swimming is growing for a variety of reasons. It imparts health benefits that increase stamina and strength, and it is a personally fulfilling activity in which camaraderie with others is easily established. Like other endurance sports and triathlons, the activity is well suited to adults who are interested in having sense of purpose while training for a unique physical challenge. It is also ideal for competitive swimmers who love the opportunity to swim beyond the confines of a pool.

The sport also provides a reason to travel. Many open water swimmers have adventurous or inquisitive minds that push them to constantly search for new locations in which to swim and challenges to meet. Many of these athletes travel out of area and overseas, seeking well-known races or off-the-beaten-path locations to swim. In fact, the number of successful swims of well-known courses, like the English and Catalina Channels, has increased exponentially over the past few decades (see figure 1.1).

In addition, the sport is growing for the following reasons:

**1.** The growth of triathlons continues unabated. This has resulted in new open water clinics, camps, races and information on open water swimming.

**2.** Online and mobile communication tools (e.g., search engines, blogs, social networks, video-sharing websites, and e-mail) have enabled more people to re-search information about open water swimming. Most races have some kind of online presence whether it is via a website, blog, or online social group. In previous decades, information on open water swims was difficult to find.

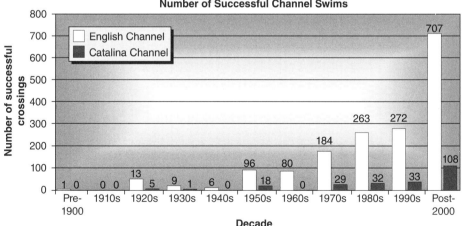

**Figure 1.1**   Growth of successful channel swims since 1875.

Using search engines, user-generated content-sharing websites, and online groups, swimmers easily share and learn information on races, water conditions, swim partners, teams, and relay possibilities with like-minded swimmers from around the world.

**3.** Technologies such as global positioning systems, Google Earth, and microweather forecasting systems, together with the increased professionalism and experience of pilots and escort teams, have led to more successful marathon swims and the ability to map out courses of all distances. The success of others has motivated even more people to realize their own dreams in the open water world.

**4.** Open water swimming remains a relatively inexpensive sport to participate in. Swimwear, a towel, and goggles, combined with affordable entry fees, do not present significant barriers to participation. Exceptions include stage swims and marathon solo swims and relays, for which costs run high because of the need for escort boats, support teams, and travel.

### Types of established annual events throughout the world

| | |
|---|---|
| Amateur swim series | Middle-distance river and lake swims |
| Channel swims[1] | Olympic 10K marathon swim |
| Charity swims | Paralympics and Special Olympics events |
| Coldwater swims | Pro marathon races-FINA Grand Prix circuit |
| Competitive swimming-sanctioned races | Pro marathon races FINA World Cup circuit |
| Expedition swims | Relay swims |
| Island circumnavigations | Short-distance beach and bay swims |
| Lifeguard competitions | Stage swims |
| Mass participation open water events | Solo marathon swims[2] |
| Masters-sanctioned | Triathlons and multi-sport events |

[1]English, Catalina, Molokai, Maui, Cook Strait, Strait of Gibraltar, Irish, Tsugaru, and Rottnest
[2]Tampa Bay Marathon, Swim Around Key West, Round Jersey, Ederle Swim, Great Lakes, and Lake Tahoe Swims

**FACT**

During her 1933 English Channel crossing, former Channel Swimming Association president Sunny Lowry's support crew did not have radios but instead used carrier pigeons to alert people interested in her progress during the 15 hours and 41 minutes that she swam.

Ann Ford

# OVERCOMING THE ELEMENTS

Olympic champion Alexander Popov (http://www.swimpsychology.com/motivational_quotes.php3) once observed, "The water is your friend. You don't have to fight with water, just share the same spirit as the water and it will help you move." In the open water, these words ring especially true. On the other hand, when you encounter wind, waves, currents, tides, jellyfish, sharks, and seaweed in the open water, Popov's words can also ring hollow.

## EXPECT THE UNEXPECTED

Open water swimming veterans expect the unexpected. They have learned to deal with Mother Nature, both in her glory and in her wrath. They know that the open water can be schizophrenic, starting off glassy calm and deteriorating to a sea of whitecaps. Like the polar opposites of Dr. Jekyll and Mr. Hyde, currents can be with you in one direction and against you in the other direction in a loop or an out-and-back course. Rather than feel fear, open water swimmers accept the conditions. Rather than experience apprehension, they welcome the challenge.

In the open water world, the expectations of land-based sports are left on the shoreline. When you run, you make progress. But forward progress is not always a given in the open water when tides, currents, and waves are involved. When you cycle, you can see around you and where your competitors are. But visual clues are significantly fewer in the open water because your eyes are alternatively looking downward toward the depths and barely breaking the water's surface.

Volunteers and officials in running and cycling races set the boundaries of the race course. But volunteers and officials at an open water swim are primarily there to protect you and minimize the risks. Open water swimming is an entirely different realm of athletic competition where the water engulfs you.

If you accidently hit a plastic bag floating in the ocean, your heart may skip a beat. If you get stung by a Portuguese man-of-war, you will remember the discomfort for the rest of your life. If you see a fin in the water near you—even if it is only that of a friendly dolphin—the moment will be indelibly etched in your mind.

Fortunately, a vast majority of open water swimming experiences are pleasant. Pick the right day and your experience will be enjoyable. As Popov says, "You don't have to fight with water." If you are fortunate enough to swim in clear, tropical waters amid colorful marine life and coral reefs, the sensations and impressions are overwhelmingly positive. If you win a close race against tough competition, the hard work makes your daily sacrifice worth the effort. If you swim farther than you ever have before, your confidence in your abilities will skyrocket.

Although it is not always possible to overcome all your fears of the open water, you can certainly minimize many of these through training, anticipation, and preparation.

## SAFETY FIRST

Anticipation requires an understanding of what you can face in the open water. Study and learn about the marine life, water temperature ranges, prevailing currents, tides, and typical boating traffic before you get in any body of water. If you do not know, there are ways to find out:

- Ask a lifeguard.
- Call a local swimmer.
- Go online and do some research.
- Pose a question to an open water swimming forum.

As is mentioned in chapter 1, nothing is as important as swimming with someone. Swimming solo in the open water presents an element of risk that you can easily do without.

If you cannot find a swim buddy, find someone who can escort you on a boat, kayak, or paddle board. If no one is available, then swim close to shore, parallel to the shoreline, so you can get out easily if trouble occurs. If you can arrange for someone to watch you or walk along the shore, ask that person to carry a mobile phone, whistle, and towel in case of an emergency. Offer a pair of binoculars so the person can keep an eye out for you from a distance. If none of these options is available, then inform someone onshore that you are going for a swim. Tell this person (a lifeguard or a family sitting next to your belongings on the shore) the estimated time, distance, and direction you will swim.

Swimming within sight of race officials is key.

Take only what you need to the water's edge during your open water workouts. Leave wallets and valuables behind to avoid tempting unscrupulous types. Alternatively, use a waterproof pouch to stick inside your swimsuit so you can carry your valuables with you in the water.

## SWIMMING IN SALTWATER

Swimming for long periods in saltwater will cause your tongue to swell and feel different. Gargle with mouthwash or a mixture of water and mouthwash to help alleviate this sensation.

Occasionally, if you swim for very long periods in very salty water, you will temporarily lose the taste sensation in your tongue. This is normal, and the sensation will soon return. Depending on the water quality, pollutants can lead to itching and skin irritation. The presence of marine organisms can also irritate your skin, which is why showering with soap as soon as possible after your swim is recommended.

## THE PHENOMENON OF THIRD SPACING

One unique physiological effect of swimming in freshwater or saltwater for long periods of time is third spacing. Third spacing causes your body to look softer and pudgier than normal. Even an open water swimmer who is fit and trim may appear waterlogged or swollen after a long time in the water. The extent of third spacing depends on the person, but it can occur in less than an hour. Fortunately, it is mainly an aesthetic concern; the body returns to normal within 24 hours.

Third spacing occurs when the body's fluids are trapped in the interstitial spaces of the brain, lungs, abdomen, and extremities. Under normal conditions, extracellular fluids are distributed in a ratio of approximately 75–25 between body tissue and plasma. But when the body's fluids collect in a "third" body compartment, you appear soft and bloated. The science of why this occurs is not entirely clear at present, but one of the causes of third spacing is being submerged in water for a prolonged period.

Sometimes, actions, such as not hydrating adequately during a cold water training session, can accentuate third spacing. Even though you may not feel like hydrating, you should do so. If you do not adequately hydrate during a long swim, the loss of electrolytes can also cause third spacing when extracellular fluids go out of your blood vessels and into your skin tissue.

## Risk of Pollution

Pollution in the open water may be in gaseous form (e.g., escort boat exhaust), liquid form (e.g., oil slicks), or solid form (e.g., flotsam, jetsam, plastic bags, floating pieces of wood, or other discarded remnants). Bacteria or unseen pollutants in the water can cause anything from an upset stomach to severe skin reactions. Although you will not be able to prevent everything from entering your system, use earplugs and try to keep your mouth as closed as possible when your face is in the water.

Rinse off soon after you get out of the water, preferably using soap. If shower facilities are not available in the area, prepare a large plastic container with tap water and rinse off as a temporary alternative before you have a chance to shower at home.

Rinsing off is also important if marine life (e.g., sea nettles) is present or if there has been a recent rainfall, especially in heavily populated areas. Rain often flushes pollutants from society's infrastructure (e.g., storm drains, canals, or city streets) into open water. The extent and amount of pollution along the shoreline increase every time it rains. In areas with much vehicular traffic, avoid swimming in the open water a day or two following a rainfall.

You can swim into almost anything in the open water. Floating junk and seaweed are the bane of open water swimmers because it often sits right below the water's surface out of easy view. You can also accidently step on seashells or something in the sand. You can get cut on rocks getting in and out of the water. Prepare by keeping up-to-date with your vaccinations (e.g., tetanus and gamma globulin shots).

If you are going to swim in water that may be polluted, ask your physician about Xifaxan (rifaximin) tablets. There may be side effects for some swimmers, but Xifaxan is used for the treatment of travelers' diarrhea caused by pathogenic *E. coli*. Some marathon swimmers take Xifaxan orally before swimming in possibly polluted water.

You can also research the relative levels of pollution in some bodies of water online. A few city, county, and state governments post information on water quality online.

## Encountering Marine Animals

Some swimmers fear what they can see. Other swimmers fear what they cannot see. Some fear both. Accept the fact that you are entering another world with innumerable aquatic denizens that consider *you* the intruder. Swimming with and focusing on a teammate or an escort as you swim side by side is one way to take your mind off whatever may be swimming below you.

The most feared predators are sharks—of any kind. Fortunately, and realistically, the chances of encountering a shark are nearly zero. According to the International Shark Attack File (http://www.flmnh.ufl.edu/fish/sharks/statistics/2008attacksummary.htm), an internationally recognized source of scientifically accurate information on shark attacks, the total number of all known shark attacks worldwide is extraordinarily low. In 2009 the ISAF investigated 61 alleged incidents of shark–human interaction that occurred worldwide and confirmed five cases of fatal shark attacks. Shark attacks have been decreasing, reportedly as a result of a declining population because of overfishing and habitat destruction.

Although sharks are talked about and feared the most, jellyfish, Portuguese man-o-war, sea lice, sting rays, and sea nettles often cause the most problems. If you are stung, simply grin and bear it until you head to shore when you can spray white vinegar on your skin or get treated by a lifeguard or medical personnel.

Dolphins, porpoises, seals, otters, schools of fish, alligators, water moccasins, sea turtles, sea snakes, and manta rays are examples of marine life that can either thrill or alarm you. You are in their world. Encounters with friendly dolphins and porpoises will create an indelible impression. Just keep swimming and these graceful mammals will playfully swim around you until something else catches their attention.

---

### Tempting Fate Among *Jaws*

Few other places on earth have as many aggressive great white sharks as the Farallon Islands, west of San Francisco Bay. Situated in the Red Triangle, the Farallon Islands are known as some of the most desolate and foreboding islands in the Pacific Ocean.

In 1967, Stuart Evans and Ted Erikson both succeeded in swimming to the California mainland from these heavily shark-infested waters where seals, sea otters, and sea lions are the protected food of great white sharks. No one since 1967 has replicated their feat.

## Humans, the Most Dangerous Creatures of All

Sharks and jellyfish can create problems for open water swimmers, but there are no more dangerous creatures in the open water than people.

Boaters, windsurfers, water skiers, Jet Skiers, rowers, kayakers, surfers, and fishermen can be oblivious to swimmers in the water. Besides being hard to see, open water swimmers often swim in places where boaters and windsurfers do not expect swimmers to be.

To protect yourself and make yourself more visible to others, do the following:

• Wear a brightly colored swim cap, either yellow, bright orange, or light green.

• Swim with a buddy.

• Be aware of the sounds of your environment, including the hum of a motor.

• Breathe bilaterally so you are aware of people on either side of you.

• Stop if a boat, windsurfer, water skier, Jet Skier, rower, or kayaker is traveling toward you. Wave your arms and yell if necessary.

• Assume that others cannot see you even if you can see them.

# SWIMMING IN ROUGH WATER

Ocean swells can be large and intimidating, but navigable when you swim in rolling seas. In contrast, small whitecaps can be punishing and demoralizing. Tides and currents can certainly push you off course, but heavy surface chop is unmerciful at all times. When the winds come up, surface chop taxes your physical limits and mental stamina.

Some swimmers are more naturally inclined to become seasick, especially menstruating women. Although some degree of acclimatization occurs as a result of practice and patience, if you experience repeated bouts of severe seasickness, you may benefit from trying the following:

• Do less sighting.

• Do the breaststroke and look at fixed onshore objects.

• Wear goggles with bigger lenses.

• Learn to breathe without swallowing water.

• Stick to glassy-flat lake swims instead of pushing the envelope in rocking seas.

## Stroke Mechanics in Rough Water

When you are constantly hit every way by waves, stay positive and try to make progress repeatedly between the waves. Focus on tiny victories while you swim against the elements. Kick harder when you are between the wave crests, and pull strongly when you swim down the face of the waves, even if it is only for one stroke and a few beats of your kick.

Ivan Torres

Conflict, collisions, and clashes frequently occur in open water competitions.

In rough water, keep as streamlined and as balanced as possible by maintaining a straight line from your head down to your hips. Use your legs as stabilizing, rather than propulsive, forces. If you have a strong core, use your strength and continue a good body rotation despite the waves. As you get pitched and rolled about in rough water, your most effective arm strokes involve using your core muscles from your entire trunk area.

Because your hand will slip in the front part of your stroke and your follow-through at the end part of your stroke will be less effective in rough water, you will gain most of your propulsion from the middle part of your stroke when your hands are directly beneath the area between your chest and hips.

If allowed, a technical swimsuit or wetsuit, especially one with full-length arm and leg panels, will create a more streamlined position that will be helpful during rough water conditions.

## TRAINING IN ROUGH WATER

There is no substitute for experience in rough water. Practice will not make perfect, but it will make swimming in rough water much easier. Instead of always training in flat conditions, occasionally swim when the winds come up so you can face heavy surface chop.

The cliché "Prepare for the worse and hope for the best" is appropriate for the open water swimmer. If you train in rough conditions, you will be ready for anything on race day. Conversely, if you train primarily in flat conditions or in a pool, you will be ready for nothing but flat conditions on race day.

Rough conditions can occur and lead to unsafe situations.

If the conditions are rough, swim parallel to the shoreline during your open water workouts. If there are whitecaps, swim in one direction for half of your swim and in the other direction for the other half so you practice with the turbulence hitting you from both sides.

It is easier to breathe away from the oncoming surface chop. Determine your most comfortable breathing pattern so you can avoid having each wave slam into your face as you breathe. Breathe farther back than normal by slightly moving your face backward as you roll your head to breathe. Position your mouth in the area under your recovering arm and armpit. Swim with your mouth closed when your face is in the water, except when you exhale moments before your head turns to breathe. This will help you avoid swallowing water. If you are not accustomed to swimming with your mouth closed and exhaling when your face is in the water, practice during your pool workouts until it becomes natural.

## FACING SURFACE CHOP

At times, you cannot see that you are being pushed by tides or currents in the open ocean. But, you can always feel the effects of wind and surface chop. From a mental perspective, surface chop changes how you feel. From a physical perspective, it can change the way you swim.

# BEAUFORT WIND FORCE SCALE

The Beaufort Wind Force Scale (table 2.1) is an empirical measurement for describing wind velocity based mainly on observed sea conditions. It is used by experienced pilots and open water swimmers to describe the conditions they face.

**Table 2.1**  Beaufort Wind Force Scale

| Beaufort number | Sea conditions (wave height in meters) |
| --- | --- |
| 0 | Flat (0 m) |
| 1 | Ripples without crests (0.1 m) |
| 2 | Small wavelets; light breeze; crests not breaking (0.2 m) |
| 3 | Large wavelets; crests begin to break; scattered whitecaps (0.6 m) |
| 4 | Small waves; moderate breeze (1 m) |
| 5 | Moderate longer waves; some foam and spray (2 m) |
| 6 | Large waves with foam crests and some spray; strong breeze (3 m) |
| 7 | Sea heaps up and foam begins to streak; moderate gale (4 m) |
| 8 | Moderately high waves with breaking crests (5.5 m) |
| 9 | High waves (6-7 m) with dense foam; strong gale (7 m) |
| 10 | Very high waves; reduced visibility; sea surface is white (9 m) |
| 11 | Exceptionally high waves; violent storm (11.5 m) |
| 12 | Huge waves; air filled with foam and spray; hurricane (14+ m) |

TRAINING TIPS

Frustration is natural when swimming in rough water. Even if you are being pushed with a current, swimming into surface chop is demoralizing and difficult. In rough water, your mental focus and determination must increase just as your physical effort increases.

When the water is choppy during a race, pay close attention to your competition. Someone can make a move on you while you are focused on fighting the elements.

You can tell that a current is with you by observing the shape of the surface chop. When the wind is blowing with the current, the wave action is smoother than when the wind is blowing against the current or at right angles to it. When the current is flowing against the wind, the waves become steeper and can turn into whitecaps quickly. As a general rule of thumb, whitecaps occur at 18 knots (1 knot equals 1 nautical mile per hour or approximately 1.15 miles per hour). If the wind speed is 15 knots and the oncoming current speed is 3 knots, the cumulative total is 18 knots, and you will face whitecaps.

## MANAGING WAVES

Ocean waves can be intimidating during onshore starts and finishes. If you do not have experience with bodysurfing, watch some online videos of bodysurfers and then go to the beach and try to repeat what you saw. When you are swimming into shore and feel the wave gaining momentum behind you, try to time your maximum speed to peak as the wave's surge picks you up and powers you forward. As the wave lifts you up and crests around you, place one hand in front of you and one hand at your side as you slide down the wave. Keep your head up and kick as you skim down the face of the wave while you allow the wave to push you forward. If you feel the wave going past you, kick harder while you swim with one arm stroking fast and one hand still in front of you. This will enable you to gain the maximum benefit from the wave and resultant whitewater. After the wave sweeps past you, start swimming again.

Before the race, examine the shore break and count the number of seconds between waves. This will give you a sense of how much time you have between the waves, what to expect, and how fast you need to keep moving through the surf zone.

If there is sizable surf as you head out, the most important thing to do is to dive under each wave and head toward the ocean bottom when you are underwater. While you are underwater, kick hard in a streamlined position with both arms held straight out in front of you. When you pop back to the surface, immediately lift your head to look for the next wave.

If the water is rough and you have to fight through the surf, you may want to put your goggle straps under your swim cap or tape your goggles to your swim cap. You can also wear two swim caps with your goggle straps between the first and second caps.

## UNDERSTANDING TIDES AND CURRENTS

Current-positive (i.e., current-assisted or current-enabled) swims, in which the currents are with you and pushing you forward, are generally easy. Conversely, current-negative (i.e., current-handicapped or current-impeded) swims are tougher to handle, especially when you are aware of their negative effects on your progress.

Swimming in rivers, estuaries or bays, in and out of coral reefs, or around islands can be tricky because of the tides and currents. In rivers, bays, reefs, and ocean coves, the water depth and flow change constantly. In general, water flows faster where it is deeper, but there are exceptions. If possible, research the conditions before every race, especially where tides and currents are significant. Experienced boat pilots are often the best source of information, but it is best to seek more than one person's opinion. Surfers, kayakers, local swimmers, and lifeguards are also helpful and generous with sound, accurate advice.

According to Tim Johnson, author of *History of Open-Water Marathon Swimming* (2004), 1 knot of current going in your direction leads to a 33-yard-per-minute advantage. That is, if you can swim 100 yards per minute in a pool and you swim that same pace in the open water with a 1-knot current going with you, you will swim 133 yards in one minute.

Pilots and coaches provide channel swimmers with advice about neap tides and spring tides (see table 2.2). A neap tide occurs twice per month during the first and third quarters of the moon when the difference between high tide and low tide is lowest. A spring tide is the opposite and occurs at the time of the new moon or the full moon when the difference between high tide and low tide is the greatest because of the collective gravitational pull of the aligned sun, moon, and earth.

Swimmers generally want to attempt channel swims on the neap tides because the lower the tide is, the slower the tidal flow will be and the swimmer will face less powerful tidal forces. Other factors can influence the decision of when to swim, however, such as the availability of pilots, weather, winds, and ocean swell direction. If the ocean swells are pushing the swimmer towards the goal, the swells present opportunities to help increase the progress of the swimmer.

Lateral currents run perpendicular or at an angle to your chosen course, and as such can push you off your straight-line tangent. Lateral currents also flow parallel to the beach and can be slow or fast.

**Table 2.2   Tide Summary**

| Type | Period | Characteristic |
| --- | --- | --- |
| Neap tide | First- or third-quarter moon | Smallest difference between high and low tides |
| Spring tide | New or full moon | Greatest difference between high and low tides |

# SWIMMING IN CALM WATER

After a few training sessions in rough water, swimming in calm conditions will feel easy. When the water is glassy, it is an ideal time to work on swimming straight. Try to limit the number of your sightings to significantly fewer than what you normally do, especially under rough conditions. Learn to swim straighter with fewer navigational sightings.

If you bilateral breathe, keep it up. If you do not bilateral breathe, then practice in calm conditions and experiment with your stroke technique. Some small stroke modifications (e.g., straighter hand pathways) may lead to an improved navigational IQ. Calm water also presents an ideal time to try different wetsuits. If you have a training partner of comparable size, exchange wetsuits to see whether another brand is a better fit for you than your current brand.

# WATER TEMPERATURE

The open water world is so vast that each condition demands a unique approach. Although most competitions and solo swims around the world are held in water between 60 and 85 °F (15.5 and 29.4 °C), some swims are held in cold water (under 60 °F) or very warm water (over 85 °F).

A water temperature difference of even a few degrees can make a significant difference in your comfort and performance levels, especially if you do not have time to properly prepare, or if you practice mostly in pools.

## FACING WARM WATER CONDITIONS

Pre-race and in-race hydration is important when you compete in extremely warm water (over 85 °F, or 29.4 °C). Drink four or five times per hour while training in warm water. You can also consume iced drinks before getting in warm water or walk around with a slushie, snow cone, or shaved ice in your bare hands before a race. Sticking your hands in an ice bucket can also temporarily reduce your core body temperature before you begin your race.

During the race, occasionally roll over on your back and do backstroke; this will feel more refreshing than constantly keeping your face in the warm water. By all means, do not wear a wetsuit in warm water or excessively push yourself; doing so can directly affect your central nervous system and rapidly lead to emergency situations such as heat exhaustion.

One easy way to know whether you are well hydrated before a swim is to check the color of your urine. It should be pale yellow or colorless.

## FACING COLD WATER CONDITIONS

Many fit swimmers can swim for long distances or overcome rough conditions, but cold water is often the largest single obstacle to success.

Your tolerance of cold water will depend on where you live, how often you swim in the open water, your level of experience, your body fat percentage, and your goals. To swimmers who live in tropical areas, swims near 68 °F (20 °C) may feel cold. Those who live in temperate climates may find water approaching 60 °F (15.5 °C) to be cold. But for hardy swimmers in traditional cold water swimming capitals (San Francisco, Boston, Dover, Cape Town and throughout Great Britain, Ireland, southern Australia, and New Zealand), under 55 °F (12.8 °C) is the cold standard.

Your relative discomfort in the cold water can also depend on weather conditions. The chill factor will play a role because fog, mist, and rain can make the water feel colder. Water at 65 °F (18.3 °C) can feel cold in windy and overcast condition, but it can feel tolerable when the sun is shining brightly during a midday swim.

## Is Weight Gain Necessary?

It is not necessary to gain weight to swim well in cold water, although extra weight will not hurt your effort. The extra weight protects your inner core and enables you to better tolerate colder temperatures for longer periods. However, excessive weight gain (i.e., over 10 lb or 4.5 kg) is not recommended, especially if you are also doing cold water training. The extra weight can be hard to take off after you have achieved your swimming goals.

If you choose to gain weight, it is better to gain weight eating healthy foods than to load up on desserts and junk food. But, the best way to swim well in cold water is simple: swim as frequently as possible in it. It may be difficult, but it is effective.

The fastest marathon swimmers are extremely fit athletes with body fat percentages not significantly higher than those of the average competitive pool swimmers. Dr. Penny Dean (USA; 7 hours and 40 minutes in 1978), Yvetta Hlaváčová (Czechoslovakia; 7 hours and 25 minutes in 2006), David Meca (Spain; 7 hours and 22 minutes in 2005), Chad Hundeby (USA; 7 hours and 17 minutes in 1994), Yuri Kudinov (Russia; 7 hours and 6 minutes in 2007) and Petar Stoychev (Bulgaria; 6 hours and 57 minutes in 2007) are among the fastest swimmers in the history of English Channel swimming. They focused on acclimating themselves to cold water rather than gaining weight.

## Cold Water Acclimatization

Cold water acclimatization (CWA) is a process of gradually increasing your resistance to cold water through regular exposure. Some people naturally tolerate the cold water better than others do because of their mental approach or physiology, but CWA is not an easy road for anyone. There is no fixed timetable. A successful formula is based on your willingness to get in cold water until you can tolerate it for long enough periods to complete your cold water swim.

If you are diligent, CWA will happen. Over the course of several weeks or months, frequent and consistent exposure to cold water is the best and fastest way to become accustomed to it. After the initial shock of your first few training sessions, you will be pleasantly surprised at how well your body adapts to the cold.

In the early stages of CWA during the colder months of the year, it may be difficult to swim longer than a few minutes. Do not be discouraged. It may be impossible to swim any significant distance at first. You may not be able to put your head in the water, but diligence and consistency will help you gradually increase from a few minutes to several miles (or kilometers) in cold water.

Get in cold water at every opportunity, no matter how unbearable it may initially feel. Consistently getting in the water is nearly as important as the duration of your practice swims. Practice on the weekends so you can focus on CWA without the pressures of work or school. If you stop training in cold water for any reason, you will quickly lose your edge. For a majority of swimmers, it is unreasonable to expect to be able to effectively adapt to cold water in the last few days leading to a cold water swim.

CWA begins before you get in the water and continues until you are fully recovered. Here are some tips:

- Be well nourished and well hydrated before you train in cold water.
- Have warm liquids ready to drink before and right after you swim.
- Arrange to take a shower, bath, or sauna within a relatively short period after you get out.
- Train in cold water after getting a good night's sleep. Test your body when you are well rested rather than when you are stressed out about work or school.

In cold water, your muscles require more energy at a faster rate. If you are shivering in the water, your glycogen stores will decrease faster than normal. Because glycogen comes primarily from carbohydrates, eat a sufficient amount of them before and after your cold water workouts. If you do not eat immediately after a cold water workout, you may feel lethargic for the rest of the day.

After you finish a cold water workout, get out of your swimsuit and dry off as soon as possible to begin the re-warming process. Get out of the wind, move to a warm area, and take a warm shower. Get into dry clothes as soon as possible: form-fitting multiple layers of clothing with a wool hat and thick socks are better than one parka and slippers. Re-warm quickly to help you recover for your next workout.

If you are shivering uncomfortably on the shore, wrap yourself in a towel and bury yourself in the sand rather than stand exposed to the elements. If a friend is with you, ask for a bear hug, get out of the wind, or go immediately to a car where you can turn up the heater. Do not drive home by yourself if you are shivering and your core body temperature is still lower than average.

Even if you plan to wear a wetsuit, it is still beneficial to train in the open water during the fall, winter, and spring. Swimming in a pool is great for aerobic fitness and technique improvement, but nothing replicates the reality of open water. A serious triathlete would not take off nine months or more from running or biking, so grab a wetsuit and maintain your edge by doing an occasional cold water training session in the cooler months.

Occasional pockets of cold water occur in many swims. Sometimes these pockets last for a few strokes; sometimes they are larger. They can sometimes take your breath away. Prepare to swim in water that is at least a few degrees colder than the average expected water temperature of your swim. If the expected water temperature is 64 °F (17.8 °C), then be ready to swim in water that is 60 °F (15.5 °C). Prepare for the unexpected, and you will not be caught off guard on race day.

## GETTING IN COLD WATER

If you get to the shoreline, but cannot handle immediately jumping in, walk or jog along the shore in your swimsuit. After a short period, start walking or jogging with your feet and ankles in the shallow water. Gradually go into deeper water until your lower legs are wet and water is splashing on your upper body. If it is still too difficult to swim, just stand or walk in the shallow water for as long as you can and then call it a day. If you are ready to start swimming, first wet your hands and splash water on your face and upper body. This will help reduce the initial shock.

CWA may take longer for you than for others. When you start swimming, your teeth may hurt. You may hyperventilate. You may feel like your body will explode, or you may get an ice cream headache. If you hyperventilate, swim with your head up or swim breaststroke take deep, long, controlled breaths. After your breathing is under control, take long, smooth arm strokes. Kick strongly to get your blood flowing if you feel your legs cramping or your feet are cold. If you start to cramp, quickly head to shore. Shivering is normal and is the body's way to generate body heat, but when your body starts to seize up, it is too dangerous to continue heading away from shore.

During your forays in cold water, think positively and focus on the details of your stroke and surroundings. Positive thoughts will help you stay focused on the task at hand and reinforce your commitment to your goals.

Cold water swimming requires a fine balance that you must determine for yourself. Push yourself hard, but not beyond what you are physically capable of. If you stop shivering and things start to get hazy, your vision starts to become impaired, or your world seems to be narrowing in on itself, you have definitely gone too far and immediately need to get out and seek help.

## GETTING OUT WHEN IT'S TOO COLD

Your coach, swim buddy, and escort should know the symptoms and effects of hypothermia (see table 2.3). Their knowledge and willingness to pull you or anyone from the water in the middle of a swim—however difficult it is—will help prevent emergencies.

**Table 2.3**  Stages of Hypothermia

| Stage 1 | Body temperature drops 1.8 to 3.6 °F (1 to 2 °C), goose bumps form, mild shivering occurs, and breathing becomes quick and shallow. |
|---|---|
| Stage 2 | Body temperature drops 3.6 to 7.2 °F (2 to 4 °C), shivering becomes more violent, and the swimmer becomes pale with lips, ears, fingers, and toes becoming blue. |
| Stage 3 | Body temperature drops below 90 °F (32.2 °C), major organs fail, cellular metabolic process shut down, and death occurs. |

As your core body temperature falls, the blood flow increases to your vital organs, including the heart, lungs, kidney, and brain, as a protective measure. The electrical activity in these organs slows in response to the cold as your thinking and reasoning are gradually affected. Confusion, slurred speech, apathy, and loss of consciousness follow if your core body temperature is allowed to drop. As your body gets colder, the brain is less able to function normally. At this point, it is very important for your escort and support crew to ask you very direct questions (e.g., How old are you? What are your children's names? What elementary school did you go to? What is your zip code?). If you cannot easily and quickly answer these questions, then they must immediately pull you from the water. You can always live to swim another day.

Jim Barber, a member of the Triple Crown of Open Water Swimming Club (people who have crossed the English Channel and the Catalina Channel and completed a circumnavigation of Manhattan Island in New York City), and Bryan Boggs compiled an Open Water Temperature Perception Scale (see table 2.4) that provides descriptions of what open water swimmers feel at various water temperatures during training, solo swims, and competitions.

**Table 2.4**   Open Water Temperature Perception Scale

| Scale | Temp | Perception | Description |
|---|---|---|---|
| 0 | >84 °F >28.8 °C | Much too warm | • Not suitable for any serious swim workout |
| 1 | 82-84 °F 27.7-28.8 °C | Too warm | • Overheating and feeling uncomfortable during moderate swims<br>• Stroke feels sluggish |
| 2 | 79-82 °F 26.1-27.7 °C | Warm | • Overheating during fast-paced swims<br>• Suitable for moderate middle-distance sets |
| 3 | 76-79 °F 24.4-26.1 °C | Neutral | • Nice temperature for all degrees of physical exertion |
| 4 | 72-76 °F 22.2-24.4 °C | Slightly chilled, comfortable swim | • Slightly chilled upon entry, but comfortable even during easy swims<br>• During warm-up period, normal stroke count is maintained without becoming chilled<br>• No shivering present during the swim |
| 5 | 69-72 °F 20.5-22.2 °C | Somewhat chilled, comfortable swim | • Initially chilled, but comfortable during moderate pace<br>• Warm-up period requires a moderate increase in normal stroke count to get warm, but normal stroke count returns within a few minutes<br>• Need to increase pace once or twice per hour to generate perceived warmth in core and arms<br>• Can tolerate up to 2 minutes for feedings before chilling<br>• No shivering during swim and only minimal shivering after swim |

| Scale | Temp | Perception | Description |
|---|---|---|---|
| 6 | 64-69 °F 17.7-20.5 °C | Very chilled, some shivers during swim though not uncomfort-able | • Initially somewhat cold, feels like an ice cream headache with some hyperventilation<br>• Stroke count is greater than normal for 5-10 minutes<br>• Need to increase pace several times per hour to alleviate some shivering during swim<br>• Fingers and toes start to curl up while swimming<br>• Can tolerate 30-second to 1-minute feedings before chilling<br>• Post-swim shivers and shakes that last less than 15 minutes |
| 7 | 60-64 °F 15.5-17.7 °C | Somewhat cold, frequent shivers during swim in what becomes a challenging swim | • Initially very cold, teeth chatter<br>• Need to do breaststroke or backstroke to prevent hyperventilation during warm-up<br>• An uncomfortable swim in which hyperventilation initially occurs upon entry<br>• Frequent shivering during swim, sometimes not alleviated by increased pace<br>• Chilled at stops, needs stops of less than 30 seconds before getting chilled<br>• Fingers and toes curl up while swimming; hands take several minutes to be useful after swim<br>• Post-swim shakes occur, but last less than 30 minutes until a sauna or warm shower is available |
| 8 | 57-60 °F 13.8-15.5 °C | Cold, un-comfortable for most of the swim | • Initial burning sensation in arms and legs, but decreases in intensity during swim<br>• Determination and perseverance required throughout the swim<br>• Must maintain fast pace continuously, though this does not fully alleviate shivering<br>• Hyperventilation and teeth chattering occurs<br>• Stops are quick—under 15 seconds to avoid chilling<br>• Fingers and toes curl up while swimming; hands take several minutes to be useful after swim<br>• Post-swim shakes unavoidable and last for over 30 minutes until a sauna or warm shower is available |
| 9 | 54-57 °F 12.2-13.8 °C | Very cold, uncomfort-able during entire swim | • Initial and somewhat continued burning sensation in arms and legs, to the point that feeling is quite diminished in arms and legs<br>• Unable to gain control of breathing pattern during warm-up; hyperventilation and teeth chattering occur<br>• Concentration is difficult because of continuous discomfort and shivering throughout swim<br>• Progressively getting colder throughout swim without a balance with heat generation and heat loss<br>• Fingers curl up while swimming; hands take several minutes to be useful after swim |
| 10 | <54 °F <12.2 °C | Too cold, numb | • All of previously listed symptoms<br>• Difficult to verbally communicate<br>• Violent shivering in water and after swim<br>• Random thoughts and incoherency require need to be pulled from the water |

## COLD WATER SWIMMING EQUIPMENT

Equipment for the cold water includes a wetsuit, a silicone or neoprene cap, and optional silicone earplugs. If you are not training for a channel swim or a marathon swim with specific rules against wetsuits, you can also use a surfer's rash guard, a triathlon speed suit, a technical swimsuit, or a neoprene surfer's cap that completely covers your ears with a strap that goes under your chin. All of these will help to keep you warm.

If you cannot use a wetsuit of any kind, try using lanolin or a mixture of lanolin and petroleum jelly to alleviate some of the initial shock of the cold water. Press the lanolin firmly into your skin especially around your neck, under your arms, and around your torso and upper legs. Do not leave globs of it hanging from your skin. Apply with rubber gloves to avoid getting it on your hands and goggles.

## COLD EXPOSURE AND BROWN FAT

In addition to training in cold water, exposure to the cold elements on land is also helpful for CWA. As your body adapts to spending greater lengths of time in cold water, you will experience physiological changes that will allow you to also better tolerate the cold on land. Your acclimatization to the cold can be a 24-hour-a-day process, if you are so motivated.

Unlike white fat, which is found under your skin, deposits of brown fat are present around your vital internal organs and along your back and sternum. In contrast to white fat, brown fat has mitochondria, is metabolically active, and generates heat. According to studies published in the *New England Journal of Medicine*, prolonged exposure to cold results in an increase in brown fat in adults. While some marathon swimmers purposefully gain weight and white fat to insulate themselves from cold water, brown fat actually insulates your core and generates heat—both of which are desirable for open water swimmers.

Brown fat is created if you expose your body to the cold elements, both in and out of the water. You can augment your CWA by taking cold showers and baths or wearing light clothing in the winter and spring to increase your tolerance of the cold. Instead of a thick jacket, wear a thin one. Forego your gloves, thermal underwear, and multiple layers of clothing to increase your exposure to the cold.

# SWIMMING AT HIGH ALTITUDE

Swimming at high altitude in freshwater lakes is more difficult than you may first imagine, even when the lakes are flat and calm. Water at 65 °F (18.3 °C) at altitude feels colder than water at 65 °F at sea level. Because of this phenomenon and the lack of density in the air, swim slowly the first few days you are at high altitude. You will feel light-headed, and you do not want to get into any emergency situations in the middle of a cold mountain lake.

# NIGHT SWIMMING

Swimming at night is usually done either for adventure or for a marathon swim. Because some marathon swims either start or finish in the dark, practicing at night is highly recommended at least a few times before your swim. Night swimming can be spooky and intimidating the first time you try it. Although there are no specific physical benefits to swimming at night, the psychological boost you receive from minimizing or conquering your fears will serve you well in the future. However, night swimming presents a significant level of risk.

Do not do night swimming alone. Always go with a swimming partner or escort. Too many things can go wrong if you night swim by yourself. Glow sticks tied to the back of your goggles or swimsuit straps are helpful so your escort or swim buddy can see you easily.

If possible, time your first night swim on a full moon. If you are lucky, it will be on a clear, cloudless night. Under these conditions, your swim will be a more enjoyable and beautiful experience.

If you do a night swim in the ocean, you may see bioluminescence, which is the production and emission of light by organisms in the water. The bioluminescence is particularly beautiful if you go under the water and look up at the surface of the water under the light of a full moon. The water's surface seems to glow magically.

You will encounter many challenges in open water swimming. The extreme conditions will tax you in ways that few other sports or activities can. You are swimming in a real-world aquarium where its aquatic denizens consider you the misplaced alien. Each challenge carries its own degree of risk that you must prepare for, recognize, train for, and overcome. Identifying the risks and overcoming these challenges takes time, effort, and focus. But a successful swim makes the journey worthwhile.

Traversée internationale du lac St-Jean

# CHOOSING YOUR EVENTS

A swimmer stretches on a shore on Maui with the warm tropical water lapping at his ankles. Another swimmer stands shoulder to shoulder with hundreds of shivering competitors as winds whip up the waters of Lake Michigan into an endless chorus of whitecaps. A third swimmer adjusts her goggles as she prepares to dive into the fast-moving waters of the Hudson below the shadows of Wall Street in New York City.

These are only a few examples of the locations where you can swim and the conditions you can experience. From warm to cold, calm to rough, tropical to temperate, seaside to lakeside, Northern to Southern Hemisphere—no two places are the same, and conditions are always in flux: seasons change, temperatures drop, winds shift. Conditions sometimes improve, and sometimes they deteriorate.

To help you focus on specific training goals, open water swimming is segmented into three general categories:

- Short-distance swims under 5K (3.1 mi)
- Middle-distance swims up to 25K (15.5 mi)
- Marathon swims over 25K

Just as swimmers prepare differently for sprint freestyle and distance freestyle races in the pool, each distance and type of open water swim requires a different type of preparation. If you are new to the sport, then you may want to start with shorter-distance races, races in warm water, or races that allow wetsuits. As you gain more experience, you may enjoy the challenge of a longer swim or a swim in colder water, or the challenge of shedding your wetsuit.

Ivan Torres

Start of an open water race near Cancun, Mexico.

## WHERE RACES ARE HELD

With 70 percent of the earth's surface covered in water, there is a vast choice of places to swim. The Daily News of Open Water Swimming, a publication found at http://www.dailynewsofopenwaterswimming.com, analyzed 2,243 open water swims in 83 countries throughout Asia, Europe, Oceania, the Americas, and Africa and found that nearly 60 percent of the world's open water swims are held in either an ocean or sea:

- Oceans or seas: 59%
- Lakes: 23%
- Rivers: 7.8%
- Bays: 7.5%
- Dams or reservoirs: 1.7%
- Canals or rowing basins: 0.9%
- Fjords: ~0.1%

# TECHNOLOGY'S PUSH TO PROMOTE OPEN WATER SWIMMING

With the advent of online communications—especially e-mail, social networks, and video-sharing websites—swimmers have been able to easily and quickly communicate with one another, and with race organizers, coaches, support teams, and escort pilots around the world. These communication tools have played an important role in expanding the sport.

Until the mid-1990s, open water swimmers primarily communicated via letters, faxes, and home telephones. Mobile phones, Facebook, e-mails, online forums, free online translation tools, and video- and picture-sharing websites have since supplanted the post office and faxes as the communication tools of choice. Instead of waiting for a letter or fax from a race director or an escort pilot, swimmers can communicate instantly with the global swimming community via smartphones, texts, tweets, e-newsletters and pokes. These benefits are immediate and profound. Contemporary real-time communications enable swimmers to enter events online and recruit relay partners and support crew members, and escort pilots from around the world via Google Groups and social online networks. Swimmers can broadcast their interests, questions, or requirements online and receive immediate responses from like-minded swimmers around the world.

GPS devices, mobile devices and online social networks also enable people from around the world to follow a swimmer's progress from anywhere in the world in near real time. This has brought the sport literally into people's homes and offices, which has generated more excitement in the sport. People interested in participating in relays, training sessions, or races around the world receive feedback from people they have never met in person. These bonds, although initiated in the virtual world, are cemented in real life when people finally meet and swim together. With a common vocabulary and common interests, swimmers in the online world do not doubt each other's intentions or abilities and tend to quickly establish a mutual trust.

The Internet also allows people to learn of water temperatures and water conditions before they head to the venue. Just as Walt Disney envisioned, it has truly become a small world.

## MEASURING OPEN WATER SWIM COURSES

Open water courses around the world are as varied as the bodies of water in which they are held. There are a few commonly used distances (e.g., 1 mile and 5K), but the actual distances and configurations of a race course are likely to be determined by the geography of the location. The exact placement of the turn buoys can differ slightly, leading to differences in race distances even on the same course from year to year. The race may start at high tide one year and at low tide another year, which can directly affect the start and finish locations. The distance of some races in lakes, dams, or reservoirs is occasionally affected by the amount of that year's rainfall.

Fortunately, modern technology can greatly help determine the precise distance of the race course and locations of the turn buoys. Global positioning system (GPS) technology is now commonly used by many race directors to provide accuracy and consistency in measuring open water swimming courses.

## THE DYNAMIC ENVIRONMENT OF THE OPEN WATER

Even when the turn buoys are anchored along the course under flat conditions, you still need to swim from point to point with a limited view. The open water always challenges your navigational IQ. If you swim off course, even in a short swim, you can add over 10 percent to your distance. Differences in water con-

Finish of the King of the Beach Challenge in Rio de Janeiro.

Pedro Rego Monteiro

ditions, winds, wave height and direction, tides, currents, and air and water temperatures render time comparisons from one year to the next over the same course nearly meaningless. However, course and world records are still maintained to provide historical perspective on the sport. Marathon records (over 25K) are archived at the International Marathon Swimming Hall of Fame website (www.imshof.org). Open water swimming records of all distances and types are archived and updated at the Open Water Source website (www.openwatersource.com).

## CHOOSING YOUR SWIM

You can select open water swims based on a variety of factors:

- Proximity to your home
- Word-of-mouth recommendations
- Positive encouragement from friends and teammates
- Location (e.g., interesting, scenic)
- Degree of difficulty

The vast majority of swimmers and triathletes enter swims in their local areas. At the opposite end of the spectrum, a small minority of swimmers travel the world proudly adding swims like collectors of prized artwork. As you become more familiar with open water swimming, you will have an easier time making decisions about races outside your immediate geographic area. Enter races that are recommended by your friends. If you do not personally know anyone who did a race that interests you, join an online forum, ask questions and read comments about different races on online forums.

Once you have set your sights on swims outside your area, target those that suit your style. If you like cold swims, research the expected water temperatures. If you want to combine travel with swimming, there are races from Alaska to Arizona, Croatia to the Cayman Islands, Ireland to Italy, Lake Michigan to Lake Windermere, and Japan to Johannesburg.

Lissa Reyden

Swimmers form a conga line during the New Zealand Ocean Swim Series.

If you like longer races, a growing number of marathon swims are offered. If you like rough conditions, ocean swims are the way to go. If you want to test your navigational IQ, enter races with challenging course configurations. Point-to-point swims in the ocean are generally more difficult than out-and-back courses in a lake.

If you are a triathlete looking to eventually do a full Ironman, look for group swims in your area. Start off with friends or teammates, including someone with a kayak who can help you navigate unfamiliar territory. Then start off your open water career with 1-miler, working your way up to 2.4 milers, even if it is an informal swim organized by your fellow triathletes. If your goal is the Ironman World Championships in Hawaii, understand that an ocean swim is part of the equation. If you do not have access to an ocean before you head out to Kona, practice along the shores in a local lake when the winds are whipping up the lake into a whitewater frenzy. The biggest reason for triathletes to pull out of the Ironman in Hawaii is seasickness, so your training experience in rough and wavy waters will be invaluable and an insurance against not even being able to hop on your bike at Ironman. On the other hand, if your goal is simply to gain muscle tone and increase cardiovascular fitness, you have selected one of the best low-impact means to become more buff and fit.

## TIME LIMITS AND HEATS

Some open water swims have time limits; that is, swimmers must reach a certain point along the race course before they are asked to leave and are pulled out by race officials. Many times, the limits are a result of safety considerations, shifting tidal flows, or time limits established by city laws or regulations governing the waterway due to boat traffic. Some races have time limits that are based on the finish of the first swimmer. In these races, swimmers must exit the water after a certain amount of time (e.g., 1 hour) has lapsed from the finish of the first swimmer.

Many races separate the field by gender, age, or speed. Larger swims around the world and the most competitive races have qualification swims or minimum time standards that swimmers must achieve. A select number of swims are so popular that either an online lottery system or a detailed selection process by committee is used (e.g., the Rottnest Channel Swim near Perth, Australia, and the Manhattan Island Marathon Swim in New York City).

## REPRESENTATIVE SWIMS AROUND THE WORLD

Tables 3.1, 3.2, and 3.3 include a very small number of representative swims held annually across the United States and around the world.

**Table 3.1** Short-Distance Swims (up to 5K, or 3.1 mi)

| Short-distance swim | Course | Description | Features |
|---|---|---|---|
| Waikiki Roughwater Swim | 2.4-mile (3.9K) swim across Waikiki Beach in Honolulu | Race across coral reefs amid plentiful marine life for swimmers of all ages and abilities | Inspiration behind the swim leg of the Ironman Triathlon |
| Big Shoulders | 2.5K (1.6 mi) and 5K (3.1 mi) course in Lake Michigan near downtown Chicago | Popular race with many of the best youth and adult swimmers from the Midwest competing | Water temperature and conditions can vary widely |
| La Jolla Rough Water Swim | 250-yard (229 m) to 3-mile (4.8K) races, north of San Diego, California | Starts and finishes in a natural amphitheater with thousands of young and old swimmers | Billed as America's Premier Rough Water Swim since 1916 |
| RCP Tiburon Mile | 1.2-mile (1.9K) point-to-point race in San Francisco Bay, California | Competitive race with many Olympians, world champions, and marathon swimmers from over 20 countries | Male and female winners receive $10,000 in a winner-take-all race |
| Cascade Lakes Swim Series & Festival | 0.5K, 1K, 1.5K, 3K, and 5K (0.3, 0.6, 0.9, 1.9, and 3.1 mi) races in Elk Lake in central Oregon | Beautiful, clear mountain lake offers five races over three days over different shaped courses | Wetsuits are acceptable, but have a 10% time penalty |
| Xstrata Nickel Swim Thru Perth | 2.2K (1.4 mi) and 4K (2.5 mi) races from Perth's Swan River to Matilda Bay | The Western Australia race hosts a mix of swimmers from 10 to 83 years old | Oldest open water race in Australia; has been held 91 times |
| Peter Pan Cup Christmas Morning Handicap Swim | 100-yard (91 m) swim in Hyde Park in London in 40 °F (4.4 °C) water | Site of the 2012 London Olympics 10K Marathon Swim where thousands will view the race | In 1838, 12 athletes swam 1,000 yards in front of 20,000 fans |
| Winter Swimming Championships | Short swims in 35-39 °F (1.7-3.9 °C) water held in various cities | Divisions include Penguins, Seals, Polar Bears, Competition, and Relays | Held in European pools carved out of frozen lakes or rivers |
| Lorne Pier to Pub Swim | 1.2K (0.7 m) point-to-point ocean swim in Lorne, Australia | Popular race that attracts Australian Olympians, celebrities, politicians, and 3,000+ swimmers | Started by lifeguards and features exciting bodysurfing finishes |
| Damme-Brugge Open Water Swim | 5K (3.1 mi) race held in a canal in Belgium | Point-to-point course offers freestyle and breaststroke races | Held 100th anniversary swim in 2010 |

**Table 3.2** Middle-Distance Swims (under 25K, or 15.5 mi)

| Middle-distance swim | Course | Description | Features |
|---|---|---|---|
| Great Chesapeake Bay Swim | 4.4-mile (7K) swim across the Chesapeake Bay in Maryland | Point-to-point race allows wetsuits but has strong currents depending on the conditions | Field is filled within 18 minutes with online entry system |
| Trans Tahoe Relay | 11.5-mile (18.5K) relay across Lake Tahoe in California | Challenging and popular non-wetsuit relay and solo race at 6,200-feet (1890 m) altitude | The six-person relays are held in sub-60 °F (15.6 °C) water |
| Swim Miami | 1-mile, 5K, and 10K warm water races in a protected saltwater stadium in Florida | Competitive swims in flat water with the Miami skyline in the background | Hundreds of swimmers of all ages and abilities take part |
| Little Red Lighthouse Swim | Current-assisted 10K (6.2 mi) river swim in New York City | Unique views of upper Manhattan Island and the George Washington Bridge | Held in the Hudson River as part of the NYC Swim series |
| Swim Around the Rock | 3.25-mile (5.2K) swim around Alcatraz Island in San Francisco Bay | Cold water, changing tides, and fast currents challenge swimmers within view of the majestic Golden Gate Bridge | A strategic race with spectacular views of the San Francisco skyline |
| Swim Across America | A series of swims of various distances held at various venues across the country | Popular charity swims that are part of the nationwide Swim Across America series | The series has raised over $20 million for cancer research |
| Bonaire EcoSwim | 1, 3, 5, and 10K (0.6, 1.9, 3.1, and 6.2 mi) swims in Bonaire in the Dutch Antilles | Races include a 2K two-person relay and a children's pier-to-pier swim for a family-fun event | Swimmers compete in crystal-clear water in pristine coral reefs |
| Cadiz Freedom Swim | 7.5K (4.7 mi) bitterly cold race from Robben Island to Cape Town in South Africa | Swimmers compete in pro, non-wetsuit, wetsuit, two- to four-person, corporate, or school relay races in 55 °F (12.8 °C) water | Robben Island, a World Heritage Site, was a prison for nearly 400 years |
| St. Croix Coral Reef Swim Race | 2- and 5-mile (3.2 and 8K) swims in St. Croix in the U.S. Virgin Islands | Swims held within a large coral reef park with endangered fish, starfish, and sea turtles | Described as having the most pristine water in the world |

*(continued)*

46

| Middle-distance swim | Course | Description | Features |
| --- | --- | --- | --- |
| Acapulco International Swim | 5K (3.1 mi) swim across Acapulco Bay in Mexico | A well-marked straightaway course along the hotel-lined shoreline in warm waters | January race date is a relief for swimmers from cold climates |
| Pennock Island Challenge | 8.2-mile (13K) swim around Pennock Island in Alaska | Circumnavigation around a rugged island that attracts cold water specialists | Race has solo, relay, wetsuit, and non-wetsuit divisions |
| Rottnest Channel Swim | 11.9-mile (19.2K) swim starting on Australia's west coast | Extremely popular race in 69-72 °F (20.6-22.2 °C) rough ocean from mainland Australia to Rottnest Island | 750 support boats escort swimmers amid strong currents |
| Maui Channel Swim | 9.6-mile (15K) six-person relay or solo swim from Lanai to Maui in Hawaii | Swimmers start on Lanai and swim toward the towering volcanoes of Maui with Molokai and Oahu visible on a clear day | Swimmers face winds, swells, marine life, and currents in cobalt-blue water |
| Boston Light Swim | 8-mile (12.9K) swim from Little Brewster Island to Boston | Strong winds up to 45 mph (72.4 km/h), cold 60 °F (15.6 °C) water and 3- to 4-foot (0.9 to 1.2 m) waves are possible | Called the Granddaddy of American Marathons |
| Swim Around Key West | 12.5 miles (20K) around the southernmost city in the continental USA | A circumnavigation around a low-lying island that can change with the shifting winds | Clear and very warm 85 °F (29.4 °C) shallow water in southern Florida |
| Distance Swim Challenge | 12.6 miles (20.3K) along Southern California coast | Course runs parallel to the coastline with seven checkpoints along the course | Cool water temperatures with potential large surf |
| Clean Half Open Water Swim | 9-mile (15K) solo swim and relay around Hong Kong | Warm water course where swimmers can face large swells, rough seas, and strong currents | Swimmers can enter a carbon-neutral relay in an outrigger canoe |

**Table 3.3** Marathon Swims (over 25K, or 15.5 mi)

| Marathon swim | Course | Description | Features |
|---|---|---|---|
| Manhattan Island Marathon Swim | 28.5-mile (46K) swim around Manhattan Island in New York | Field is limited to qualified and experienced solo swimmers and relay teams | Quickly reaches its maximum number of swimmers |
| Highlands Lake Challenge | Five-day 16-mile (25.7K) staged race across five lakes near Austin, Texas | 4.2 miles (6.8K) in Lake Buchanan + 2.6 miles (4K) in Inks Lake + 2.6 miles (4K) in Lake LBJ + 3 miles (4.8K) in Lake Marble Falls + 3.6 miles (5.8K) in Lake Travis | Swimmers can enter five-day staged race or individual races on each day |
| Tampa Bay Marathon Swim | 24 grueling miles (38.6K) in Tampa Bay on the west coast of Florida | Solo and relay swimmers face tides, surface chop, and currents in a large estuary | Celebrates Earth Day and the revitalization of Florida's estuary |
| St. Vincent Medical Center's Swim Across the Sound | 25K (15.5 mi) solo and relay race from New York to Connecticut | Solo and relay swimmers come from many states and several countries | Annually raises $350,000 for cancer prevention programs |
| Maratón Acuático Rio Coronda | 57K (35.4 mi) professional race downstream in Argentina | Field is limited to competitive swimmers who navigate currents and eddies for over 9 hours | Part of the FINA Open Water Swimming Grand Prix circuit |
| Maratona del Golfo Capri-Napoli | 22-mile (36K) sea race from Capri Island to Napoli in Italy | Swimmers are at the mercy of the elements including large swells and heavy surface chop | Swimmers have visited Napoli for this race since 1954 |
| Traversée internationale du lac St-Jean | 19.9-mile (32K) cold water race across Lac St-Jean in Canada | Multiple races (1K, 2K, 5K, 10K, and 32K) held for both amateur and professional swimmers | Town explodes in size during weeklong event; has been held since 1955 |
| Kalamata-Koroni Long Distance Swim | 30K (18.6 mi) across the Messiniakos Gulf in Greece | Calm, protected, clean waterway of 16.5 nautical miles | International field of swimmers of all abilities and ages |
| International Self-Transcendence Marathon Swim | 26.4K (16.4 mi) in cool Lake Zürich in Switzerland | Swimmers can experience significant surface chop in a beautiful setting | Field quickly reaches its maximum number |

Traversée international du lac St-Jean

Swimmers round the turn buoy at the Traversée internationale du lac St-Jean.

# OCEAN'S SEVEN

The Seven Summits are the highest mountains in each of the seven continents. As of 2010, 275 climbers have achieved this mountaineering challenge. Open water swimming's version of the Seven Summits is the Ocean's Seven:

1. North (Irish) Channel between Ireland and Scotland
2. Cook Strait between the North and South Islands of New Zealand
3. Molokai Channel between Oahu and Molokai Islands in Hawaii
4. English Channel between England and France
5. Catalina Channel in Southern California
6. Tsugaru Channel between the islands of Honshu and Hokkaido in Japan
7. Strait of Gibraltar between Europe and Africa

No human has yet completed the Ocean's Seven—but dozens of marathon swimmers are planning, plotting, and training their way to history.

Achieving the Ocean's Seven requires an ability to swim in both very cold and very warm seas. It demands that the swimmer be physically and mentally prepared to overcome every condition known to defeat open water swimmers, from strong currents to stiff winds, in seven completely different parts of the world—each with its own challenges and requirements. Like its mountaineering cousin, the Ocean's Seven requires a tremendous amount of planning, time, and financial resources, as well as a multinational support team of knowledgeable local experts.

1. North (Irish) Channel
   - Location: Channel between Ireland and Scotland.
   - Reasons for difficulty: Heavy seas, cold water, thunderstorms, and strong currents are among the natural elements that must be overcome in the 21-mile (33.8K) channel.
   - Window of opportunity: July through September.
   - Hazards: Considered to be the most difficult channel swim in the world with a water temperature of 54 °F (12.2 °C), normally overcast days, and tremendous difficulty in accurately predicting weather and water conditions. Swimmers face large pods of jellyfish if conditions are calm.
   - Description: Has been attempted at least 73 times since 1924, but only 15 successful solo swims have been achieved by 11 swimmers to date. Most of the attempts have been abandoned as a result of difficult conditions and hypothermia.
   - Additional information: Swim crossings are governed by the rules set by the Irish Long Distance Swimming Association. The first attempt was made in 1924, and the first success was in 1947.

2. Cook Strait
   - Location: Channel between the North and South Islands of New Zealand.
   - Reasons for difficulty: 16 nautical miles (25.7K) across immense tidal flows in icy water conditions among jellyfish and sharks; for only the most capable and adventurous swimmers.
   - Window of opportunity: November through May.
   - Hazards: One in six swimmers encounter sharks on their crossings. Sharks come around only to be nosey. No one has ever been attacked during a swim. Both sides of the strait have rock cliffs. Water is cold (57-66 °F, or 13.9-18.9 °C), distance is over 26K (16 mi), and surface chop is heavy.
   - Additional information: To date, only 77 successful crossings have been made by 64 people from eight countries. Hypothermia and changes in weather conditions during the swim are the most common reasons attempts fail.

3. Molokai Channel (or the Kaiwi Channel)

- Location: Channel between the western coast of Molokai Island and the eastern coast of Oahu in Hawaii.
- Reasons for difficulty: 26 miles (41.8K) across a deep-water (701 m) channel with extraordinarily strong currents in the middle of the Pacific Ocean; aggressive marine life.
- Window of opportunity: As conditions permit.
- Hazards: Extremely large rolling swells, strong winds, tropical heat, and very warm salty water offset the incredibly beautiful views of the Hawaiian Islands and deep-blue underwater scenery.
- Additional information: This deep-water channel with beautiful views of the Hawaiian Islands was first crossed in 1961 by Keo Nakama in 15 hours and 30 minutes and has been crossed 15 times by only 13 people to date.

4. English Channel

- Location: Channel between England and France with the narrowest point being in the Strait of Dover between Shakespeare Beach, Dover, England, and Calais, France.
- Reasons for difficulty: An international waterway of 21 miles (33.8K) at its narrowest point, cold water temperatures, strong currents, and ever-shifting water and weather conditions.
- Window of opportunity: June to September.
- Hazards: Failures due to strong currents and tidal flows, strong winds, and whitecaps caused by changing conditions and hypothermia.
- Additional information: 1,189 individuals have conquered the world's most famous channel with 1,648 crossings. Considered to be the standard for channel crossing with the rules and traditions significantly influencing the worldwide open water swimming community.

5. Catalina Channel

- Location: Channel between Santa Catalina Island and Los Angeles, California, USA.
- Reasons for difficulty: Cold water (especially near the coast), strong currents, potential for strong winds, marine life, and distance. Shortest point-to-point course is 21 miles (33.8K) from Emerald Bay on Santa Catalina Island to the San Pedro Peninsula.
- Window of opportunity: June to September.
- Hazards: A deep-water channel that is comparable to the English Channel in terms of water conditions, difficulty, distance, and physical and mental challenges. Marine life seen on occasion includes migrating whales, sharks, and large pods of dolphins.

- Additional information: Since the first successful swim in 1927 when Canadian George Young won $25,000 in the Wrigley Ocean Marathon Swim in 15 hours and 44 minutes, 199 people have crossed the channel.

6. Tsugaru Channel
   - Location: Deep-water channel between Honshu, the main island of Japan where Tokyo is located, and Hokkaido, the northernmost island of Japan.
   - Reasons for difficulty: An international waterway, 12 miles (19.3K) at its narrowest point. Swimmers must cross an extremely strong current between the Sea of Japan and the Pacific Ocean and will encounter large swells and abundant marine life. English and other Western languages are not spoken in the area. The water can be between 62 and 66 °F (16.7 and 18.9 °C).
   - Window of opportunity: July and August.
   - Hazards: Swimmers are swept long distances as a result of the extraordinarily strong currents flowing from the Sea of Japan to the Pacific Ocean. Swimmers face large blooms of squid during the night. Swimmers are challenged by occasional patches of cold water that flow up from the depths and are caused by the screws of the large oil tankers from the Middle East traveling to the West Coast of the United States. Only four confirmed solo crossings, two confirmed double crossings, and one confirmed triple crossing have been achieved to date.

7. Strait of Gibraltar
   - Location: Strait between Spain and Morocco that connects the Atlantic Ocean to the Mediterranean Sea. Shortest point is between Punta Oliveros in Spain and Punta Cires in Morocco.
   - Reasons for difficulty: 8.9 miles (14.32K) across an eastern flow of water from the Atlantic Ocean to the Mediterranean Sea with an average current of 3 knots (5.6 km/h). Heavy boat traffic, logistical barriers, and surface chop confront swimmers throughout the crossing.
   - Window of opportunity: June to October.
   - Hazards: The boundaries of the Strait of Gibraltar were known in antiquity as the Pillars of Hercules, and the currents have his strength. Because of the unpredictability of the water conditions and high winds, only 297 people have succeeded in crossing.
   - Additional information: Most attempts are made from Tarifa Island because of the influence of strong currents; this is a distance of 11.5 to 13.7 miles (18.5 to 22K).

The world is so vast and the waterways are so numerous that every possible open water swimming goal can be fulfilled, from short ice swims to long channel swims. The number of opportunities to do all kinds of open water swims of various lengths and degrees of difficulties is nearly endless. You can swim just for fun, in competition, to set a record, or to make history. The choice is yours. Enjoy the experience.

Steven Munatones

# THE OPEN WATER TOOL KIT

As swimmers prepare themselves on the shoreline to face the rigors of open water swimming, they truly stand exposed to the elements. Confident in their own skin, they do not need much equipment or many tools. At its very core, open water swimming is a primordial contest in which athletes are stripped nearly bare and asked to test themselves against Mother Nature.

Before, during, and after these events, some athletes use a wide variety of relatively simple and inexpensive tools and equipment. Others keep it simple and stick to just a swimsuit and goggles. The gear listed in this chapter is separated into four categories: gear used in the pool, in open water training, during races, and in marathon swims.

If you did every type of swim from short lake swims to solo channel swims and wanted to stock up on everything, your equipment list may include the products and services included in table 4.1 on page 56. The importance of each piece of equipment is for you to decide. Keep in mind, too, that new equipment is always being developed by and for the open water community.

## EQUIPMENT FOR POOL TRAINING

The primary purposes of the equipment and tools used in the pool are to improve your speed, swimming technique, and strength with each having a specific use and purpose.

**Table 4.1**  Types of Swim Equipment

| Pool training | Open water training | Racing | Marathon swims |
|---|---|---|---|
| Fins | Air horn or whistle | Cup and water bottle | Cameras |
| Goggles | Binoculars | Feeding stick | Escort boat |
| Pull buoy | Earplugs | Gel packs | Flashlights |
| Hand paddles | GPS unit | Rubbing alcohol | Fluids and food |
| Kickboard | Kayak | Correction fluid | Illumination |
| Pace clock | Paddle board | Waterproof bag | Inoculations |
| Snorkel | Lanolin and skin lubricants | Wetsuit | Shoe holder |
| Sunscreen | Petroleum jelly | Swimwear | Marine chart |
| Swim cap | Rubber gloves | Transponders | Medicines |
| Turn buoys | Small towel | Safety device | Mobile phone |
| Video camera | Online surf forecasts | Safety vest | Mouthwash |
| Stroke analysis | Vinegar | Waterproof tape | Mylar blanket |
| Training log | Water thermometer | Scissors | Whiteboard and markers |

# FINS

Fins are especially useful for improving your kicking strength, speed, and ankle flexibility as well as the position of your legs and body. Fins can be used by themselves, with snorkels, or with kickboards, depending on the set. Although fins are rarely allowed in a race, they benefit your training by increasing your kicking strength.

Fins are available in many sizes, shapes, materials, and fastenings. Borrow different pairs of fins from your teammates before deciding on the model that best suits you.

One of the benefits of fins is to help correct a crossover kick. When you use fins, kick fast to work on your aerobic conditioning and concentrate on your leg and lower body positions to improve your kicking mechanics and leg strength.

If you are new to wearing fins, try ones made of softer materials; these are less stressful than more rigid fins. Stiffer fins place more stress on your ankles and joints. Similarly, fins with shorter blades place less pressure on your joints and muscles than fins with longer blades and enable you to maintain a kick closer to your normal freestyle kick. The longer the fin blades are, the slower and more powerful each leg kick is. Longer fins can improve ankle flexibility and correct a crossover kicking action, both of which will result in greater kicking efficiency.

# Goggles

Goggles are among your most important pieces of equipment. Goggles range in size (child or adult), shape (of lens and eye socket), field of view (wide or narrow), color (clear, tinted, or metalized), type (hypoallergenic, prescription, optical, anti-fog, and UV protected), and adjustment fittings. A comfortable, non-fogging, good-fitting pair of goggles makes your swim a much more enjoyable experience. If your eyesight is not good, a pair of prescription or optical goggles will greatly enhance your enjoyment and navigational abilities, especially if you are swimming in a particularly scenic location or you are nearsighted and must navigate from objects in the distance.

Some open water swimmers enjoy larger goggles with wide lenses that provide a wider field of vision. These goggles also cover a larger area of your face, an important benefit if the water is cold.

Experiment with several models before you decide on the best pair of goggles for you. Borrow goggles from friends to learn how other models fit. When you test a pair of goggles, wear them over your eyes for at least an hour. When testing in a pool, do not move the goggles from your eyes to your forehead during breaks because goggles that might feel comfortable in the first few minutes might not be as water-tight after an hour.

When you find a pair of goggles that you like, buy several pairs of that model. The sizes, shapes, and color of goggles change because manufacturers occasionally discontinue models and launch new models without warning. You always want to have your favorite pair of goggles ready even if your preferred model is no longer commercially available.

Also, purchase clear or lightly tinted goggles as well as dark or metallic-tinted goggles of the same model, if available. Clear goggles are good to wear during the early morning or evening hours, or when visibility is low (e.g., when it is foggy or raining). Darker or tinted goggles are well suited to bright, sunny days or when you are swimming into the sun.

If your goggles get foggy, use commercial defogging products or baby shampoo to clean them. Wash your goggles in fresh water after every pool and open water training session. Keep them in their protective case between workouts. Commercial products such as Foggle also help to reduce the residue and fog in your goggles. One trick is to keep the Foggle wet wipe in a zip-lock bag for multiple uses.

# Pull Buoy and Hand Paddles

A pull buoy is a foam flotation device that comes in various shapes. The pull buoy is placed between your upper thighs to immobilize your legs and eliminate your kick while it naturally elevates your legs and body position.

Pull buoys are an excellent training device to develop upper-body strength that give you the opportunity to focus on your arm strokes and bilateral breathing. When using a pull buoy, focus on your proper head position, breathing rhythm, and hand pathways. You can use elastic bands around your ankles to keep your feet from splitting and legs from kicking.

You can also use pull buoys with hand paddles. Hand paddles come in numerous shapes and sizes, each with its own benefits. The primary purposes of hand paddles are to build strength from your arm through the shoulder and chest down to your core and to help you achieve correct stroke pathways (i.e., pulling straight back, not in an S-shape pattern).

Paddles increase your speed as well as help make some stroke flaws more obvious. If your hand improperly enters the water, your stroke will be interrupted. If you do not follow through properly, your hand paddle can come off.

Large hand paddles result in a reduced stroke tempo for many swimmers. If you know that one arm is weaker than the other, use a smaller paddle on the hand of the weaker arm, or do not use a hand paddle on your stronger hand to equalize the strength in both arms.

Pulling is easier than regular swimming, so do not become overly dependent on pulling with buoys and hand paddles. You can lose your feel for the water, it is less taxing aerobically if you do not go fast, and too much pulling can lead to shoulder problems. On the other hand, if you race with a wetsuit, use a pull buoy to gain more buoyancy, which is what you experience with a wetsuit.

## KICKBOARD

A kickboard allows you to focus on your legs. Although kicking tends to have the lowest priority for triathletes, do not overlook kicking if you are a competitive open water swimmer.

Although there is a tendency to relax or talk with teammates when using a kickboard, kick hard enough to elevate your heart rate to nearly its maximum. Avoid crossing over your centerline with your feet (crossover kick), and focus on kicking your entire leg straight up and down with only slightly bent knees and pointed feet, instead of simply bending your legs at your knees.

Kicking without a kickboard is also beneficial. Freestyle kicking in the vertical position for 30 seconds or more with your hands out of the water or arms straight above your head in a streamlined position is a more physically demanding exercise than traditional kicking with a kickboard. Butterfly kicking in the vertical position helps to build abdominal strength, which is very helpful, especially if you swim long distances.

## PACE CLOCK

Every competitive swim club has an analog or digital pace clock on the pool deck visible from the water. The pace clock (see figure 4.1) allows you to do interval training so you can keep track of your times and pace. With a pace clock, you can separate your workout into sets and repeats. A set is a group of swims or repeats with a specific purpose (e.g., ten 200-yard swims at an interval of three minutes or, in swimming vernacular, 10 × 200 at 3:00). A repeat is an individual swim within a particular set. The pace clock is used for the following reasons:

- To time the individual repeats in any given set
- To tell you when to start on your next repeat within the set
- To separate the individual swimmers in your lane (usually starting 5 to 10 seconds apart)

Swimmers use a special lingo that is based on the pace clock. During the beginning of a set, the coach may say, "Go on the top" or "Go on the 60." Both

**Figure 4.1** Digital and analog pace clocks used at the pool.

of these phrases mean that the first swimmer in the lane will start when the pace clock's second hand reaches 60. "Go on the bottom" means start when the second hand hits 30. When the coach says, "Go five seconds apart," the second swimmer will leave five seconds after the first swimmer. Other swimmers in the lane will then subsequently start five seconds apart with everyone swimming in a circular pattern. When there are several swimmers in a lane, swimmers swim on the right side of the lane's centerline at all times. Swimming in a circular pattern allows more swimmers to efficiently and safely use a single lane in a pool.

If you start first, simply read your time as you would with a stopwatch or clock. If you start a 100-yard swim on the 60 and finish at the 15, your time is 1 minute and 15 seconds. If you start at the 30 and finish at the 50, your time is 1 minute 20 seconds (or 1:20). If you are the second, third, or fourth swimmer in the lane, calculate your time based on the time you started.

The pace clock is also used when you do best average sets, descend sets, lactate tolerance sets, and threshold endurance sets. On a large team with swimmers of various speeds, swimmers are generally segregated by lanes according to their ability to maintain a certain pace (i.e., faster swimmers can maintain a pace at 1:10 minutes per 100 yards and slower swimmers swim at a pace of 2:00 minutes per 100 yards).

| | |
|---|---|
| Best Average Sets | Try to maintain your fastest average time per swim within the set. |
| Descend Sets | Start off slowly and swim increasingly faster until the last swim is the fastest repeat of the set. |
| Lactate Tolerance Sets | Swim at 90-95% of your maximum heart rate with three to five minutes' rest between the repeats within the set. |
| Threshhold Endurance Sets | Swim at 80-85% of your maximum heart rate with minimal rest (10-30 seconds) between the swims. |

## SWIMMER'S SNORKEL

A swimmer's snorkel is a great tool to use. It can be used with a pull buoy and paddles. When using a snorkel, look straight down to the bottom of the pool and focus on a straight-arm stroke path from the time your hand enters the water to the time it exits the water past your hip. A snorkel enables you to concentrate on body balance, body rotation, head position, and arm stroke technique.

## SUNSCREEN

Open water swimmers are exposed to the elements, especially to the harmful ultraviolet rays of the sun. When outside, wear the longest-lasting, highest SPF (sun protection factor) sunscreen you are comfortable with. For the best protection, use sunscreen with zinc oxide, which provides the most complete sunblock available. When a sunscreen is defined as water-resistant, it has been tested to remain effective for at least 40 minutes in the water.

Apply your sunscreen to every exposed area on your body, even to areas that are covered by your swimsuit. Because swimsuits can ride higher on the hip or move around your shoulders during a swim, the skin near the edges of your swimsuit are often exposed while swimming. When a sunscreen is defined as very water-resistant, it has been tested to remain effective for at least 80 minutes in the water.

It is best to apply sunscreen before you leave home and then reapply it right before you start to swim. In the water, some marathon swimmers reapply sunscreen during their swim by using a spray bottle or a small plastic sandwich bag. They place the sunscreen inside the sandwich bag and then turn it inside out, using the dry side of the bag as a sort of makeshift applicator. They can then wipe the sunscreen on their skin without getting anything on their hand.

## SWIM CAPS

Swim caps come in a variety of materials including silicone, latex, Lycra, and neoprene. Because upwards of 30 percent of your body heat is lost through your head, use neoprene caps, bubble caps, or insulated swim caps during cold water swims to retain body heat. Caps with chin straps and that cover the ears are helpful when swimming in cold water, although the straps add another area of potential chafing. Silicone caps offer slightly more insulation than latex caps, which are the thinnest types.

Some races permit the use of two swim caps, but some races do not allow neoprene caps. Confirm you know the race rules regarding swim caps. If you are worried about your goggles being knocked off in a crowded field, place your goggle straps over one swim cap, but underneath a second cap. Alternatively, if two swim caps feel too tight on your head, place waterproof tape over your goggle straps to better adhere your goggles to your swim cap (see figure 4.2). If you have long hair or your swim cap tends to come off in open water races, do not wash your hair or use conditioner in the days leading up to your race.

Dr. Jim Miller

**Figure 4.2** Taping over goggle straps helps avoid losing them in a race.

Some races and many triathlons require participants to wear race caps. If the cap that is provided on race day is hard to keep on, use hair pins to help hold it in place. Generally, the thicker the cap is, the longer it will last in chlorinated pools. Just as with your goggles and swimsuit, make sure to practice with the same cap you will use on race day and have more than one comfortable fitting swim cap ready to go.

## REGULATIONS ON SWIMWEAR

The traditional channel swimming organizations have strict rules on swimwear and swim caps. For example, the Channel Swimming & Piloting Federation states:

> *No person in a Standard attempt to swim the [English] Channel shall use or be assisted by an artificial aid of any kind, but is permitted to grease the body before a swim, use goggles, wear one cap and one costume. The word "costume and cap" shall mean a garment, not made of neoprene or rubber or any other material considered by the Federation to give a similar type of advantage, and not in any way designed to contain body heat, and aid buoyancy (http://www .channelswimming.net).*

## TURN BUOYS

Turn buoys—even small ones—are an integral part of any seriously competitive open water swimmer's tool kit. Whenever possible (especially during the winter months when there are fewer open water races and most training is done in pools), use turn buoys in the pool for pool open water (POW) workouts. POW workouts keep you sharp in the off-season. Once the water gets warm enough to do open water training, take your turn buoys to your ocean or lake workouts and practice turns, navigation, and sighting.

# EQUIPMENT FOR OPEN WATER TRAINING

The tools used in the open water are just as important as the tools used in swimming pools. However, tools related to safety are particularly important in the open water. These tools range from whistles to boats.

## AIR HORN OR WHISTLE

There is always a possibility of injury, accident, or emergency in the open water, regardless of your level of experience and ability. Not only do you face the natural elements, but windsurfers, Jet Skiers, and fishermen do not always expect or look out for swimmers.

Take a whistle or air horn with you to open water practices. If a coach, friend, or family member is with you, either in a kayak or watching from the shoreline, you can alert that person of an emergency with a whistle or air horn—whether it is you or someone else who is having problems. Quick blasts of an air horn or loud whistles will help get attention when help is needed.

If you are escorted by a kayaker or paddler, that person can use a whistle to alert you to partially submerged flotsam or batches of seaweed that you do not see. Whistles are also good to get your attention if you are doing a marathon swim at night or if you need to stop for a scheduled feeding break.

## BINOCULARS

Binoculars are indispensible for viewing the course before a practice or a race. Your coach, teammates, or family can use the binoculars to watch you while you are in the water. If you swim far from shore or alone, binoculars are truly an essential piece of equipment for your coach and support team.

## EARPLUGS

Tightly sealed earplugs decrease the exposure of your middle and inner ear to cold water and lessen the dizziness and discomfort that can accompany exposure to cold water if you are not acclimated.

Earplugs, either the moldable silicone type or the premolded rubber type that comes in various sizes, also protect the inner ear from water that can occasionally lead to problems such as swimmer's ear. Swimmer's ear, also called acute external otitis or otitis externa, is a painful infection of the ear canal usually caused by bacteria in the thin layer of skin lining the ear canal. It is easily treated, and prompt treatment can help prevent more serious complications and infections.

In addition to earplugs, commercial ear drops or a few drops of isopropyl alcohol placed in your ear with a medicine dropper after each workout will help dry out your ears and prevent bacteria from growing.

## GLOBAL POSITIONING SYSTEM (GPS) UNIT

Open water swimmers use the same GPS devices (see figure 4.3) and technologies that generate a plethora of information for cyclists, runners, boaters, and race drivers. GPS enables you to review your open water workouts and calculate your pace and navigational lines in the open water. Experiment with a GPS unit and document your training sessions, including analyzing various parameters of your open water swims.

Following is a common set of tools use by marathon swimmers:

- Garmin Forerunner 305
- Computer
- Specialty software (Ascent or GPS TrackMaker)
- Swim cap
- Waterproof bag

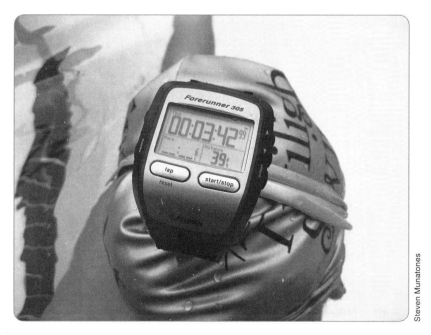

**Figure 4.3** GPS units can be worn on your head, under or over a swim cap.

Many GPS devices and software programs are available, but the Garmin Forerunner 305 can provide data and a visual map showing exactly where you swim, your split times, your average pace in minutes per mile or kilometer, and your average speed in miles or kilometers per hour. To use this device, follow these steps:

1. Remove the wrist strap of the Garmin unit.
2. Place the strapless unit in a waterproof bag.
3. Put the waterproof bag under your swim cap, on the back of your head.
4. Face the Garmin unit skyward for optimal satellite reception.
5. After you enter the water, switch the unit on and swim as you normally do.
6. After you get out of the water, turn off the unit.
7. Download the information to your computer and analyze your workout and navigational course with your swim buddies and coach.
8. Compare your pace in certain time intervals (e.g., first hour versus last hour), the distance you covered, and the route you actually swam.
9. If you train regularly in the same location, compare the course and swimming speed data.

## KAYAK AND PADDLE BOARD

Rent, borrow, or purchase a kayak or paddle board if you train frequently for long distances in the open water. Ask your coach, friends, or family members who are comfortable on the water to escort you during your training swims. Your escort can carry drinks, food, and other equipment (e.g., extra goggles, a swim cap, earplugs, a whistle, mobile phone, camera or GPS unit) in the kayak or on the paddle board.

An experienced escort can be a great help in providing course direction, feedings, and vocal support during your swim, especially if the person also knows the local waters well. Remind your escort to be ready for a range of weather and water conditions and to stay in reasonable physical shape to be able to assist if problems occur. You can focus on swimming while you place your trust in your escort's judgment and visual perspective.

Ask your escort to be positioned along the side on which you predominantly breathe. He should paddle parallel to you so you can easily see him when you breathe. If you have to lift your head up and around to locate your escort, then he is not in the optimal position. If you position yourself at mid-kayak, then you will always remain in eye contact with your escort. Eye contact with your escort is very helpful and comforting in a sport where your visual perspectives are extremely limited.

## LANOLIN AND SKIN LUBRICANTS

Many marathon swimmers use lanolin, either in anhydrous (without water) or hydrous (with water) form as an alternative to petroleum jelly. Some swimmers prefer to use a mix of lanolin and petroleum jelly, sometimes referred to as channel grease. Because opinions and preferences vary widely, determine what is best for you based on the amount of body hair you have, your tolerance of cold water and the amount of chafing that usually occurs.

Lanolin is processed from the glands of sheep and is also called wool wax, wool fat, anhydrous wool fat, or wool grease. It is a thick, greasy, sticky substance that appears white on the skin and stays on much longer than petroleum jelly. You can purchase lanolin at medical supply stores and some pharmacies, although you may have to special order it.

Lanolin will not only minimize chafing, but will also lessen the immediate impact of cold water, helping alleviate some of the sting and shock of cold water. As many open water swimmers appreciate, anything—psychological or physical— that helps alleviate the impact of cold water is useful. Lanolin will not, however, decrease heat loss or prevent hypothermia over the long haul.

Firmly press the lanolin onto your skin with a flat, gloved hand or a small plastic sandwich bag, especially around your back (figure 4.4), neck (figure 4.5), under your arms, around your torso, and on your upper legs. Some swimmers put on a thick, uneven coat of lanolin and petroleum jelly; however, thick gobs come off in the open water and may inadvertently get on your hands or goggles.

**Figure 4.4**  Lanolin on the back.

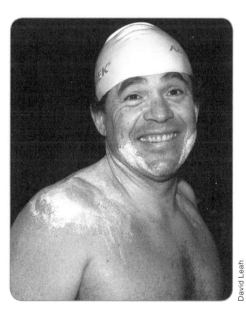

**Figure 4.5**  Lanolin around the neck.

Lanolin is more easily applied to your skin by first heating it to a viscous liquid before smearing it on your body. The downside to lanolin is that it is difficult to remove, even after being in the water over six hours. It is usually more difficult to apply on swimmers with lots of body hair than it is on swimmers with smoother skin and less hair.

After your swim, remove the lanolin by initially using Popsicle sticks or other flat items to scrape off the remaining gobs where the lanolin has coagulated on your skin. Wash off the remaining lanolin with a soap that includes ground pumice, or with baby oil.

Other antifriction skin lubricants include products such as TRISLIDE and BodyGlide. These lubricants are made from natural ingredients, are hypoallergenic, and are water resistant. Some are aerosol sprays (e.g., TRISLIDE), and others are gel balms (e.g., BodyGlide). These non-petroleum-based products are convenient to apply by yourself, are not greasy or oily, and are easy to wash off with soap and water. BodyGlide uses special waxes that adhere to skin cells and offers longer protection compared with petroleum jelly. TRISLIDE can be sprayed around your ankles and wrists to increase the ease and speed with which you remove your wetsuit in the swim–bike transition during triathlons.

Take care to avoid chafing when you swim for prolonged periods, especially in salt or polluted water. If chafing is severe and the water is less than pristine, treat the lacerations of your skin with antibacterial topical agents that have antistaph and antistrep properties.

## Petroleum Jelly

Use petroleum jelly to prevent chafing under your arms, around your neck or chin, between your thighs, and underneath your swimsuit straps. The chafing is a result of constant friction caused by your body parts rubbing together or by the repeated contact of your swimsuit against your skin.

Petroleum jelly comes off your skin relatively quickly in the open water, especially in salt water, but it effectively minimizes chafing at the various friction points on your body for short-distance swims. Lanolin can stay on longer for marathon swims.

## Rubber Gloves

If you put on petroleum jelly or lanolin by yourself, put on a pair of rubber gloves or use a plastic sandwich bag to prevent the ointments and lubricants from getting on your hands. A friend or coach who puts lubricants on you will especially appreciate the availability of rubber gloves to use. If the lubricants get on your hands, it may also get on your goggles, which will significantly impair your vision in the open water.

## Small Towel

If you do not have rubber gloves, carry a small terry cloth towel with you. If something gets on your hands or if you bump into another swimmer coated with skin lubricants or lanolin, you will appreciate the ability to wipe your hands clean. You can also use a throw-away or paper towel.

## Online Surf Reports

Real-time information, including data and images, is available online for thousands of beaches and lakes around the world. If you have Internet access, research the water and weather conditions of the water before you leave for the shoreline. Because the open water is a dynamic environment, this information—unavailable to previous generations of athletes—is especially helpful.

Online surf reports (www.swellwatch.com, www.surfline.com and www.magicseaweed.com are three great examples) provide historical, actual, and forecasted wind direction and speed, air and water temperature ranges, wave height, general water conditions, and time of sunrise and sunset. These information sources also offer webcams that broadcast real-time images of the water so you have an idea of what conditions to expect before you head out. Some of this information is also available via mobile alerts or text messages.

The National Oceanographic Data Center (NODC) provides real-time and monthly average water temperatures on its NODC Coastal Water Temperature Guide. The water temperature is taken from year-round stations that are moored in the water at coastal locations including the Hawaiian Islands, Pacific Islands, Great Lakes, Gulf of Mexico Coast, Atlantic Coast, and Pacific Coast. The National Oceanic and Atmospheric Administration's online resource also provides an RSS feed that allows you to receive updates on the water temperature. Other services around the world also provide similar information (in °C) in multiple languages depending on the country.

## Vinegar

A spray bottle with household white vinegar is useful when jellyfish are present. Jellyfish tentacles contain small nematocysts that release toxins upon contact. Regular white vinegar sprayed on the skin helps deactivate these nematocysts and the venom release, although the initial vinegar spray may irritate freshly stung skin.

Spraying on vinegar is more effective than rubbing the jellyfish tentacles off with your hands. If you do not have vinegar, wash your skin off with ocean water and remove the tentacles with a towel if that is all you have.

If you are stung by anything in the open water and, as a result, experience shortness of breath, vomiting, an allergic reaction, or other signs of shock, ask someone to immediately take you to a doctor.

Meat tenderizer and other local remedies are occasionally used, but vinegar is the gold standard for relief recommended by medical and scientific communities worldwide. Commercial products, such as StingMate Neutralizing Spray, are useful and conveniently packaged in spray bottles. StingMate, a vinegar gel with menthol, helps suspend the stinging cells left on your body. The cells can then be scraped off and the gel reapplied, then rinsed off for a very effective treatment.

## WATER THERMOMETER

An inexpensive water thermometer can help you precisely learn the water temperatures and weather conditions in which you swim best and those that are outside your comfort zone. Alternatively, a waterproof watch with a built-in thermometer can also help you compare water temperatures from day to day and location to location. Over time, as you repeatedly record and experience different water temperature ranges, you will be able to accurately estimate within 1 or 2 degrees (Fahrenheit or Celsius) what the water temperature is by merely sticking your feet or hands in the water.

# EQUIPMENT FOR RACING

On race day, special types of equipment can help you compete faster and more safely. Some of these products are widely available at retail stores; others are custom-made products that are unique to the open water swimming world.

## CUPS AND WATER BOTTLES

For competitive races over 5K, there are generally opportunities for feedings. Use wide-mouthed water bottles or paper or plastic cups to quickly consume your feeds. A clothing pin can be used to clip a gel pack to the cup, or a simple rubber band can hold a gel pack, chocolate, energy bars, or whatever you desire to the cup.

## FEEDING STICK

Because you cannot be touched or aided by others during an open water swim, and you cannot hold on to a boat or kayak during a marathon swim, a feeding stick (also called a feeding pole) is an ideal tool. Most feeding sticks are home-made devices that enable your coach or your support crew to hand you a drink, bottle, or some kind of food or medicine from an escort boat, pier, pontoon, or feeding station while you are in the water (see figure 4.6).

A professionally designed feeding stick is an extendable pole (generally up to 12 feet, or 3.7 meters) with single or double cup holders and gel pack clips so you can easily grab what you need quickly and easily.

Ann Ford

**Figure 4.6** Taking fluids during an open water race.

## FEEDING FAST: TWO SECONDS OF PRESSURE

At the Olympics, world championships, World Cup, and other professional events, swimmers are assisted by coaches who only have a few critical seconds to hand the swimmer fluids during the race.

Unlike marathon runners, who have frequent water stops available along the race course and volunteers handing them cups of water on land, marathon swimmers in competitive races have only a handful of momentary opportunities to receive fluids during a race.

Unlike race car drivers, who know precisely where their pit crews are located, swimmers do not always know where their coaches are positioned at the feeding station. As swimmers battle for position coming into the feeding station, they expect the end of their feeding sticks to be slightly above the water's surface and facing at an optimal angle, so they can quickly grab their own cup without breaking their stroke rhythm.

Despite the coach's best efforts and years of experience, swimmers sometimes grab or inadvertently hit other swimmers' feeding sticks and the coaches spill the contents. If a pack of swimmers race shoulder to shoulder and come into the feeding station together, even the longest feeding stick cannot reach the swimmer who is positioned on the outside.

So the pressure is on . . . the coach.

On the other hand, some coaches simply tie string or rope to a water bottle and toss it to the swimmer in the water. Many swimmers prefer this. Others prefer feeding sticks, which are useful when the conditions are rough and getting close to a boat is risky.

Swimmers pass their coaches on a floating station and have only a few brief moments to grab their cups. The swimmer and coach duo must be synchronized to time their feeding right, with very little room for error. If there is a missed hand-off, the swimmer's chances of victory drop. If the coach–swimmer teamwork is successful, the swimmer reaches up for the cup, rolls over back, gulps the drink and resumes swimming within five seconds.

## GEL PACKS

Gel packs are small, easy-to-use, individual squeeze packages that contain simple and complex carbohydrates, electrolytes, antioxidants, and amino acids to provide an energy boost during a swim. You should consider taking at least one gel pack if you swim over 45 minutes, even for triathletes who are doing a 2.4-mile (3.9K) swim leg. There is no need for triathletes to get dehydrated before they have to head off on their bike leg. You can stick one or two single-serving pouches somewhere in your swimsuit or wetsuit. The pouches are usually available at sporting goods stores and come in a variety of flavors. The compact packages contain a semi-liquid gel that is fast acting, easy to digest, and scientifically formulated. The gels should ideally be taken with water, but this may not be possible in a competitive situation.

Numerous commercial brands of gel packs are available. Experiment to find which are best for you. Gel packs provide the fuel you need, but they can be difficult to open in the water, especially if you are cold or have very little time to open them because of the competitive situation. Before your race, cut a very slight hole near the package opening. Use scissors so the cut is sharp. This pre-race preparation enables you to easily open the gel pack during races instead of having to tear them open with your hands or teeth in the water. Squeeze hard so your hand forces the contents of the gel pack into your mouth.

Competitive swimmers stick the prepared gel packs in their swimsuits before the race. Many experienced athletes take up to five gel packs with them to consume at their convenience during their race or training, especially if they will be swimming over two hours.

## RUBBING ALCOHOL AND CORRECTION FLUID

During the check-in period, your race number is written in black marker ink or large block stamps on the side of your shoulders, the back of your shoulders, or the back of your hand. Remind the race volunteer to write in very large, thick strokes because it makes it easier for the race officials, race announcer, your coach, family, and friends to spot you (via your number) during the race.

If you put sunscreen on before your race number is written on your skin, the black ink tends to run and become unreadable in the water. One way to prevent this is to clean the area where your race number will be written with rubbing alcohol.

If you want your race number to stand out, outline your number in correction fluid (Wite-Out). The white border makes the black ink more visible to others who are watching or judging the race.

If you want to make it easier for your coach, teammates, or friends to identify you in a race, apply lightly colored zinc oxide on one or both of your forearms so you visibly stand out in the crowd in the open water.

## TRANSPONDERS

Other than a swimsuit and swim cap, the only mandatory piece of equipment in some races is transponders worn on your wrists or ankles.

Each swimmer is given transponders for timing and placing purposes. Wrist transponders are the weight and size of a waterproof wristwatch. Ankle transponders attach with Velcro. You can be disqualified—or at least not officially recorded—if your transponders are lost during the race, so make sure they are on tight enough but not too tight to make you uncomfortable.

**Figure 4.7**   Transponders taped to both wrists so the straps do not flap in the water.

To keep your transponders snugly attached to both wrists, ask your coach to tape the straps with waterproof tape (see figure 4.7). Tape the wrist straps down to prevent them from flapping, which can cause unnecessary frustration during the race.

## SAFETY VEST

A neon-colored traffic safety vest helps your coach stand out at a crowded feeding station. Reflective vests are also helpful for your support crew to wear on kayaks or on your escort boat during night swims or marathon races. You can easily see your support crew from the water when they wear brightly colored neon traffic safety vests or place glow sticks on their clothing.

## WATERPROOF BAGS

Waterproof bags (or boxes) for your clothes and gear are always useful, especially on escort boat or kayaks during a marathon swim If the conditions are rough, rainy, or stormy, you do not want soggy clothes after you have finished swimming. In a short- or middle-distance race, bring a permanent marker to mark your bag with your race number. On race day, the best way to identify your bag is with your race number.

## WETSUIT

A large number of wetsuits are available, each with its own benefits and price point. Each brand has various models and styles that will result in a different feel as a result of the thickness, construction, and materials of the wetsuit; your swimming technique; and your body shape.

Specialty triathlon wetsuits, first developed in the 1980s, brought a buoyancy, warmth, and skin protection factor not available to previous generations of athletes. Not surprisingly, the total number of wetsuit-clad triathletes quickly grew and outnumbered the open water swimming traditionalists within a relatively short time period. When buying a wetsuit, focus on a proper overall fit. Look for a wetsuit that provides sufficient flexibility throughout your shoulders so your normal swimming stroke is not impaired. It should fit comfortably around your neck to keep cold water out, but not so tightly as to cause significant chafing. Because you will be aerobically taxed, you do not want your wetsuit to be too tight around your chest. An ideal wetsuit enables you to kick normally while providing the warmth and additional buoyancy necessary for performing well.

Once you have decided to wear a wetsuit for your open water swim, make sure to practice with it in the open water. If you do not have many opportunities to wear it before race day in the open water, wear it at your pool so you understand exactly where it chafes your skin. Put a sufficient amount of skin lubrication on areas where the wetsuit chafes. Because petroleum jelly is damaging to neoprene, commercially available skin lubricants are a good bet.

Before you purchase a wetsuit, do your research and try on several before making your final decision. Consider the thickness of the wetsuit, which can directly affect your arm stroke, and its cut, which will directly affect where it may produce friction against your skin.

Occasionally practice with your wetsuit during your pool workouts, especially sessions in which you will swim for longer periods. Also, if you will be swimming in very warm bodies of water where the heat is expected to be close to unbearable, use your wetsuit during pool training sessions as part of your warm water acclimatization process. In these workouts in which you are purposefully mimicking warm water conditions, make sure to hydrate frequently, and always monitor yourself carefully to avoid heat exhaustion.

# SWIMWEAR

All kinds of swimwear are used by open water swimmers, from board shorts and bikinis to sophisticated technical swimsuits and wetsuits of various thicknesses and materials. Competitors at open water swims use various types of swimwear depending on their goals and budgets.

At most open water competitions, the water is generally between 65 and 85 °F (18.3 and 29.4 °C). Depending on the regulations, males wear full-body swimsuits, jammers, legskin suits, or regular swimsuit briefs. Females generally wear legskin, kneeskin, or traditional racing suits.

If you know you may be exposed to jellyfish or other types of stinging creatures in your race, a technical swimsuit or wetsuit may be your best bet. If you are female, consider a swimsuit that rides high and tight up near your neck. For women, shoulder straps are a key design element to consider. During a 1-mile (1.6K) swim, the average swimmer takes a minimum of 1,800 arm strokes (i.e., 60 strokes per minute for 30 minutes); that amounts to 1,800 times for your swimsuit to chafe against your shoulders and back.

Advanced manufacturing processes, new fabrics, and well-placed compression panels have changed the type and functionality of traditional swimsuits. Different races allow different types of swimsuits. Comfort and safety should be your primary concerns when deciding what to wear during an open water swim.

Technical swimsuits provide buoyancy and skin protection against the sun and stinging creatures. These have drawn opposition from purists who remain true to their non-neoprene roots. The sport continues to navigate its way between the wishes of traditionalists and those of people who consider technological advances to be a part of any sport. As the debate rages on and regulations change, the introduction of neoprene has led to thousands of newcomers trying and enjoying the sport. Many of the world's races cater to the athletes' desires by offering wetsuit and non-wetsuit divisions, each with separate divisions and awards. The race directors are, wisely, doubling the fun—not halving the alternatives.

# SAFETY DEVICE

Convenient, lightweight, waterproof floats solve a number of problems, especially for those who are visiting an unfamiliar stretch of water or who are training alone. These brightly colored plastic bags tie to your waist and float on the water while creating minimal drag and serving as an emergency float in case of emergencies. The bag enables you to swim point-to-point with all your personal items (mobile phone, towel, shoes, money) dry and safe with you.

# WATERPROOF TAPE

All-around handy waterproof tape can hold goggles to your swim cap, food to your feeding bottle, repair feeding sticks or solve a variety of other problems at the shorelines and feeding station.

## Scissors

Scissors are another tool that may come in handy to cut a variety of items on race day including rope that may be used on a boat or feeding station or even to poke holes through cans of powdered drinks.

# EQUIPMENT FOR MARATHON SWIMS

Because of the length of time marathon swimmers are in the water and the various risks they face, they often use a variety of costly and specialized equipment that short-distance and middle-distance open water swimmers may never need or even know about.

## Cameras

Personal cameras (video and still) enable you and your escort crew to document your marathon swim. Ask your crew to take close-up photos of you before and after your marathon swims to show the psychological changes that occur over the duration of a marathon swim. Videos taken during various parts of the swim will help you understand how your stroke tempo changed—or didn't. You will always treasure images that capture the last few strokes of your swim and the first few steps onto the shore.

## Escort Boat

A seaworthy escort boat, a knowledgeable support crew, and an experienced pilot are essential for the success of any marathon swim. Because so many things can go wrong in marathon swims, experienced hands are truly worth the effort you may have to put out to find them and engage their services.

Get to know your pilot and support team. Make sure they clearly understand your goals and capabilities. Do not simply show up on the day of your marathon swim, bring your personal items on board, and then expect everything to go as you want. Expectations must be discussed and mutually understood.

Visit with your pilot and the support crew on their boat before your swim. Understand the facilities on the boat and how much room there is. Exchange key information with your pilot such as your preferred time intervals to feed and what side you primarily breathe on. Tell your pilot of your swimming experience and speed so you can plot, plan, and work together to achieve your goal. Show your feeding stick or feeding system to your pilot before swim day so you both can estimate how close you can get to the sides of the boat in both flat and rough water. Observe how high the sides of the boat are and what angle your feeding stick will be placed at. Discuss the lighting on the boat and the hanging of glow sticks from the sides of the boat with your pilot before the day of your marathon swim. Determine the details of your swim before you get in the water—not during your first feeding or during the first few hours of your swim.

## FLASHLIGHTS

Flashlights, with plenty of backup batteries, are always useful to take on marathon swims that start or finish at night, especially when starting or finishing on a rocky point. Flashlights provide light on the boat or onshore whenever necessary and can be used to signal the official start and finish of a marathon swim done at night.

## FLUIDS AND FOOD

A successful open water swimmer is a well-hydrated one (see figure 4.8). If you are swimming more than 45 minutes at a time, hydrate before, during, and after your training sessions to properly prepare for, perform in, and recover from your workouts. If you swim longer than one hour, take gel packs that contain carbohydrates and electrolytes.

If an average gulp is assumed to be about 1 fluid ounce (30 ml), take 2 cups (16 oz, or 473 ml) of fluid about two hours before your workout and one half of a cup (4 oz, or 118 ml) 15 minutes before. During the workout, drink about 6 to 12 ounces (177 to 355 ml) at least every 20 minutes.

You never know how calm or rough the water will be during a marathon swim. You may even experience the extremes: calm at the start and rough at the end, or vice versa. In rough seas, your crew may find smaller bottles and cups more convenient to handle than larger ones during feedings. Premix your drinks before you get in the water. If you need warm drinks during your swim, an experienced crew will be able to handle that.

**Figure 4.8**   Taking fluids during a marathon swim.

If you provide food for your support crew to eat during your swim, bring energy bars, fruit, or bread rather than foods they have to prepare. You are best served by being the focus of their undivided attention and unwavering eye contact throughout your swim.

The most important thing about fluids and food is for you to practice repeatedly. If you want energy bars, candy, water, carbohydrate drinks, gel packs, electrolyte drinks, banana slices, cookies, fig bars, peach slices, pieces of chocolate, or tea during your swims, then practice consuming these same fluids and foods during your training. Train yourself to take nutrition and fluids while performing at a high level—not just once, not just the week before, and not just the month before. Constantly and repeatedly integrate fluids and foods into your training sessions. If you are a newcomer, this will allow you to experiment with various formulations, tastes, and amounts so you know what is optimal. Some swimmers prefer only liquids, some prefer a mix of liquids and gels, and some prefer solids.

Although many English Channel swimmers use Maxim Energy Drink, other marathon swimmers prefer Cytomax, Gatorade, defizzed sodas, or their own homemade concoctions. Preferences are completely individual. Things taste differently in fresh water than they do in salt water. Drinks even taste slightly different the longer you stay in the water. If the water is cold, take liquids that are warmed to your preference. Conversely, if the water is warm, take liquids that are cooled or iced if that is what you practiced with. In very warm water conditions, consume a snow cone or drink an iced drink before a swim as long as you know it does not lead to stomach cramping.

Practice with whatever tools (e.g., feeding sticks, paper cups, water bottles, gel packs) you will use to receive fluids and food during a swim. Taking small sips of water from a water bottle between sets while resting on the wall or standing up in the pool is not the same as practicing in the open water.

## ILLUMINATION

Many marathon swimmers start or finish their swims in the evening hours. Swimming at night can be either an extremely fascinating activity or an entirely frightful situation depending on the circumstances and your outlook. In either case, various types of illumination can help you remain safe and calm at night.

Lamps, lights, glow sticks (see figure 4.9), strobe lights, and LED lights are all used by swimmers, kayakers, paddlers, and escort boats during open water swims at night for safety purposes. These types of illumination can be attached to the back of your swim cap, your goggles, or swimsuit straps with safety pins to make you more visible to your support crew on the escort boat.

Pencil-shaped glow sticks can be the single-use chemical type in translucent plastic that are often used during Halloween or at concerts, or narrow, battery-powered illumination. Multi-use compact flashing strobe lights or small half-dome-shaped disc lights are easily affixed to your swim cap, goggles, or swimsuit with safety pins or ties. Some swimmers and escort crews like the strobe setting, and others like the non-strobe setting. Glow sticks are approximately 6 inches (15.2 cm) long and can be purchased in bulk from hardware, outdoor, or marine products stores. Although various colors are available (pink, purple, or blue), green is recommended.

## INOCULATIONS

**Figure 4.9** Glow sticks (as indicated by the arrows) under a light-colored surfer's vest can be seen at night.

The world and its waterways are, unfortunately, becoming more polluted. If you swim in any area with a sizable population, rainfall can cause an immediate deterioration of the water quality. There are many ways to get sick or become injured: you can swallow polluted water, step on glass onshore, run into sharp rocks in the water, or get cut brushing against piers and floating debris.

Check with your physician to see whether the following inoculations are recommended: hepatitis A, typhoid (sometimes combined with hepatitis A), hepatitis B, yellow fever, tetanus, diphtheria and polio (combined), and gamma globulin. Each of these can be taken as a precautionary measure. If you must, get inoculations in different arms over time and well before your swim so any soreness or resultant illnesses will not be a factor in your training. If you travel internationally, these inoculations are also good preventive health measures and should always be updated.

## SHOE HOLDER

An inexpensive plastic shoe holder with multiple pockets is an excellent product to hang on your escort boat so your crew can organize and quickly grab anything you may need during your long marathon swim. You can store things such as gel packs, extra goggles, plastic bags of lanolin, aspirin, extra laminated instructions for feeding, and spray bottles of vinegar. The shoe holder should be hung somewhere convenient on the boat within easy reach of your coach and crew members and tied down so it will not swing during rough conditions.

## MARINE CHARTS

Marine charts (including nautical, coastal, and GPS marine charts) are maps of the water and its surrounding areas. British Admiralty, C-Map, Transas, and Maptech cover most of the earth. Charts by the National Oceanic and Atmospheric Administration and SoftChart covers American waters. Maptech's ChartPack covers most of Europe, the Mediterranean Sea, and all of the Caribbean Sea.

Marine charts provide information that you cannot gauge by simply viewing the course from shore. A chart tells you of the channels, water depths, and other marine information. Water depths help you understand and appreciate the flow of water during the tide cycle.

Marine chart information is significant for understanding a channel, ocean, or river swim. You can swim during an ebb tide or a flood tide. Knowing, for example, that water moves through the deepest channels can make an important difference in a race or solo swim.

Additionally, marine charts are great as a memento of your accomplishment especially if your entire support crew signs the chart.

## MEDICINES

Some marathon swimmers take aspirin, pain killers, and antihistamines (for jellyfish stings) when they swim. Carefully consider the benefits and downsides with your coach and your doctor.

Your escort boat will travel at your swimming speed, so every wave felt onboard is amplified. Seasickness does not affect everyone, but it may affect those who are on your escort boat.

Ask your escort crew whether they want to take seasickness pills or anti-motion sickness pills in advance. They may consider taking non-drowsy, anti-motion medicine or homeopathic seasickness tablets. Help your support team avoid seasickness during your marathon swim. You do not want crew members who are either vomiting or too ill to lend a supporting hand.

If you have adequately trained in the open water before your marathon swim, including doing some training swims in very rough water, seasickness medicine is generally unnecessary. However, if you are taken to your starting point in rough seas on a boat, then you may consider it.

## MOBILE PHONE

A mobile phone is always useful for your coach and support crew to have. They can send tweets on Twitter, updates to Facebook, blog entries, or text messages to those who are not on location. The information can be uploaded automatically to websites and blogs so your family and friends are informed of your progress during a long marathon swim.

Alternatively, various GPS services are available so others can keep track of your progress. Confirm with your escort pilot what services are available and how you can integrate these services for the benefit of people who are interested in the progress of your swim in real-time.

## Mouthwash

Use mouthwash to remove the salt taste from your mouth if you have been in the water a long time. Dilute your preferred mouthwash with water and practice in the open water with various solutions well in advance of your swim.

## Mylar Blanket

After a long swim, you may feel cold and re-warming quickly is important. A Mylar blanket (also called a space blanket or aluminized blanket) is useful and comes in handy in emergencies and before you are ready to put on your clothes. Also, bring a warm hat and remember that your body may still have gobs of lanolin coagulated under your arms, between your legs, and around your neck after a swim. Your clothes will not be the same after they have been smeared with lanolin.

## Whiteboard and Markers

Bring a pack of nonpermanent markers and a whiteboard on your escort boat so your coach and support crew can provide you with information periodically. The information should be written in large, clear uppercase letters and in short, easy-to-understand phrases. The information can be motivational (e.g., "Husband is waiting at finish"), whimsical ("Dolphins can't keep up"), instructional (e.g., "Kick harder—against tide") or directional (e.g., "Angle right").

Your coach should hold the whiteboard steady for at least five breathing cycles or until it is obvious when you have read the message. You can acknowledge that you have read the information with a head nod, hand wave, or verbal shout.

Permanent markers are good for numbering bags and bottles, such as C for chocolate or M for mocha. At night, it may be difficult to see, so little clues like this can help your support crew avoid mistakes after a long night out in the open water.

## Miscellaneous Equipment

Rubber-soled slip-on shoes or neoprene socks are useful, especially if you have to scramble on slippery rocks, walk down to the beach on hot sand, or walk on a wet boat deck, especially if it is raining.

Use small stickers to label goggles or bags of food. On a night swim, label substitute goggles and thermos bottles so your support crew knows the sequence in which to provide these essential items.

The Shark Shield is a long-tailed shark deterrent system used by marathon swimmers who venture in areas where sharks congregate. The Shark Shield can be fitted to your support kayak. It emits a pulsing three-dimensional electrical wave form that is detected through sensory receptors and induces spasms on the snout of predatory sharks, including great whites, tigers, bulls, makos, and bronze whalers. Shark Shield was invented by the South African government's Natal Shark Board and is used by the Australian military, the South African navy, and the U.S. Coast Guard.

Training equipment such as surgical tubing and physio balls have a variety of uses both in and out of the water. Surgical tubing can be used for resistance training to develop a connection between your arm, hand, and lower abdominal muscles. Do pulling exercises on land with surgical tubing while you are on an unstable surface (e.g., physio ball) to develop a strong core.

A compass is also useful to give to your kayakers so they can head in the proper direction if your escort boat temporarily gets out of position.

## SOPHISTICATED TOOLS FOR THE COMPETITIVELY MINDED SWIMMER

The most serious athletes and coaches use a variety of more sophisticated equipment and services—some unusual and some expensive—to help them reach their potential.

### UNDERWATER VIDEO CAMERA

You can arrange to have yourself periodically videotaped so you can have your stroke technique analyzed by an experienced coach or at a swimming camp or clinic that offers these services.

You can be filmed both above and below the water with one of the lightweight, portable, and easy-to-use underwater video systems that work with any camcorder. You can better appreciate and visualize how to improve after viewing yourself underwater and listening to a coach's advice.

### STROKE ANALYSIS

Competitive swimmers and triathletes undergo sophisticated velocity analyses in their quest for increased speed and efficiency. Services such as SwiMetrics (www.swimetrics.com) offer these underwater video analyses of swimming technique.

Similar to a wind tunnel test for cyclists, the underwater analysis quantifies your stroke's strengths and weaknesses by measuring the real-time velocity of your arm stroke and kick. The data are superimposed on an underwater video. An analysis shows you how, why, where, and how much you slow down (or speed up) at every point in your swimming stroke. The peaks and valleys of the velocity data indicate the increases and decreases in velocity as you kick

---

### CASE STUDY OF IMPROVING AN OLYMPIC CHAMPION'S STROKE

Background: In 2008, 41-year-old Dara Torres attempted an Olympic comeback. Could the mother and retired Olympic champion improve her times and win a medal in Beijing against some of the world's fittest women—who were half her age?

Test: Dara was tested in a series of 20-meter swims that measured her swimming velocity. The results opened her eyes to new discoveries of her swimming inefficiencies and the real possibility of making the Olympic team for a record fifth time.

Discovery: Small flaws—unseen by the naked eye—in Dara's swimming stroke were identified and quantified. She learned that her speed was slightly reduced when she breathed to her left as compared to when she breathed to her right.

Analysis: Dara focused on her key weaknesses and started breathing only to the right despite the fact that she had bilateral breathed throughout her entire career.

Outcome: Dara did her personal bests at the age of 41, made the Olympic team, and won three silver medals in the 2008 Beijing Olympics. She missed a gold medal by one one-hundredth of a second in the 50-meter freestyle to become one the world's most heralded athletes in 2008.

---

and pull. By comparing the average and peak speeds of your left arm and right arm, you can compare the relative speed of one arm with the other. This data shows what parts of your arm stroke generate the most speed and what parts cause you to decelerate. The integration of video and data leads to awareness and, ultimately, translates to speed improvement.

Triathletes also use the SwiMetrics analysis to test and compare the drag forces caused by various wetsuits. This can help you learn precisely which wetsuits are slower and which are faster based on your swimming technique, your body type, and how the wetsuits interact with your body in the water. The more drag forces there are on your body, the less efficient and slower the wetsuit is for you.

## TRAINING LOG

Getting organized lays the foundation to success in any endeavor, but laying out a year-round training program based on the the Pyramid of Open Water Success philosophy (explained in chapter 6) takes time and is important for a seriously committed swimmer. Both you and your coach should plan for every type of condition in the open water and keep track of the specific training methodologies used. A log will help you keep track of your workouts.

A training log (many are available online), consistently used, helps you keep track of distances, times, and other key parameters of your training. The most sophisticated programs allow you to modify your current and future training plans on the fly and to record your resting heart rate, quality of sleep, length of sleep, willingness to train, mood, fatigue level, level of muscle soreness, and ability to recover from a workout. It also helps you keep track of any effects on workout performance of illness, pain, or injury; the start and finish of your menstrual cycle; and your total swimming volume and total dryland workload volume, times, and stroke counts during both your pool and open water workouts.

Open water swimming can be a simple endeavor that you can do yourself for exercise or enjoyment, or quite a sophisticated undertaking that requires a large team of supporters during a channel swim. The amount and type of equipment you chose to use reflects these extremes. You can limit yourself to a swimsuit and goggles—or you can outfit yourself with GPS units and an expensive wetsuit and be escorted by a pilot with sophisticated marine equipment and an expensive boat filled with a support crew of experienced people. As the sport continues to develop new products and you gain experience in various bodies of water, you will find additional tools, equipment, and services that will enable you to swim faster, more efficiently, safer, and more intelligently.

Dr. Jim Miller

# BUILDING A FASTER FREESTYLE

Open water swimming techniques have dramatically changed since Captain Matthew Webb first crossed the English Channel in 1875 swimming breaststroke.

Rather than the slow and steady beat of the breaststroke commonly used in the 19th century, modern-day open water swimmers and triathletes use freestyle. Freestyle was first used by swimmers in the Solomon Islands and later adopted by the resourceful Australians, who popularized the more efficient stroke in the rest of the world.

In the early part of the 20th century, freestyle became the stroke of choice among open water enthusiasts and was constantly refined by each new generation of swimmers who had the twin goals of saving energy and improving speed.

## IMPROVING SPEED

Constantly evolving training methodologies and imitations of the fastest swimmers has led to a continuous improvement in the speed of the average swimmer. Large workout volumes, increasingly more difficult interval training, tapering, and lactic threshold sets are just a few concepts that have spread globally. Just as on land, imitation in the water is the sincerest form of flattery. When an Olympic champion did an S-shaped pull in the 1960s, other freestylers endeavored to do the same. When a world-record holder shaved his legs and swam faster as a result, the other athletes followed suit. When an English Channel–record holder incorporated more frequent, albeit brief, feeding stops in his swims, this changed the mind-set of other marathoners.

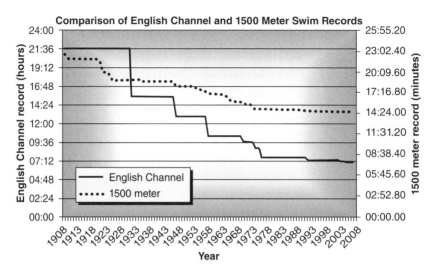

**Figure 5.1** World record times in the 1500 meter freestyle and the English Channel (1908 – 2008).

Figure 5.1 shows the constant improvement in freestyle speed by plotting the world-record times for the men's 1500 meter freestyle in the pool against the English Channel world-record times (from England to France) between 1908 and 2008. During this 103-year period, these two sets of world records were held by people from over a dozen countries.

But no swimmers are in both demographic groups. Only one world-record holder in the 1500 meter freestyle, American John Kinsella, crossed the English Channel, but he did not set a record. None of the English Channel–record holders ever qualified for the Olympic 1500 meter finals, although the current English Channel–record holder, Petar Stoychev, has competed in the Olympic 1500 meter freestyle three times for his native Bulgaria. Therefore, the similar rates of improvement by swimmers of two completely different demographic group in two separate freestyle disciplines over 103 years reveal how swimmers quickly adopt any demonstrable improvements in speed and efficiency—regardless of their country, origin, venue, or era.

## THE WORLD'S BEST FREESTYLERS

The best freestyle swimmers are very fluid and powerful in the water with every part of their bodies coordinated to generate forward propulsion. They are symmetrical and streamlined, maintaining a balance between their left and right sides as well as between their lower and upper bodies. "He swims like a dolphin" is a compliment often heard of champions in the pool and open water, which refers to their streamlined grace. Swimmers introduced to the sport later in life can achieve a similar level of kinetic elegance in the water.

In a pool, the combination of symmetry, grace, and strength is important. In the ocean, the symmetry becomes even more important because dynamic forces such as tides, currents, waves, surface chop, and wind constantly affect technique and speed. Even in a glassy, flat lake, the water temperature, choice of swimwear, and proximity to other swimmers play a part in either negatively or positively affecting stroke technique, balance and speed.

This chapter's information is based on observations, scientific testing, and empirical analyses of the world's best freestyle swimmers. Olympic pool medalists and world-record holders share many commonalities with channel swimmers, professional marathon swimmers, and professional triathletes renowned for their swimming skills.

# PROPULSION FROM THE UPPER AND LOWER BODY

Based on propulsion data measured by SwiMetrics developed by Dr. Genadijus Sokolovas, Director of Physiology for the 2000, 2004, and 2008 USA Olympic swim teams, 89-93 percent of the propulsion in very good competitive swimmers in the pool is generated by their arms with the remaining 7-11 percent generated by their legs. As distances increase from 50 meters in pools to longer swims in the open water, the percentage of propulsion generated by the legs decreases; the amount of force generated by the kick of world-class marathon swimmers is less than 5 percent. Although none of the marathoners have been measured empirically during actual marathon swims, they mostly depend on a two-beat kick with a relatively high stroke turnover of between 73 and 85 strokes per minute.

However, the importance of an open water swimmer's kick goes beyond mere propulsion. A constant, balanced kick with pointed toes and flexible ankles— even without generating significant propulsion—leads to balance between the left and right lateral body rolls, a high hip position, and a streamlined body position, all of which reduce frontal resistance. This position, in which the body rides high in the water, is the secret of the world's best open water swimmers.

But there are exceptions to this upper- and lower-body propulsion ratio. Like a race car driver, you must be able to shift gears several times within your race. You have to know when it is advantageous to slow down, speed up, turn, draft, and veer off in different directions. Those gear changes are driven by your arm stroke tempo and a corresponding increase in your kick. These surges and shifts in speed are necessary at various times during races, as noted here:

- A significant increase in kick propulsion during a surge in a race
- A significant increase in kick propulsion during a sprint to the finish
- An increased kick speed to take advantage of advantageous river currents or ocean swells

- A decrease in kick while drafting
- A decrease in arm stroke turnover and an increase in arm stroke length while drafting
- A significant increase in kick and arm stroke turnover while trying to catch an ocean wave
- A sustained kick when riding an ocean wave, especially as the wave starts to dissipate
- A sustained kick and increased arm turnover when fighting against a current or tidal flow

If you simply want to complete a swim from point A to point B without the need to tax yourself aerobically, your ratio of arm-to-kick propulsion can remain comfortably low (i.e., 95 percent arms and 5 percent legs). To swim most efficiently, do not drop your kick and let your legs float behind you. Even without a strong kick, maintain as streamlined a position as possible with your feet pointed and your hips riding as high as possible in the water. A smooth two-beat kick with a small amplitude enables you to swim through a narrow imaginary cylinder. You do not want to create additional resistance by not kicking and having a low hip position.

## ESTABLISHING GOOD BODY ROTATION AND SYMMETRY

One of the fundamental characteristics of a fast and efficient freestyle is good body rotation. The shoulders, torso, and hips of great freestylers rotate smoothly around a fixed axis centered on the spine. There is very little lateral movement of the head, torso, hips, and legs, including when they breathe. They keep the left arm and left leg on the left side of the central axis and the right arm and right leg on the right side of the central axis.

In the open water where there are no lines, lanes, or walls, a streamlined and symmetrical body position is essential. From turn buoy to turn buoy, symmetry helps you to swim straight. Symmetry in your technique in turn reduces the number of times you lift your head to navigate. Symmetry also enables you to maintain the same speed and distance per stroke whether you breathe on the left side or right side. In fact, swimmers with excellent symmetry often do not need skin lubrication because they rarely chafe anywhere on their bodies no matter how far they swim or what conditions they swim in.

In the open water, you will occasionally face waves coming at you laterally or head on. Other times, you may want to breathe to the other side because of the position of your competitors, the glare of the sun, landmarks onshore, or the irritating exhaust from an escort boat. Decide on a breathing pattern during workouts so you can swim equally well while breathing on either your left or right side. For example, occasionally swim half of your workouts breathing to the left side and the other half breathing to the right even if you are not a bilateral breather. If you do not normally bilateral breathe, try swimming 100 yards on your predominant side for every 25 yards on your weak side. Mix it up because you never know what race day will bring.

## BODY ROTATION DRILLS

Various drills in the pool will help you develop a better feel for a good body position, although you may feel unbalanced or uncoordinated when you first try them. With practice, you will begin to feel more balanced and coordinated. Among the number of body rotation drills, here are three that can help your technique:

1. Kick with both your arms at your side. Breathe to one side and then the other.
2. Kick on your side with one arm extended in front of you for half the pool or 10 kicks. Then rotate arms and breathing sides for the other half of the pool or 10 kicks.
3. Pull with your pull buoy positioned between your ankles or calves.

Rotate from your hips when you roll into your breath. A good, coordinated hip rotation will generate more power in every stroke. If you rotate primarily from your shoulders, your arm stroke will be inefficient.

If your body moves laterally left or right with your arm stroke, focus on rotating your core around your spine when you swim. Swim slowly and concentrate on getting it right. Be patient. It will take time. Ask your coach or teammate to occasionally watch you and give you some feedback. Watch videos of great swimmers and visualize yourself swimming similarly. This continuous neurological focus will help you reduce your body's lateral movements.

To keep a streamlined body position and stay as horizontal as possible, keep your body slightly tense. Your increased body tone will reduce the total drag forces in the water and engage your core muscles in your arm stroke.

## BODY SYMMETRY DRILLS

Here are three drills that can help you improve your body symmetry:

1. Use a swimmer's snorkel. Observe your hand path under the water as you try to catch the water early in your stroke and pull straight back.

2. Use a swimmer's snorkel in your swimming sets. As your hand enters the water, point your fingertips straight down while you keep your wrists firm and palms flat. While your eyes are looking straight down, pull straight back without crossing your centerline. If you have a crossover kick, do this drill with fins on. Do this drill slowly, but as perfectly as possible. Then gradually increase your speed.

**3.** Swim with one arm at your side with your eyes looking straight down. Swim with only one arm, breathe to the opposite side of your arm stroke, and time yourself for a set of 100s. Then do the same drill using your other side. If your average times are different, work on your weaker side by using a small hand paddle on that side.

# ESTABLISHING GOOD HEAD POSITION

As your shoulders, torso, and hips ideally rotate smoothly around your central axis while you swim, keep a stationary head position. If your head remains in alignment with your spine, you will effectively eliminate lateral (left and right) and vertical (up and down) head movements with every arm stroke. By firmly extending your neck forward and looking straight down in the open water, you will streamline your profile in the water and decrease the resistive forces against your forward progress.

In the pool, most swimmers tend to look forward under the water so they can avoid swimming into people who share their lane. In the open water, most swimmers tend to look forward because they are sighting so much. In both cases, the water level tends to be at their forehead. But when your eyes scan forward or the water level is at your forehead, you create greater resistance than when you are looking straight down. Keep your neck straight, not bent upwards and slightly tensed. Looking straight down will minimize your resistance in the water.

## THE IDEAL BREATHING MOTION

Do not twist your head to the side when you breathe. Do not lift your head up to turn and breathe. Rather, your head should naturally move to its proper position when your shoulders and torso rotate to your breathing side. As your torso rotates 30 to 45 degrees, your mouth will be repositioned above the surface of the water, enabling you to easily breathe in the trough created under your armpit.

If your head is out of alignment with your spine or moves independently of your torso, your overall streamlined position is compromised. Think about how fish move and are shaped. Without humanlike necks, fish are streamlined by nature. When fish move through the water, their heads are in perfect alignment with the central axis of their bodies. We are certainly not fish, but we can try to imitate the wonders of nature.

The bow of a boat is another example of something that cuts efficiently through the water. If the bow of a boat moved laterally or vertically in the water, the efficiency of the boat is reduced. You want to maintain a firm neck position, so you slice through the water efficiently like the bow of a boat.

A simple, but physically difficult, drill can help you learn what your optimal head position should be in the water. Swim holding a ball that is slightly larger than a tennis ball between your chin and chest. This will cause your eyes to face downward. The top of your head will be perpendicular to the surface of the water, and your head and neck will be in line with your spine. If the ball falls from your chin when you swim and breathe, then your head is not in the optimal position. Initially, keeping the ball in place will be very difficult. But, with more practice, you will be able to swim and breathe to both sides with the ball in place.

## EXCEPTIONS OF PROPER HEAD POSITION IN THE OPEN WATER

In open water swims, there are exceptions to the ideal head position described in the preceding section. Consider the following scenarios:

- If jellyfish, seaweed, or flotsam is present, swim with your head up to avoid getting stung, tangled, or cut on your face.
- When you bodysurf down a wave, keep your head up with one arm slicing the water with an outstretched arm.
- Take a quick glance ahead or behind you to check landmarks or buoys.
- Twist your head forward or back to check your competition along the course.
- When you swim in very cold water or hit a cold patch, you may prefer to swim with your head up until you feel more comfortable putting your head down.
- When lifting your head at night when your kayaker and escort boat are more difficult to see.
- When you are in the middle of a pack, lift your head to check for opportunities to escape.
- When you are on a marathon swim and you think your escort boat is out of position (i.e., you are not between the bow and stern of the boat), swim with your head up and request (yell) instructions to your support crew. Your boat may be angled in the correct position, and you may be swimming in the wrong direction, but you want to confirm this as soon possible.

## HEAD POSITION WHILE SIGHTING

The most efficient way to sight in the open water is to lift—or reposition—your head as one hand enters the water in front of you. Imagine an alligator with its eyes barely breaking the surface of the water: It is very still, very smooth, and streamlined. You want to replicate the head position of an alligator when sighting.

Lift your head out of the water only high enough to see your target (a landmark, turn buoy, or competitor) with a slight downward push (not an outward sweep) of your front hand and a corresponding snap of your hips when your eyes are above the surface of the water. Kick more quickly than normal as you try to keep your body as streamlined as possible.

Before your eyes break the surface of the water, exhale. As your eyes break the surface and scan the area in front of you, mentally take a snapshot of your position, your direction, and the target(s) in front of you.

Do not lift your head too high, and do not breathe when you are looking forward. If you are able to breathe when you are looking forward, then your head is too high. After you look forward, rotate your body slightly to your breathing side. At this point in your stroke, your head is near your normal breathing position. Breathe when your eyes are facing to the side. This sequence minimizes drag and helps you maintain a good body position while you sight. If water conditions are rough, lift your head higher to clear the surface chop.

A typical swimmer sights between 200 and 300 times in a 2.4-mile (3.9K) swim. Triathletes sight 282 times if they lift their heads an average of every 15 yards in a full Ironman swim leg distance. Swimming straighter or sighting less will result in time and energy savings.

**Steps for Efficient Sighting**

1. Exhale.
2. Your front hand recovers over the water's surface and enters the water.
3. Lift your head forward.
4. Push your front hand down backwards.
5. Kick harder.
6. Look forward to take a mental snapshot of the course.
7. Rotate your body to the side as your head moves to its normal breathing position.
8. Take a breath.
9. Rotate your torso and shoulders back to a position parallel with the water surface.

# PRACTICING OPTIMAL ARM AND HAND MOVEMENTS

Figure 5.2 illustrates proper arm and hand movements. Ideally, you should move your arms in a straight-line path once they enter the water. Based on Newton's third law of physics (i.e., for every action, there is an equal and opposite reaction), push the water straight back—not in an S-shaped curve—to maximize your forward speed.

Have your hands enter the water just slightly outside your shoulder line. If your hands enter the water too wide or cross your central axis, your body will fishtail. This movement may be only slightly perceptible to the naked eye, but when repeated on each stroke cycle, the cumulative effects result in significant inefficiencies and slower speeds. As your relaxed hand enters the water, point your fingertips downward. Do not cup your hand, but keep it flat with your wrist firm. As your hand moves deeper and pulls the water in the early part of your stroke, keep your elbow higher than your hand for an optimal catch.

© Human Kinetics

**Figure 5.2** (*a*) Start pointing your fingertips down once the head enters the water; (*b*) sweep your hand straight back with a high elbow position; (*c*) pull straight back while eyes continue to face down; (*d*) push your hand past your hip and maintain a streamlined, balanced head and body position.

This will take considerable practice and is best seen with an underwater video shot from a straight-on angle.

Accelerate your hands through your stroke as they move under your body. You can learn to accelerate your hands underwater by doing drills in the pool in which you minimize the number of strokes per lap. Count the number of arm strokes per lap. Then take fewer strokes on the next lap, but keep the same pace, to increase your distance per stroke. Focus on pushing the water backwards on every stroke. Try to have good follow-through in your pool workouts, but realize that your follow-through will be less effective in the open water.

You can swim optimally with your fingers slightly spread apart and held in a comfortable position rather than being tightly closed or widely spread. Research studies have shown that spreading the fingers slightly (0.32 cm, or .1 in., between fingers) allows your hand to create a more optimal propulsive force in the water.

As you hand pushes the water under your body, your elbow should be closer to the surface of the water. With high elbows, your hands and forearms will be in the optimal position. When your hand is under your body in front of your chest, continue to push the water straight backward. You should feel a connection between your core muscles and your arms as you push the water through your stroke.

With the proper head position and high elbows throughout your stroke, you may feel as though you are swimming over a barrel or swimming downhill, especially when you kick hard. When you hold this position consistently in the open water, you will experience less frontal drag and will be able to swim faster.

In the early part of your stroke when your hand first enters the water, avoid pressing your arm and hand straight down. Because the weight of your head needs to be supported by something when you sight, most swimmers tend to press their hands straight down or sweep them outward in the early part of the stroke. This bad habit keeps the head elevated over the surface of the water, but is not conducive to swimming faster.

This tendency to press your arms down or to sweep your hands outward beyond the width of your shoulders usually becomes more pronounced when the water conditions get rougher, the surface chop gets larger, or the race gets longer. Resist this urge and continue to focus on swimming through a narrow imaginary cylinder no matter how turbulent the conditions become in the open water.

## PROPER ARM RECOVERY

As one arm is pushing underwater straight back, your other arm (positioned with a high elbow) is recovering over the surface of the water in the recovery phase. As your arm recovers over the water, keep your arm and hand relaxed. Smoothly move your arms over the water, parallel to your centerline. Ideally, what you do on your left side is exactly mirroring what you do on your right side.

Additionally, keep your arm's recovery during your non-breathing strokes and your breathing strokes the same. Do not swing your straight arms over the water. A wide arm recovery may result in a sideward counter-reaction. This frequently leads to a crossover of your centerline with your hands, decreasing your forward velocity.

---

### NORMAL CATCH-UP DRILLS

In normal catch-up drills, one arm remains stretched in front of you while the other arm moves through the entire stroke. After one arm completes its stroke cycle, the other arm begins. As you alternate arms, concentrate on pulling and pushing the water back in a straight-line path under the water and symmetrically over the water.

### REVERSE CATCH-UP DRILLS

In reverse catch-up drills, one arm remains stationary at your side at all times. Keep one hand near your thigh when your other arm is moving through its stroke cycle. After one arm completes a stroke cycle, the other arm begins. This reverse catch-up drill requires a higher degree of body and breathing coordination than the normal catch-up drill does.

---

## HAND AND ARM STROKE DRILLS

Practice your recovery and straight-line arm path in the water by using normal and reverse catch-up drills in the pool.

## MAINTAINING THE PROPER ARM STROKE TEMPO

The tempo (arm strokes per minute) of world-class open water swimmers is slightly higher than that of pool swimmers. World-class male swimmers generally swim between 72 and 84 strokes per minute (SPM) in the open water until they start to sprint at more than 90 SPM. Female world-class open water swimmers generally swim between 78 and 88 SPM in the open water until they start to sprint and sometimes get over 95 SPM. Ask your coach to count your arm strokes per minute during a race and in an open water workout so you can become familiar with your own SPM pace.

This difference in tempo between the pool and open water is partly due to the fact that world-class pool swimmers are swimming, at most, 45 meters straight at any one time in a pool; they rely on a significantly faster kick and lengthy push-offs from the pool walls (where they pick up much momentum) over short periods (seconds or minutes). On the other hand, open water swimmers swim long distances over long periods (hours) under constantly changing conditions with no place to pick-up momentum like pool swimmers. The elements in the open water (e.g., wind, waves, currents, tides, surface chop, and crowded swimming conditions) have many negative effects on the forward velocity of open water swimmers and impacts a swimmer's uncertainty as to where exactly to swim due to limited visibility.

Your optimal tempo in the open water is the fastest pace you can maintain without shortchanging the power phase of your arm pull. The power phase of most open water swimmers occurs when the hand is pulling underwater between their head and a position near their hips.

If you know that one arm is stronger than the other arm through empirical testing, strengthen the weaker arm by swimming with a small paddle on that arm for some portion of your pool workout (e.g., during your pulling sets). Developing symmetry in your stroke and strength on both sides will help you swim straighter.

There are exceptions to these arm stroke recommendations. If you are swimming in choppy water under windy conditions, either with or against whitecaps, you may want to lift your arms higher out of the water to avoid having them be hit by the waves. This will require greater energy expenditure and may lead to frustration. Either raise your elbows higher or swing your arms over the turbulence.

## ESTABLISHING PROPER BREATHING IN THE OPEN WATER UNDER ROUGH CONDITIONS

A wave can hit you at any time. A mouthful of salt water is always an unwelcomed surprise and can lead to subsequent problems. Some swimmers have a natural ability to sense the water's movement and enjoy uncanny timing when they breathe. But many others must work on their breathing in the open water.

Fully exhale through your mouth and nose when your head is down in the water (see figure 5.3). When you rotate for a breath, inhale quickly. Do not first exhale and then inhale when your face is above the water surface. (*Note:* You should follow these steps in both open water and pool swimming.)

© Human Kinetics

**Figure 5.3** Exhale fully with both your mouth and nose while underwater.

When you exhale underwater, do so as fully as possible. This not only enables you to get the maximum amount of air when you inhale, but also helps calm you under competitive or stressful conditions.

Breathe to both sides, if possible. Although your forward velocity is slightly lower when you breathe on one side compared with the other, the benefits of bilateral breathing far outweigh those of single-sided breathing. If you breathe exclusively to one side, you may develop a less-than-ideal body rotation. Your stroke may also be less symmetrical than bilateral breathers. If you do not breathe bilaterally, then you must focus on your symmetry even more.

Try to first overcome this one-sided dependency in a pool. One-sided dependency becomes a larger problem in the open water where there are no lines, lanes, or walls. The less symmetrical your stroke is, the more likely you will be to veer to one side. Then you compensate for this inability to swim in a straight-line tangent. This leads to lifting your head more often to sight, which causes your hips and legs tend to sink lower in the water and to your expending more energy, decreasing speed. Figure 5.4 shows the domino effects of poor symmetry.

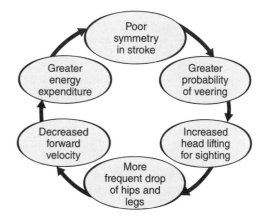

**Figure 5.4**  Effects of poor symmetry.

## EXCEPTIONS UNDER ROUGH CONDITIONS

There are exceptions to the preceding open water breathing recommendations. If you are swimming in choppy water under windy conditions, either with or against whitecaps, you may have to change the position of your head when you breathe (see figure 5.5).

Breathe away from the waves and surface chop. Breathe under your armpit with a little more body rotation

**Figure 5.5**  Breathing mechanics can change during rough water conditions.

than normal so your body is acting as a shield for your mouth. Also, you may have to turn your face and mouth toward the sky a little more so you do not swallow water.

## ENGAGING YOUR CORE

World-class swimmers engage their core when they swim. A strong and stable torso from the upper back to the abdominals enables them to stay streamlined and helps drive their arm strokes.

Engage your upper back (latissimus dorsi), chest (pectoralis major), and core muscles (abdominals and low back) during your body rotation to drive momentum in your arms. If your body position is too flat, your stroke will be powered by your shoulders. Over long distances, especially in the open water, you want to rely not only on your shoulders, but also on the larger muscles of your core, back, and chest areas.

With a strong core, your body will be straighter with a minimal bow in your low back. A reduction in the bow of your back will keep you more streamlined and reduce or avoid low back discomfort. Unlike swimming in a pool where you can reorient yourself every lap and take pressure off your low back at every turn, your low back enjoys no rest in the open water.

When the water conditions are rough with surface chop, the best swimmers continue to engage the core, using their larger muscles to keep good body rotation. On the other hand, inexperienced swimmers rely on their shoulders and primarily use their legs for balance while they swim flat to stabilize themselves in the rough water. The sagging bow in their body position occasionally results in an aching or sore back.

### DRILLS FOR YOUR CORE

Strengthen your core by occasionally doing pulling sets with your pull buoy around your ankles or calves instead of in the traditional position between your thighs. This unusual position will help you develop better hip-and-body rotation and establish a better connection between your lower abdomen and legs.

Another drill for your core is to keep one arm extended forward underwater with your other arm held above the water surface in a bent recovery position. Kick strongly in this position and then rotate from your hips to breathe. You can also swim in a pool with a small weight belt (1 to 2 lb, or 0.45 to 0.9 kg) on your hips to increase the strength of your core.

Also, try to maintain a good posture out of the water. Good posture on land helps you swim straighter in the open water. Good posture enables you to use your core—from your upper back down through your abdominals—to power your arm stroke, which is essential, especially when the water conditions are rough.

If you want to strengthen your upper chest and upper back, finish each swim repeat during your main set with a partial deck-up. That is, immediately after you finish each swim, place both hands flat on the pool deck. Pull yourself up until your arms are fully extended and your elbows are locked. Then slide back into the water for your next swim.

# USING YOUR LEGS AND FEET PROPERLY

Elite open water swimmers generate propulsion from their kick, which also eliminates the significant drag that would come if they simply let their feet and hips drop. A constant, tight two-beat kick, albeit not necessarily a propulsive kick, helps your body rotate more naturally because it lifts your legs and gives you a better body position.

Using your legs throughout your open water swim will also prepare your legs for an onshore finish or swim–bike transition in a triathlon. If the water is cold, you can use your legs to keep you warmer. In these cases, try not to bend your knees too much. Kick from your hips to engage the larger muscles of your upper legs, which will help prepare you for an onshore run or transition as well as keep you a bit warmer.

Use your legs more forcefully when you lift your head to sight. As you lift your head to sight, kick slightly more quickly so the weight of your head and upper body is partly supported by your legs. But keep the amplitude of your kick small. Increasing the depth of your kick will only create additional resistive forces.

Kick your feet enough so only your heels break the water's surface with a minor knee bend. If your entire foot comes out of the water, you generate no additional propulsion. If your feet come high out of the water, it is likely that you will drive your feet too deeply on your down-kick.

## CREATING THE OPTIMAL KNEE BEND

Imagine that you have no knees. Try to keep your legs as straight as possible when you are swimming. This is humanly impossible, but theoretically desirable. Kick from your hips with only a minimal bend in your knees. Point your toes on both your down-kick and up-kick. This will help prevent a cross-over kick. When one foot crosses over the other during the kicking sequence, the lower your propulsion will be.

Keep the angle in which your legs separate (i.e., your kicking amplitude) to a minimum. In the open water, where many dynamic forces are working against your forward momentum, reducing your kicking amplitude is important. Deep leg kicks will only lead to drops in forward velocity, especially if your toes are not pointed. A large kicking amplitude will only increase the drag forces on your body.

To learn how little to bend your knees, do vertical kicking in the deep end of a pool. When you kick in the vertical position, keep your back as straight as possible with your neck aligned with your spine. Move your entire leg as one unit with as little knee bend as possible. For greater aerobic conditioning, keep your hands and elbows out of the water or hold them straight over your head.

Kick by engaging your lower abdominal muscles. Also, try kicking sets with a Thera-Band Loop, which will keep your legs from separating too much. Alternatively, you can kick with tennis shoes or socks on, which makes kicking with a large amplitude much more difficult.

You can also use fins in the pool to reduce your kicking amplitude. Kicking with fins will also help correct cross-kicking. Although cross-kicking may keep you balanced in the open water, crossing your feet in your kick motion usually results from other stroke inefficiencies rather than serving a particular benefit.

## THE IMPORTANCE OF ANKLE FLEXIBILITY

Fast swimmers have excellent ankle flexibility. When they point their toes, the angle between the top of their feet and their calves is greater than 180 degrees. In contrast, triathletes and runners often have poor ankle flexibility because of the repetitive motions they use in running and cycling.

You can work on your ankle flexibility by flexing your feet underneath you (see figure 5.6). Sit on your feet with the tops of your feet flat against the floor. Lean straight back, keeping your back straight, as you keep the tops of your feet and knees flat against the floor. While leaning back as far as possible, feel the stretch on the top of your foot. Do this stretch at least three times per week. Even if you cannot achieve a competitive swimmer's level of extreme flexibility, this exercise will increase your ankle flexibility over time.

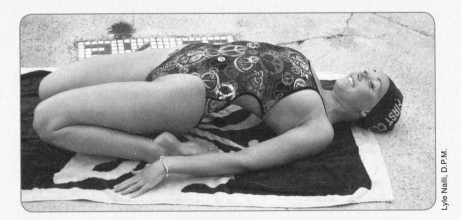

Lyle Nalli, D.P.M.

**Figure 5.6**   Try to increase your ankle flexibility through frequent stretching.

# Kicking Tempo

Kicking tempo is the number of kicks (i.e., beats) per arm stroke. In a two-beat kick (2BK), there is one leg kick for each arm stroke. In a four-beat kick (4BK), there are two leg kicks for each arm stroke. In a six-beat kick (6BK), there are three leg kicks for each arm stroke. World-class open water swimmers use a range of kicking tempos at different points in an open water race depending on the situation.

A strong 6BK is common during the very first part of a race. Swimmers then settle back to a 2BK during the majority of the race. A 4BK is used when the pace picks up during the race, whereas a 6BK is usually reserved for the very last sprint.

For most triathletes and open water swimmers most of the time, a 2BK is the most comfortable tempo because more energy is conserved for the upper body and a slower tempo fits into their natural rhythm of the stroke. Anything less than a 2BK will drop your legs and hips to a suboptimal position. For some, especially those with a faster arm tempo, a 4BK is a more natural cadence. Table 5.1 lists some common swimming technique problems and the recommended solutions.

**Table 5.1   Common Swimming Technique Problems, Solutions, and Training Drills**

| Body part | Problems | Solutions and reasons why | Training drills |
|---|---|---|---|
| Head | Eyes are looking forward | Eyes should be looking straight down to straighten out the spine and place the body in an ideal streamlined position. | Use swimmer's snorkel during training. Look straight down at bottom of pool to keep head lower and in line with body. |
| | Head moves with each arm stroke | Extend neck and look down while not breathing. Keep stronger neck to stabilize lateral head movements. | Swim with a tennis ball between chin and upper chest while swimming in a pool. Do catch-up and reverse catch-up freestyle drills. |
| | Head is too high while breathing | One goggle lens should be in the water while breathing. Head is too heavy to keep it high in the water. | Swim with a tennis ball between your chin and upper chest. Use swimmer's snorkel while looking straight down. |
| Neck | Head moves laterally | Keep neck rigid and extended from spine to reduce frontal drag. | Use swimmer's snorkel during training and look straight down at bottom of pool. |
| Shoulders | Body moves laterally with each arm stroke | Drive arm stroke from hips, enabling the shoulders to rotate automatically with hips. | Focus on hip rotation while swimming with a snorkel. Do not cross arms over central axis while doing catch-up drills. |

*(continued)*

**Table 5.1** *(continued)*

| Body part | Problems | Solutions and reasons why | Training drills |
|---|---|---|---|
| Elbows | Elbows are lower than hands | Keep fingertips points down throughout the entire stroke. | Swim more with paddles to develop a feeling of an early catch with high elbows. |
| Arm | Arm pull is not strong | Establish a high elbow position at the beginning of your stroke. Use core muscles to pull hand and forearm straight backwards. | Do the first half of the arm stroke only, trying to establish a high-elbow position early in the stroke. Always point fingertips straight down. |
| Hands | Hands do not catch the water early | Point fingertips down after hands enter the water at the beginning of the stroke. | Do catch-up stroke drills where fingertips are pressed down at the beginning of each stroke. |
|  | Hands move laterally in an S-shape pattern | The straighter the hand pathway, the more powerful the stroke. If hand moves in an S-shaped path, swimming velocity drops. | Do reverse catch-up stroke drills. Start with both arms at your sides. Do not begin one arm stroke until the other arm has finished and touched your thigh. |
| Body | Torso is not streamlined | Develop stronger core in order to create better posture in water. | Swim with a pull buoy between calves or ankles or exercise on a physio-ball. |
|  | Body moves laterally with every stroke | Rotate your core around the spine to avoid lateral movements. | Do land exercises on physio-balls or other unstable platforms to strengthen core. |
| Knees | Knees are bent too much | Most of kicking propulsion comes from lower leg. Reduce knee bend. | Do vertical freestyle kicking with arms above surface of water. |
| Legs | Kick amplitude is too great | Kick more shallowly and increase kicking tempo. | Point toes and keep feet shallow while kicking with a kickboard. |
|  | Kicking is weak | Improve power of flutter kick. | Kick vertical freestyle with straight legs. |

Ann Ford

# 6

# PREPARING FOR SHORT-DISTANCE SWIMS

To optimize your performance in the open water, plan your pool and open water training on the Pyramid of Open Water Success (see figure 6.1), a philosophy used by many successful open water swimming coaches. The Pyramid of Open Water Success includes optimal training recommendations for short-distance, middle-distance, and marathon swims. The amount of time you spend on each area of the Pyramid depends on the time of year, the amount of time you have to train, and your swimming background.

The foundation of the Pyramid includes base training, speed training, and distance tolerance. These training fundamentals are rooted in the competitive pool training philosophies that were born in the 1950s.

The open water swimming–specific components of the pyramid are at the next level and include race-specific training, skills training, and open water acclimatization. These three fundamentals are less well known, but are important to incorporate in your training regimen.

Tactical knowledge is at the apex of the pyramid. This refers to the knowledge and understanding of what to do in a dynamic environment in which your competitors, the climatic elements, and the water conditions can change at a moment's notice. To perform well in any open water swim, you need to anticipate, adapt, and respond to moves by your competition during races and to the

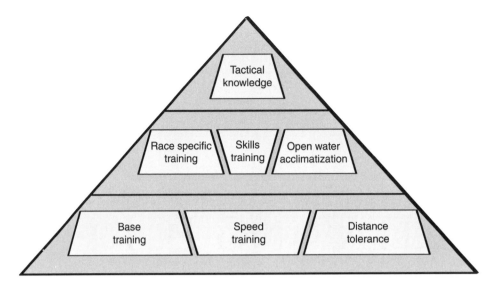

**Figure 6.1** Pyramid of open water success.

natural environment during any of your swims. Tactical knowledge includes the study of everything from the elements (tides, currents, waves) to the tendencies of competitors during the final sprint. You can obtain and enhance your tactical knowledge from observation, study, and real-world experiences.

The pyramid does not include a nutritional component, which is a separate, but essential, component of preparation for competitive athletes. It also does not include preparations related to your support team, another essential component for marathon swimmers.

## BUILDING A TRAINING BASE

Base training gets you in good physical shape during your preseason and mid-season training cycles and includes swimming repeated aerobic training sets in the pool. Base training is a fundamental component of competitive pool swimming programs for age-group, collegiate, and adult swimmers. It includes stretching and strength training exercises, often referred to as dryland training. If you have limited time, you can focus your dryland training on flexibility work (using yoga, Pilates, or other forms of calisthenics for your shoulders and ankles) and strengthening your abdominal muscles, which is critical if you enter competitive races or do marathon swims.

Depending on your experience, the amount of training time you have, and the distance of your swim, base training can range from 2,000 yards three days per week if you are a working adult swimmer to 14,000 meters per day six days per week if you are a highly competitive swimmer.

An important element of base training is consistency. Consistency will build a solid foundation for your optimal performance. If you consistently swim a third of your total race distance in a pool, then you can develop a base strong enough to do well in short- and middle-distance races. That is, if you aim to do a 10K race, regularly swim at least 3K per workout.

Table 6.1 includes base training examples specific to training in a 25-yard pool. They can be modified according to your level of experience and speed.

Following are some particularly tough base training sets actually performed by world-class swimmers:

- World 5K champion Melissa Gorman: 3000 meters + 2000 meters + 1000 meters at 1:10 pace per 100 meters
- World 25K champion Brendan Capell: 21 × 500 meters alternating 1 × 500 at 6:10 + 1 × 500 at 6:00 + 1 × 500 at 5:50
- World championship 5K and 10K silver medalist Ekaterina Seliverstova: 6 × 2000 meters at 1:13 pace per 100 meters + 10 × 1000
- World 5K champion Eva Fabian: 50 × 100 meters at 1:10 + 1-hour straight swim
- Pan American Games medalist Bob Placak: 10 × 500 yard swims
- Olympian Chloe Sutton: 30 × 100 meters at 1:15
- RCP Tiburon Mile champion Kane Radford: 10000-meter swim as fast as possible

**Table 6.1** Examples of Base Training in a 25-Yard Pool

| | |
|---|---|
| **Short-distance swims** | 3 × 500 pulling with a pull buoy and snorkel + 3 × 500, descend 1-3 (meaning that each 500 swim in the set gets increasingly faster) |
| **Middle-distance swims** | 2000, descend each 500 within the 2000 + 3 × 500 + 2 × 100 + 2 × 50 + 4 × 25 |
| **Marathon swims** | 10 × 800 at 12:00 (meaning 10, 800 yd swims done on an interval of 12 minutes), descend 1-5 |

# DEVELOPING SPEED

Speed training improves your speed through up-tempo swims. It includes anaerobic training sets that last up to two minutes in which you perform brief, near-maximal muscular activity, another traditional component of age-group, collegiate, and adult swimming teams. In contrast, the longer aerobic swims last beyond two minutes.

Even though marathon swimmers are endurance athletes with well-developed slow-twitch muscle fibers, they still need to do speed training (see table 6.2 on page 104). At times during an open water swim, they may need to pick up their speed to cross a current or catch a wave.

**Table 6.2**   Examples of Speed Training

| | |
|---|---|
| **Short-distance swims** | 150 swim + 30 s vertical kicking + 100 swim + 20 s vertical kicking + 50 swim + 10 s vertical kicking + 25 + 20 s vertical kicking |
| | 400 swim with every fourth lap fast + 300 with every third lap fast + 200 swim with every second lap fast + 100 all fast |
| **Middle-distance swims** | 4 × 300 with first 100 freestyle, second 100 individual medley, third 100 fast freestyle. 1 min rest between each 300. |
| **Marathon swims** | Three-person relay. Only one person swims at one time in one lane. Your rest interval is the time it takes for your teammates to complete their swims. Each person swims 4 × 50, then 4 × 100, then 4 × 200, then 4 × 10, and then 4 × 50. Select and maintain a goal pace to maintain for the entire set. |
| | 10 × 100 + 50 all-out swim after each 100 |

Vertical kicking helps build leg strength. When you kick freestyle straight up and down in the water, do not bend your knees too much and keep your back straight. Start with your hands at the surface of the water; then progress to rest your hands on your head. Later, hold your arms straight up in the air with straight elbows.

# ESTABLISHING A TOLERANCE FOR DISTANCE

Distance tolerance develops your ability to swim the specific distance of your chosen open water event (e.g., 1K or 25K). It is important to develop your ability to swim 130 percent of your target swim distance. You do not have to swim this entire distance at race pace. Rather, you simply should be able to swim this distance nonstop. By building up to a distance 30 percent longer than your swim, you are prepared to swim well—even if the water is colder than what you are accustomed to, the currents are running against you, or the waves are higher than expected. The extra 30 percent gives you a buffer to cover the unexpected conditions and intangibles that inevitably happen in open water races.

If your aim is to compete in a 1-mile swim, prepare to swim 1.3 miles without a problem. If your goal is a 10K swim, then prepare to comfortably swim 13K.

The distance tolerance guideline is appropriate for both short-distance and middle-distance swims, but it should be modified for marathon swimming. For swims up to and beyond 25K (15.5 mi), build up to at least one swim that is 60 to 80 percent of your expected marathon distance. Depending on the conditions and opportunities, your longest-distance training swim can be done two to four weeks before the anticipated date of your swim. If you are training for a marathon (i.e., swims over 25K) including channel swims like the 21-mile (33.8K) English Channel, gradually build up to a six- to eight-hour swim performed in the same expected water temperature of your marathon attempt.

If you can do a 15-mile training swim, then you are physically prepared to cross a 21-mile channel, especially if you are psychologically strong and are guided by an experienced pilot and escorted by a good team. Table 6.3 provides examples of tolerance levels for various swims.

**Table 6.3**   Examples of Distance Tolerance

| | |
|---|---|
| **Short-distance swims** | 3 × 1000 with 30 s rest between swims |
| | 2 × 1500 with 1 min rest between swims |
| **Middle-distance swims** | 10 × 800 + 200 hard after each 800 |
| | 50 × 200, alternating sets of 10 swimming and pulling |
| **Marathon swims** | 15 × 500, with each swim gradually getting faster within a set of 5 (i.e., "descend 1-5") |
| | 100 × 100 swims |
| | 15 × 1000 at an even pace |

# SIMULATING RACING CONDITIONS

Race-specific training is overlooked by many pool-oriented coaches, but it simulates open water racing conditions in a pool and helps acclimate you to open water races in which physical contact, running in and out of the water, drafting, and positioning are major components. Practice these aspects of open water swimming in the pool and do not wait until race day to experience them.

## PACELINE SETS

Paceline sets are drills in which groups of swimmers (generally three to five) closely draft off one another, changing leaders, the pace, or both throughout the set. Swim immediately behind the swimmer in front of you while doing a circular pattern within the lane (i.e., always swimming on the right side of the lane).

For 100 paceline sets (done in either a 25-yard or a 50-meter pool), the leader of the group swims a 100 at a set pace. The other swimmers follow closely behind, similar to a group of cyclists in a peloton. After the first 100, the leader stops, pulls over, and waits at the side of the lane out of the way as the other

**FACT**

The Channel Swimming & Piloting Federation requires solo swimmers who attempt the English Channel to complete a certified swim of six hours in water under 61 °F (16 °C) or to provide proof of completion in a recognized event considered an acceptable alternative by the Federation. English Channel relay swimmers must supply proof of a two-hour swim in water under 61 °F or of completion in an event recognized by the Federation. The North (Irish) Channel requires that a swimmer complete the English Channel as a prerequisite.

swimmers continue swimming pass. The swimmers keep the same order as the new leader (who was previously the second swimmer in the peloton) takes over and leads the group for the next 100. This pattern is repeated until everyone has led the group for two to four rotations. The pace can be slow or fast, depending on your group's goal.

If each leader swims at a fairly good pace, the entire set provides the following benefits:

- You get a very good aerobic workout.
- You practice drafting on the feet of your teammates.
- You learn how to conserve energy while drafting at a good pace.
- You increase your focus and awareness of the swimmers around you during every moment of the set because you must be careful to avoid hitting them at the turns and avoid tapping them on their feet.
- You practice increasing and decreasing your pace in the middle of a training set.

If the paceline distance is 50 yards or meters, then your group's pace will get faster because the lead swimmers can maintain a faster pace for a 50 than they can for a 100. Because the leader is going faster, the entire pace of the aquatic peloton gets faster. Conversely, if the pace is increased to 200, the group pace becomes slower for the opposite reason (i.e., the lead swimmers cannot maintain a faster pace for a 200 compared with a 50 or 100.

## POOL OPEN WATER (POW) TRAINING: INITIATION FOR THE UNINITIATED

Even if you train far from an open water swimming venue, you can still prepare by replicating open water racing conditions with pool open water (POW) training. POW training provides many benefits and excellent training for the rigors of open water swimming, enabling you to learn the following:

- Swimming without lane lines
- Swimming without following the black lines on the bottom of the pool
- Swimming in a pack of swimmers in all positions: lead, middle, back, left, and right
- Executing quick turns around buoys in traffic with both left- and right-shoulder turns
- Swimming without pushing off the walls
- Using competitive open water racing tactics, including defensive and offensive maneuvers
- Positioning in a dynamic environment

- Drafting in various positions
- Dealing with physical contact
- Sprinting to the finish

## What Is POW Training?

POW training is done in a pool and is a safe, easy-to-implement, educational, and enjoyable introduction to open water swimming. It can lead to increased confidence and is a fun change for many swimmers. Coaches using POW training can be confident that they are providing a great aerobic workout for their athletes while acclimating them to open water racing.

POW training is conducted in a pool after removing the lane lines and setting four turn buoys near the corners of the pool. If all the lane lines cannot be removed because other swimmers are simultaneously using the pool, remove only a few lane lines and set two turn buoys near both ends of the pool. This reduces the area necessary to hold a POW workout, but provides the same benefits. POW course configurations are flexible and can be determined as your situation allows.

## POW Configurations

An eight-lane, 50-meter pool is preferable for a POW workout, but smaller pools of any dimensions can also be used. In a 50-meter pool, place four turn buoys near the four corners of the pool, enabling a total distance of approximately 120 meters for each loop (see figure 6.2 on page 108).

In a standard POW course, the four turn buoys are anchored at the intersections of the outside lanes and the backstroke flags. If only a few lanes are available because of crowded conditions, then anchor two turn buoys at the end of the pool near the backstroke flags to create a cylindrical course (see figure 6.3 on page 108).

## POW Training

Once a POW course is set up, swim around the course in a clockwise and then counterclockwise direction, practicing both left- and right-shoulder turns around the buoys. Your ability to skillfully make turns in either direction is important because there are no standard open water courses or turns. Entire workouts can be conducted using a POW configuration (see table 6.4 on page 109).

## POW Tips

If you have never seen or participated in a POW workout, here are some tips:

- POW workouts can be conducted in any direction, but initially, counterclockwise is recommended because most swimmers are right-handed and most find left-shoulder turns a bit easier than right-shoulder turns.

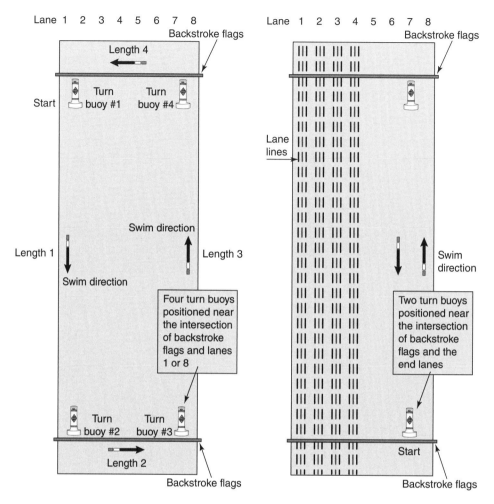

**Figure 6.2** 50-meter rectangular POW configuration.

**Figure 6.3** Cylindrical POW configuration while sharing pool time.

- When you and your teammates become more accustomed to POW swimming, add different configurations to your workouts. Do X-shaped or Z-shaped patterns in the pool (see figure 6.4), or follow the leader to become equally adept at doing any type of turn in the open water.

- Practice turns at various angles, not only 90-degree and 180-degree turns.

- Ask your coach to use a whistle and issue yellow and red cards in practice to simulate the actions of a referee in a race. A yellow card is a warning; a red card is a disqualification if you pull anyone back or commit unsportsmanlike conduct.

- POW is also useful when you train in a shallow pool. Not only are more waves created when there are no lane lines in the pool, but you can also practice your dolphining technique.

• Practice onshore finishes by doing deck-ups. Instead of finishing by touching the wall or turn buoy, swim to the end of the pool and then pull yourself out of the water and onto the pool deck (i.e., perform a deck-up). This sudden change from swimming in a horizontal position to standing in the vertical position simulates onshore finishes in open water races.

**Table 6.4    POW Workout Example**

| Warm-up | Swim two loops around the course in a clockwise direction and then two loops around the course in a counterclockwise direction. |
| --- | --- |
| Preset | Swim length 1 of the course at a comfortable pace, length 2 at a medium pace, length 3 at a fast pace, and length 4 all-out. Repeat each stroke twice. |
| Pulling | Pull two loops with a pull buoy. |
| Kicking | Kick two loops with a kickboard. |
| Main set | Paceline Swim: 4 × 1 loop where everyone swims immediately behind the feet of the swimmer in front of them. Each person has an opportunity to lead the group for one loop. Sprint Paceline Swim 3 × 2 loops where three swimmers swim abreast for the first loop at a comfortable pace and then race on the second loop. Swimmers switch positions (left-middle-right) after each loop.<br>Descend Swim: 4 × 1 loops at three minutes, gradually getting faster on each swim. |
| Sprint work | Relay: 4 × 1 loop where each relay member does one loop.<br>Open Water Starts and Finishes: Dolphin one length all-out + one length easy freestyle. Repeat five times. |
| Cool-down | Swim in an X- or Z-shaped pattern in the POW course for five minutes. |

Steven Munatones

**Figure 6.4**    POW training in a Z-shaped pattern.

- If many swimmers do a POW workout together, different groups can be set off at different times to maximize the number of people using the course (see figure 6.5). For example, when the first swimmer of group one reaches the first turn buoy, the second group can start, so dozens of swimmers can swim the POW course at the same time.

- Paceline sets work well in POW training when swimmers closely follow each other, swimming right behind the feet or the hips of the swimmer in front of them. This proximity to other swimmers, and the occasional physical contact that occurs, are practical training experiences that introduce you to the real world of competitive open water racing.

- To become familiar with various positions that you will encounter in competitive open water swimming, switch positions within any given POW paceline set to experience the following:
  - The difference between swimming on the inside and on the outside
  - The difference between swimming in the front in the lead and drafting behind
  - Being boxed in, in the middle of the pack
  - Swimming two body lengths behind the group

- Remain alert for physical contact. Impeding, obstructing, and interfering with other swimmers is not the goal of POW training, but it will happen on occasion.

Steven Munatones

**Figure 6.5** Starting a POW set with groups at different times.

## POW PACELINE SETS

The level of swimmers in each POW group should be as evenly matched as possible. This is an excellent way to create a situation where you push each other. However, if the swimmers' individual abilities are different, they can still push the pace while in the lead.

POW paceline sets provide the best combination of aerobic training and race-specific training in a pool. To best simulate an open water race in a pool, sprint the last part of each set (e.g., 50, 100, or 200 yards) or time (e.g., 1 to 3 minutes) and have everyone try to win. The coach can blow a whistle to signal the start of the final sprint in a POW set.

The race-pace POW finish is particularly helpful for race-specific training (see table 6.5). Although the leader of the pack has the initial advantage, the trailing swimmers often have the momentum to catch and pass the leader as a result of their drafting position. Of course, with three to five people swimming all-out in a paceline POW set, exercise caution. Arms may cross or become entangled. But, this kind of all-out closing sprint under slightly confusing, crowded, and stressful conditions is as close as you can get to experiencing real-world open water racing in a pool.

**Table 6.5**   Examples of Race-Specific Training

| | |
|---|---|
| **Short-distance swims** | Standard paceline with four swimmers: Swim 2 × 800 with a leader change every 100 yd and 1 min rest after each 800. |
| | Standard paceline with three swimmers: Swim 1 × 450 with a leader change every 50 yd so each swimmer leads the group three times. |
| | POW paceline with four swimmers: Swim 16 loops with a leader change every two loops. |
| | POW paceline with three swimmers: Swim six loops with a leader change every loop. |
| **Middle-distance swims** | Standard paceline with three swimmers: Swim 3 × 1000 with a leader change every 100 yd and a 20 s rest after each 1000. |
| | Standard paceline with four swimmers: Swim 4 × 800 with a leader change every 200 + 1 × 100 fast sprint for time. |
| | POW paceline with four swimmers: Swim 16 loops with a leader change every two loops + a two-loop closing sprint with everyone swimming to win. |
| | POW paceline with five swimmers: Swim 18 loops with a leader change every loop + a three-loop closing sprint with everyone swimming to win. |
| **Marathon swims** | Standard paceline with two swimmers: Swim 4 × 1500 with a change of leader every 500 yd. Odd-numbered swims are pulling; even-numbered swims are regular swimming. |
| | POW paceline with three swimmers: Leaders change every 10 minutes over a 1-hour time period. |

## DECK-UPS

Deck-ups are another essential race-specific training drill for open water swimmers and triathletes (see table 6.6). They are ideal for onshore finishes and for the swim–bike transitions in triathlons (called T1). In deck-up sets, immediately pull yourself out of the pool after every swim and dive back into the pool to start the next swim. Your body position change from horizontal to vertical simulates on-the-beach finishes and T1 transitions.

Deck-ups assist your open water racing preparation in a number of indirect ways. Because deck-ups increase your heart rate, especially if you swim at a good pace, they are an excellent way to train yourself to respond to surges by your competitors. Also, in channel swims, you must "clear the water" with no assistance from others to officially finish. This means that after you have swum for several hours in the horizontal position, you must go vertical by walking onshore.

**Table 6.6   Example of Deck-up Training**

| Short-distance swims | 10 × 50 deck-up swims with even-number swims hard at 1:30 |
|---|---|
| Middle-distance swims | 12 × 200 deck-up swims, swim progressively faster in each set of 3 swims ("descend 1-3") at 2:30 |
| Marathon swims | 5 × 1000 swims with deck-ups at the end of each 1000 |

# DEVELOPING TECHNICAL SKILLS

Skills training teaches the finer technical points of open water swimming, including feedings, sighting, starts, turns, positioning, and navigation, all of which can be simulated in a pool. The term *feedings* can occasionally be a misnomer. Most feedings are actually hydration stops in which swimmers only drink.

## SIMULATING FEEDINGS

Drink from a water bottle and place gel packs in your swimsuit to practice feedings in the pool. Drink from your water bottle and consume your gel packs while you are treading water—not while hanging on the wall or standing on the pool bottom.

Ask your coach to bring a feeding stick to the pool, if available. Practice open water feedings by briefly stopping in the middle of the pool in the outside lanes. Grab your bottle from the feeding stick, stop to drink, and then resume swimming. If you do not have a feeding stick, set your water bottle set at the edge of the pool and practice quickly grabbing and drinking from it.

Practice fast feedings. You can always drink comfortably and slowly before and after practice, but practice consuming drinks in the pool quickly, preferably up to 6 fluid ounces (177 ml) within five seconds if possible. With practice, fast feedings will become second nature.

If you are a marathon swimmer, the discipline of keeping to relatively short feedings is important. In marathon swims, feeding breaks tend to get longer and longer as the swim progresses and the swimmer tires or the conditions worsen. An additional 20 or more minutes spent feeding and not moving forward can lead to problems, especially if the winds come up or you miss the tides.

## PRACTICING NAVIGATION

Practice navigation and sighting (see figure 6.6) in the pool by lifting your head and looking forward every fourth lap while you do your regular interval training sets (e.g., 6 × 400). With practice, effective sighting can become second nature. It is critical to continue kicking and not drop your hips or lower your legs when you lift your head to sight. Also, remember to push the water backward—not downward—in the first part of your arm stroke to maintain your maximum velocity during sighting.

Your coach can set an orange traffic cone at the end of the pool in various locations every 100 yards or every few minutes. Your goals are to quickly sight and find the new position of the traffic cone (e.g., at the end of lane 2 or under the starting block in lane 6). Your coach can then move the traffic cone to a different location when you swim in the opposite direction.

**Figure 6.6**   Navigation—alone and in a pack—must be practiced in all conditions.

If a traffic cone is not available, but a small portable pace clock is, your coach can move the pace clock to a different location at the end of the pool every few minutes. The purpose of this drill is to check your split times every 100 yards by locating not only the pace clock itself, but also the second hand on it. This can be difficult if you are nearsighted, but it does force you to learn how to sight efficiently, especially when looking for distant turn buoys in the open water, which can be difficult to spot.

Do not continue to swim with your head up if you do not see the traffic cone (or pace clock) on your first attempt. When you swim head-up for several consecutive strokes to find your target, your hips will drop and your speed will decrease. If you cannot see your target the first time you lift your head, put your head back down, take a few more strokes, and look up again.

Incorporate bilateral breathing (also called alternate-side breathing) in your pool training sets, even if you traditionally favor left- or right-side breathing. Bilateral breathing will help you balance your stroke. It will also enable you to check on your competition, landmarks, and navigational points in the open water on both sides.

## Contra-Flow Lanes

Contra-flow lane patterns are best done in a pool without lane lines. Without lane lines, the pool will become more wavy and more closely simulate the open water. Instead of everyone swimming up the right side of the lane and down the left side of the lane as usual, the swimmers in the even-numbered lanes can continue with this traditional configuration while the swimmers in the odd-numbered lanes swim in the opposite direction. With this configuration, everyone is swimming alongside swimmers in the lane immediately adjacent to them.

## Rounding Buoy Turns

Nothing is better than POW sets for simulating open water turns in the pool. But even without turn buoys, you can practice open water turns by swimming to the ends of the black lines on the bottom of the pool. Without touching the wall or making a flip turn, turn around to head back in the opposite direction without pushing off the wall. Do this no-wall turn in various ways to practice various ways to get around a turn buoy. How you get around a turn buoy is often dictated by the number of swimmers near you and the angle of the turn (see chapter 9).

In the first type of no-wall turns, do a regular flip turn at the end of the black line without touching your feet to the wall. Build momentum by taking a few quick arm strokes augmented by a strong freestyle or scissors kick.

In the second type of no-wall turn, do an open turn in which you change direction by swiveling over your hips and turning on your side using a crossover arm stroke with your outer arm and a scissors kick.

Do these no-wall turns on every lap or every other lap when you are swimming at a comfortable pace or, even better, during the last four laps of a set when you are swimming fast. No-wall turns are more difficult when you are swimming fast because your momentum carries you in the opposite direction to where you want to go. This training simulates turns in the open water because you have to change direction without the benefit of using the pool walls, which is exactly what happens in the open water.

## REFINING DRAFTING SKILLS

There are plenty of ways to practice and simulate drafting and positioning in the pool (see table 6.7). The most practical and beneficial way is doing a POW training set with partners. But you can also swim with other swimmers in your lane in various formations.

You can swim one behind each other paceline style, so you are nearly touching your teammate's feet. Alternatively, three swimmers can swim abreast shoulder to shoulder in the same lane. In this case, the middle swimmer takes the lead and the other two swimmers draft on either side of the leader's feet, knees, hips, or shoulders.

## PRACTICING STARTS AND FINISHES

A shallow pool is a great place to practice the dolphining technique that is used during onshore starts and finishes (see table 6.8 on page 116). If you swim in a shallow pool (e.g., 3 ft, or 1 m, deep), practice dolphining by placing both hands above your head and pushing off the bottom of the pool at a shallow angle. When you reach bottom, grab (or hold) the bottom with both hands, pull your legs

**Table 6.7** Examples of Drafting and Positioning

| | |
|---|---|
| **Short-distance swims** | 9 × 100 at 1:30, in which three swimmers swim together. The middle swimmer starts a half body ahead. The head of the drafting swimmer is at the waist of the middle swimmer for the first 75 yards. Keep this formation until the final 25 yards, when it then becomes an all-out sprint. Rotate positions (left, right, and middle) after three swims so each swimmer practices in each position. |
| **Middle-distance swims** | 9 × 300 at 4:00 with every third 300 fast. Swim immediately behind one another, nipping at each other's heels, but collectively descend your swim times in groups of three. The final time is the time of the last swimmer. The first swimmer leads for the first three swims. the second swimmer leads for the second three swims, and the third swimmer leads for the final three swims in the set. |
| **Marathon swims** | 3 × 1000 with three swimmers together in one lane. Swimmers swim straight in the lane, not in a circular pattern. Each swimmer leads the other two swimmers for one 1000. Swimmer 1 swims at the waist of Swimmer 2. Swimmer 2 swims at waist of Swimmer 3. Rotate swimmers in the lead. This formation may be difficult to maintain, but it is a great exercise to develop mental focus and position awareness. |

**Table 6.8**   Examples of Dolphining

| Short-distance swims | 10 × 75 at 1:30 with the first 50 normal freestyle and the last 25 doing fast dolphining |
|---|---|
| Middle-distance swims | 10 × 200 at 3:00 with dolphining on the first and last 25 |
| Marathon-distance swims | Not necessary |

under you, and immediately push off the bottom at an approximate 45-degree angle to head toward the surface.

As you slightly clear the water, arc yourself gracefully over the surface of the water as you take a breath of air and begin to dive back down into the water. Repeat the dolphining motion the length of the pool. Remain as streamlined as possible during the push off the bottom as you break the surface and reenter the water. As you dolphin, place one hand over the other and keep both arms pressed tightly against your head. Kick hard throughout your dolphining sets to maintain the highest possible velocity, which will be helpful when you race in the ocean and fight through oncoming waves. You can also incorporate starts and finishes into sets when you practice in a shallow pool and time yourself to measure your improvement.

In short- and middle-distance swims, swimmers are usually surprised at the speed of the pack to the first turn buoy. Simulate race starts in your pool practices by sprinting side by side in one lane with two other swimmers for 50 yards. The more competitive you want to become, the more important it is to practice this drill with teammates. Although you may feel a bit uncomfortable and crowded, this type of skills training simulates the conditions of triathlons and open water swims.

You may not have ever played water polo, but you can think like a water polo player at the start and finish of competitive open water races by protecting your space and swimming defensively, offensively, or perhaps even aggressively. Swimming defensively means that you protect your space and maintain your position when you get bumped or brushed against. Do not move or get veered out of your preferred navigational line by a competitor.

Swimming offensively means that you literally move into, or toward, the space of your competitors. Usually only the most competitive swimmers do this at key points in swims or triathlons.

Swimming aggressively means that you intentionally bump or veer your competitors in a direction you wish them to swim. You can still legally influence the positioning of your competitors by not crossing the line of good sporting behavior. Like short-track speed skaters who maneuver around the ice rink at incredible speeds, open water swimmers frequently come into contact with each other. If you swim very close to your competitors, most likely, they will move, giving you an edge.

If you decide to swim offensively or aggressively, you may bump, touch, or brush up against the torso, feet, legs, or arms of your competitors. This takes experience and skill for two primary reasons: (1) Your most experienced or aggressive competitors will similarly protect their own positions and may retaliate in some way, and (2) you must be careful not to impede the progress of your opponents (see figure 6.7). Of course, impeding the progress of your opponents is a matter of interpretation and perspective, but it is generally observed that the more aggressively you swim, the more likely you will generate bad feelings in a local race or draw the attention of referees in a major race.

One way to practice offensive or aggressive swimming in a pool is to swim shoulder to shoulder with two teammates in the same lane. You will likely brush against your teammate; you may even bump each other, but this kind of physical contact is better to experience in practice so you learn to not get frustrated or intimidated during a race. You must be prepared when unanticipated physical contact occurs at the start, around turn buoys, or toward the finish (see figure 6.8 on page 118). If you really want to get accustomed to the physical contact that occurs at the start of triathlons or large swims, swim butterfly with a partner in the same lane at the same time side by side.

Of course, if you simply aim to finish a race or swim from point A to point B, then offensive or aggressive swimming is completely unnecessary; most swimmers do not find it enjoyable. Keep in mind, though, that aggressive swimmers are not the only ones who initiate physical contact in the open water. Often, inexperienced swimmers or those with a low navigational IQ are just as guilty of bumping into and frustrating other swimmers. The result is the same; the only difference is the intent.

**Figure 6.7**   Swimming offensively while not impeding the progress of opponents.

Dr. Jim Miller

**Figure 6.8** Unintended physical contact is unavoidable, and you must be aware of your surroundings at all times.

## EXPECTING THE UNEXPECTED: RECOVERING YOUR EQUIPMENT

Accidents do happen, and you can prepare for the inevitabilities with simple drills. You can start a set of 5 × 200 with your goggles tucked inside your swimsuit. On the middle of the first lap of each 200, take your goggles from your swimsuit and quickly put them on. Try to swim as close as possible to your normal 200 pace as you learn how to put on your goggles quickly.

For an even more difficult drill and to simulate the confusion and stress that may occur if you lose your goggles in a crowded race, start each 200 with your goggles already on. During the first 50, remove your goggles and let them float in the lane while you continue swimming. During the second 50, locate your goggles and quickly put them back on. With practice, you will be surprised at how quickly you can put your goggles on.

Sometimes, you will accidently get skin lubricant, sunscreen, or lanolin on your hands or arms by brushing up against a greased competitor before or during a race. To prepare for this unusual sensation, purposefully put some petroleum jelly on your hands and forearms to learn what it feels like. You can also put a dab of petroleum jelly on an old pair of goggles and learn to swim with impaired vision.

Your swim cap may occasionally fall off during a race and you will not find it. To prepare for this, purposefully take off your swim cap during a practice—even if you have long hair—and learn how it feels to swim without one.

# ACCLIMATING TO THE OPEN WATER

Open water acclimatization, especially if you are new to the sport, is required to familiarize yourself with the marine environment, which can be very cold, warm, rough, polluted, or filled with marine life. The water may be very deep and clear, permitting you to see everything below you, or it may be the exact opposite. Either situation can be a psychological barrier that can be just as difficult to overcome as the physical challenges. Practicing with a patient, experienced teammate will help you cross these barriers.

Open water acclimatization also includes learning to deal with jellyfish and sea nettles; swim through surface chop, boat fumes, oil slicks, kelp, fog, pollution, flotsam, and jetsam and race despite waves, chop, and currents. If you experience any of these conditions for the first time in a race, you may be surprised, frustrated, or alarmed. Your heart can begin to pound unmercifully or feel like it skipped a few beats. In order to increase your level of comfort in these difficult situations, you can lift your head and look around to see other athletes, stop and do a few strokes of breaststroke, or call over the water safety personnel.

Cold water often presents the most difficult barrier in open water swimming. Cold water acclimatization (CWA) takes significant time, effort, sacrifice, and commitment. Depending on where you live and what your goals are, give yourself months to prepare for a non-wetsuit cold water swim of significant length. Preparing for a marathon swim in water below 60 °F (15.6 °C) often takes several months. It is not an easy process; there are no shortcuts. Start swimming in cold water as early in the spring if reasonable. You may only be able to withstand the cold water for one minute when you first jump in. But practicing consistently and frequently in cold water will help you naturally acclimate to the environment.

The opposite is true for warm water swims. You may want to practice occasionally with a wetsuit in a pool to simulate the stress of swimming in uncomfortably warm conditions.

It is also possible that you will get stung by jellyfish, be bothered by sea nettles, get tangled in seaweed, run into floating plastic bags, or choke on fumes from boats or Jet Skis. The experience will be frustrating and unpleasant, but the good news is that the sensations will be temporary and you will be stronger and less surprised the next time.

# DEVELOPING TACTICAL KNOWLEDGE

As open water swimming becomes more competitive, tactical knowledge is often the most overlooked training component. But with enhanced tactical knowledge, you can enjoy improved performance and a greater understanding of what it takes to achieve success in the open water.

Tactical knowledge refers to your understanding of the dynamics of open water racing. Because literally thousands of conditions and situations occur in races, gaining tactical knowledge is an ongoing process that takes years—and is never over because the sport and competition continue to evolve. It includes learning why packs of swimmers form, how they get formed along various points in the race (including straightaways and turns), and why they take on certain shapes. You can develop a greater understanding of how to tactically place yourself in the pack at various points during the race and of the importance of hydration and feeding techniques.

Some people want to win, but many others simply want to finish or do better than before. Tactical knowledge comprises a unique spectrum of information for each swimmer. At the simplest level, it includes only knowledge about the course. At the highest level, it includes course information; how to use the elements; and an in-depth knowledge of the strengths, weaknesses, and expected tactics of competitors. Figure 6.9 illustrates the hierarchy that tactical knowledge takes when assessing your race goals.

## STUDYING YOUR PERFORMANCE AND YOUR OPPONENTS' PERFORMANCES

Many races are posted online on video-sharing services such as YouTube and Vimeo. You can review these videos to learn the tactics of successful open water swimmers and triathletes. You can also study your opponents by watching videos of previous races. Research your competitors' best pool times. Go to clinics, camps, and presentations where you can directly talk with top athletes and coaches. Ask them about various scenarios and their recommendations. Experienced open water swimmers, coaches, and triathletes enjoy talking about their sport, so getting valuable information from them is often only a matter of asking questions.

Athletes in a variety of sports watch videos of themselves and their opponents to learn how to gain an edge or make up for a weakness. For example, the best

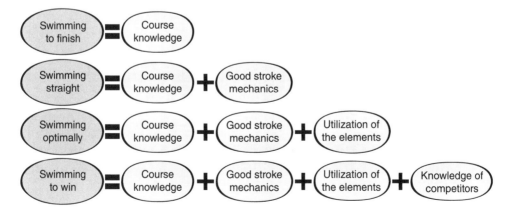

**Figure 6.9**   Range of information needs for success.

---

### POOL TRAINING TIPS

In addition to paceline training, deck-ups, and POW workouts, the following pool training tips will help you perform well in the open water:

- Do a main set without touching or pushing off the walls—just swim from backstroke flag to backstroke flag.
- Change tempo and pace periodically though your workout.
- Occasionally remove all lane lines to create abnormally wavy conditions in the pool. Use a contra-flow circular pattern in these cases.
- If possible, drop the water level in the pool a few inches (or centimeters) and then remove all the lane lines. This will create very wavy conditions.

---

race car drivers, runners, and cyclists know what their strengths are relative to those of the competition and when to slow down or speed up. These athletes develop a competitive mind-set and the physical tools to put themselves in a position to win. You can do the same in the open water world.

Before you jump in the water, learn how to deal with a variety of scenarios that can occur during a swim. This tactical knowledge will come with experience and will boost your confidence. After every race, conduct a post-race analysis in which you objectively think about and review your performance.

## INCORPORATING OTHER STROKES

The ability to swim straight is one of the best assets of an open water swimmer. In addition to bilateral breathing and having an efficient freestyle stroke, you can help yourself become more symmetrical by adding butterfly, backstroke, breaststroke, and individual medley sets to your pool swimming workouts.

Incorporating other strokes into your workouts has the following benefits:

- Butterfly builds strength, is good for your abdominal muscles, and is aerobically challenging.
- Butterfly and breaststroke require bilateral symmetry with both left and rights sides moving together at the same tempo. As a result, these strokes help establish more muscular symmetry.
- Backstroke also develops bilateral symmetry over time. When you share your lane line with other swimmers, you will quickly learn to swim straight using backstroke out of necessity.
- Because backstroke can be considered an inversion of freestyle, it works your arm and leg muscles in the opposite directions, which builds overall strength.
- Your hip rotation in backstroke can improve your hip rotation in freestyle.

- If you have a relatively weak freestyle kick, working on other strokes, especially backstroke, will build leg strength. Also, many swimmers often kick more in backstroke than they do in the freestyle.

- Learning and working on all the swim strokes helps you become more kinetically aware of your body's movements in the water. This will help you improve your freestyle.

- Individual medley (butterfly + backstroke + breaststroke + freestyle) sets are aerobically challenging. Finishing an individual medley set with fast freestyle splits is a great way to work on your finish sprints.

- By incorporating other strokes, you can add significant variety to your pool workouts while enabling you to be less dependent on hand paddles, pull buoys, and kickboards.

Following are a number of individual medley (IM) sets:

- 100 IM + 200 IM + 300 IM + 400 IM

- 100 IM + 200 IM + 300 IM + 400 IM in reverse order (i.e., freestyle + breaststroke + backstroke + butterfly)

- 1 × 25 easy freestyle + 1 × 25 hard butterfly

- 1 × 25 easy freestyle + 1 × 25 hard backstroke

- 1 × 25 easy freestyle + 1 × 25 hard breaststroke

- Then increase the hard 25s to 50 yards on the second set, to 75 yards on the third set, and to 100 yards on the fourth set.

- 5 × 100. The first push-off from the wall on lap 1 is either one underwater breaststroke pull or two underwater butterfly or backstroke kicks. The rest of the first lap is freestyle. The second push-off on lap 2 is either two underwater breaststroke pulls or four underwater butterfly or backstroke kicks. The rest of the second lap is freestyle. The third push-off on lap 3 is either three underwater breaststroke pulls or six underwater butterfly or backstroke kicks. The rest of the third lap is freestyle. The fourth push-off on lap 4 is either four underwater breaststroke pulls or eight underwater butterfly or backstroke kicks. The rest of the lap is freestyle.

## STRENGTHENING YOUR CORE WITH ABDOMINAL WORK

You need a strong core to assist with body positioning and stroke efficiency in open water swimming. The following set will help you build your core, especially if you maintain a small amplitude with your feet as you kick from your core and maintain a streamlined body position with a strong kick during head-up freestyle:

- 1 × 25 butterfly kick on your back + 1 × 25 head-up freestyle
- 2 × 50 butterfly kick on your back + 2 × 50 head-up freestyle
- 3 × 75 butterfly kick on your back + 3 × 75 head-up freestyle
- 4 × 100 butterfly kick on your back + 4 × 100 head-up freestyle

## LEARNING HOW TO SWIM STRAIGHT

Swimming straight is not simply the ability to sight well or sight frequently in the open water. Swimming straight requires a streamlined body position and a balanced, symmetrical freestyle stroke that must be constantly worked on during practice. If you do not swim straight, find out whether you tend to veer to the left or to the right, and by how much.

A series of simple self-tests in the open water can show you whether you tend to hook (i.e., swim to the left) or slice (i.e., swim to the right). Start near the shoreline and identify one or two landmarks behind and ahead of you such as buildings or piers. Take 50 to 100 strokes straight out from shore with your eyes closed. Try to swim as straight as possible. After you stop, note where you are and confirm your position relative to the starting point. Repeat this test a few times at various speeds (slow, medium, and fast). You will learn whether you naturally hook or slice. Once you know your natural tendencies, repeat the test, trying to compensate in some way to see whether you swim straighter. Repeat this exercise every few months to confirm whether you are improving your navigational IQ.

## LEARNING PROPER SIGHTING

Swimming straight requires sighting, in which you lift your head to take a quick look at the course ahead. Following are the fundamentals of sighting:

- Incorporate sighting into your natural arm stroke rhythm.
- Slightly increase your kick to support your head and upper body while sighting.
- Take a breath to the side every time you sight.
- Look for landmarks, trees, turn buoys, piers, buildings, intermediate buoys, safety boats, or other swimmers to create a mental picture of where to swim.
- Adjust your bearings according to what you see.

When sighting, lift your head forward, capture the mental picture, and then rotate your head to the side to breathe. Lift your head only until your goggles are barely breaking the surface of the water. This may not be possible when there is heavy surface chop or large surf. If you cannot see where you are going because of a wave, boats, or surface chop, do not stop or keep swimming with your head up. Instead, put your head back down in the water, take a few more strokes, and then sight again. If there are waves or heavy surface chop, time your sighting to occur at the crest of the wave and not in the trough where your view is blocked.

Keep in mind that your head, hips, and legs will sink slightly every time you sight. To understand the negative impact of sighting on your swimming speed, compare your normal race-pace 100 freestyle time and your race-pace 100 freestyle time when you sight once every 25 yards. In this test replicated among swimmers of various ages and abilities, many swimmers are at least two seconds slower when sighting, which amounts to an additional 0.5 seconds per sighting. If you are an average swimmer, sighting this often will add 1 minute and 24 seconds to the 2.4-mile (3.9K) Ironman swim leg.

## Avoiding Heavy Lifting

You will always have to sight in a race, but if you can swim relatively straight and limit the number of sightings, you will save time and energy. If you sight an average of once every 25 yards, then you will lift your head approximately 169 times in a 2.4-mile (3.9K) Ironman swim. If you sight once every 15 yards, as many swimmers are taught, then you will lift your head 282 times in a 2.4-mile (3.9K) swim.

If the weight of your head is 11 pounds (5 kg), then you will theoretically lift the equivalent of nearly 1 ton (2,000 lb, or 907 kg) during a 2.4-mile swim if you sight every 25 yards and 1.54 tons (1,397 kg) if you sight every 15 yards. That's a lot of heavy lifting. If you minimize your sighting frequency, you can use your energy for other actions in the open water.

## Taking Advantage of Sighting Alternatives

Sighting forward is not the only kind of sighting you can use in the open water. You also want to sight to your left and right during your natural breathing sequence. You can easily gain navigational clues from swimmers and landmarks on either side when you take a breath, using peripheral vision. Another option is to sight by looking diagonally forward or diagonally behind you. For diagonal sighting, you do not have to do a complete head lift, but only a modified shift of your head and range of vision.

You can also get a good idea of where you are by first sighting forward and then sighting behind you. Alternatively, quickly turn over on your back and take one or two strokes while you look behind you, a useful move if you are swimming back to shore when there is surf. Having a good idea of where you are going and where you came from will definitely give you a better idea of where you are.

## Pre-Race Preparations

Swimming straight requires that you understand the course before you get in the water. Learn where all the possible landmarks and course buoys are, as well as the number of buoys on the course, their size, positioning and colors. You also need to know the approximate distance to shore at every point in the race and the direction and approximate force of the oncoming currents or tides.

Ask the race director whether there will be a lead boat or whether the lead swimmer will be swimming blind (i.e., without an escort). Everyone swims straighter when there is a lead boat or kayaker. Conversely, without one, swimmers must navigate the course themselves.

If you are swimming parallel to the shoreline, know whether there are any hotels, houses, buildings, lifeguard towers, tall structures, piers, or boat launches that you can use to approximate the distance you have covered. For example, knowing there is a lifeguard tower located near the halfway mark will help you pace yourself in the race. If you are heading back toward shore for the finish in an out-and-back course, know the relative angles between the turn buoys, visible landmarks, and the finish line. This information can provide valuable clues so you can triangulate your position throughout the race.

## USING THE ELEMENTS

Swimming optimally requires everything explained thus far: having good stroke mechanics and comprehensive course knowledge. In addition, you should know how to best use the elements such as wind, surface chop, waves, currents, and tides. Even if wind, waves, and currents are against you, use them to your advantage relative to your competition. If the wind, waves, and currents are moving in the same direction as you are swimming, use them to your advantage.

You may sometimes want to swim off the straight-line course to take advantage of the elements. For example, if the ocean swells are hitting you at an angle on your right hip, you can offset your course slightly to the left when you feel the ocean swell lift you forward. Use the power of the waves to push you closer and faster to your goal even if you are not necessarily going in a straight line. Then, in the trough of the swells, re-correct your course to head straight for the next turn buoy. Continue to take advantage of the swells even if you temporarily head slightly off course; you can always correct between swells.

Surface chop due to wind, ocean waves, currents, or a tidal pull is highly unlikely to be going parallel or perpendicular to your straight-line course. With this information, think like a mariner and compensate for the elements. For example, if the currents and surface chop are hitting you at a 45-degree angle, modify your orientation so the net effect is that you swim optimally from point to point or from turn buoy to turn buoy.

## COMPENSATING AND NAVIGATING

Navigational compensation for the elements takes various forms in the open water. When you are swimming into shore and the waves are pushing you, but not exactly to the finish line, continue to ride the waves to the finish, using their power to get you to shore faster. Once you hit the shore, run to the finish because it is faster to run on land than it is to swim in the ocean.

If your swim is near a pier, jetty, or seawall, it is often advantageous to swim off the straight-line tangent. Water often flows most quickly along a pier, jetty, or seawall than elsewhere. Take advantage of swimming along a fast-flowing portion of the waterway even if it is not the straightest path to the finish or next turn.

The velocity of water flow in a river or along a shoreline generally increases with the depth of the water. If you know where a river or ocean channel is deeper than average, you can swim off the straight line to take advantage of these faster currents.

### DEVELOPING YOUR NAVIGATIONAL IQ

The ability to compensate for the elements is based on your navigational IQ. Compensating in the open water is second nature for some swimmers. Others are less comfortable in the open water. If you fall among the second group, practice and learn through experience and observation. Practice in rough water conditions when waves, surface chop, and currents are present. Ask your coach to video-record your training swims and races so you can analyze your navigational abilities. If you practice only when the water is calm, facing rough conditions on race day will lead to frustration and disappointment.

## SWIMMING TO WIN

Swimming to win is the ultimate competitive approach to open water swimming, but is not necessarily everyone's goal. Winning can result in handshakes and hugs from your competitors to thousands of dollars in prize money. But as famed UCLA basketball coach John Wooden stated, "Success is a peace of mind which is a direct result of self-satisfaction in knowing you did your best to become the best you are capable of becoming" (http://www.coachwooden.com/index2.html).

Dr. Jim Miller

# PREPARING FOR MIDDLE-DISTANCE SWIMS

Open water swimming is experiencing a revolution unlike anything it has seen in its history since Gertrude Ederle brought worldwide acclaim to the sport with her English Channel crossing in 1926.

Besides the emergence of triathlons, which have introduced millions of multi-sport endurance athletes to open water swimming, the Olympic 10K Marathon Swim's introduction at the 2008 Beijing Olympics and the dramatic 10K courses in Hyde Park planned for the 2012 London Olympics and at Copacabana Beach for the 2016 Rio Olympics have served as catalysts for global growth. As a result, middle-distance races are held in bodies of water around the world. Swimmers compete in various point-to-point and loop courses with water temperatures ranging from a low of 55 °F (12.8 °C) to a high of 85 °F (29.4 °C).

For some swimmers, simply completing a middle-distance swim is their primary goal. But for an increasing number of competitively oriented swimmers, a thoughtful approach to performing well is important. This chapter is written primarily for these competitive athletes.

# INCORPORATING THE PYRAMID OF OPEN WATER SUCCESS

A strategic, comprehensive, year-round approach is required to perform well in middle-distance races. Integrating the Pyramid of Open Water Success outlined in chapter 6 is critically important to establishing a well-rounded training program.

Although environmental conditions (e.g., winter) and logistical issues (e.g., lack of access to open water) may prevent you from fully integrating all of the pyramid elements during some months of the year, work on each area when circumstances allow. At the very least, incorporate different elements into each week's workout because you will use these skills at some point during your races.

A focus on the pyramid elements lead to increased workout creativity and a well-rounded holistic approach to open water swimming. This creativity will eliminate the boredom that may come from an overreliance on only base training and distance tolerance. For example, if you work on distance tolerance during a pool workout, concurrently work on skills training (e.g., sighting and feeding) by incorporating one or two sightings on every fourth lap during a 4 × 1000 swim paceline set and taking a feeding during each 1000.

# FUNDAMENTAL RACING STYLES

Although every competition and body of water is unique, there are four fundamental competitive styles of racing at the world-class level. Each is named after the country of an accomplished athlete: the Dutch Style, the Russian Style, the British Style, and the German Style.

Whether you are a world-class athlete or a newcomer, you can adopt one of these racing styles to fit your level of fitness and strengths. Most importantly, determining your racing style will help you decide your training goals so your training is more purposeful.

## DUTCH STYLE OF RACING

The Dutch style is epitomized by world champion and 2008 Olympic gold medalist Maarten van der Weijden. Van der Weijden recovered from leukemia and dramatically won the 2008 Beijing Olympics 10K Marathon Swim and was known for sitting back in the early parts of the race until he forged his way through the lead pack with a tremendously fast closing sprint.

Swimmers using the Dutch style swim relaxed during the first half of the race. They stay toward the back in the lead pack, avoiding confrontation, drafting, and conserving their physical and mental energies. They think strategically about their position and pace and know the tendencies and abilities of their competitors. They are patient and tactical thinkers, skillfully biding their time to charge to the front in the late stages of the races. They hydrate well during the race and have the energy to sprint fast when others are fading.

Physically, the Dutch style requires a strong foundation of base training combined with frequent speed training and comprehensive tactical knowledge of one's own strengths and the weaknesses of competitors. The Dutch style requires swimmers to constantly monitor and modify their position relative to that of their opponents during the race. It is a relatively risky style because conserving energy throughout the race can result in being too late in the final charge.

The Dutch style demands patience and a tremendous closing speed. It is best suited to cerebral swimmers who enjoy tactical moves as they make their way through the pack to open water at the front.

## RUSSIAN STYLE OF RACING

The Russian style is epitomized by multiple world champion and Olympic gold medalist Larisa Ilchenko. Ilchenko was undefeated in world championship events between 2004 and 2008. She is well known for protecting the number two position throughout her races and then dramatically sprinting to victory at the end.

Swimmers using the Russian style generally maintain a one-body-length distance behind the leader. The degree of separation from the leader rarely increases to two body lengths. They aggressively protect their position in the pack by constantly sticking right on the feet of the leader, mirroring the leader's every navigational move and change of pace. They efficiently draft off the leader and largely depend on the leader to navigate, trusting in that person's judgment. If the leader veers left, they veer left. If the leader speeds up, they speed up. If the leader slows down, they slow down. This style requires an acute awareness of the swimmers around them and a high level of physical toughness. By drafting off the leader, Russian style swimmers eliminate navigational worries and essentially make the race a two- or three-person race rather than a competition against many swimmers in a large pack.

Physically, the Russian style requires a strong foundation of base training combined with frequent speed training and skills training, especially drafting and positioning. Tactical knowledge of competitors' strengths and weaknesses and the dynamic conditions of the race is highly developed in swimmers using the Russian style. It requires a swimmer to be cunning and strategic while waiting for the optimal time to make the final move.

The Russian style demands confidence in one's sprinting speed and an acute sense of timing. It is best suited to alpha swimmers who prefer being in control of the situation and who can use the element of surprise to outsprint their competitors to the finish.

## BRITISH STYLE OF RACING

The British style is epitomized by world champion and Olympic silver medalist Keri-Anne Payne, who is known for sprinting to an early lead. She sets the pace and direction for the field throughout the race while having sufficient speed to hold off everyone at the finish.

Swimmers using the British style sprint to the front, supremely confident that they can set the pace for the field. They are fearless as they constantly push the pace from the front and confident in their ability to navigate well. Their leadership position enables them to avoid the physical contact and mental stress that comes from swimming in the pack. Even if they do not get the benefit of drafting, they conserve physical and mental energies by swimming alone and focusing on their own pace, stroke, and strategy without having to react to others.

British style swimmers know that the field will instinctively follow their direction and pace. By forcing the pace, they also effectively eliminate or minimize the threat of being outsprinted at the end of the race and turn the race into a two- or three-person race rather than a more risky competition against a larger field.

Physically, the British style requires a strong foundation of base training combined with frequent speed training and race-specific training to cover all kinds of dynamic racing conditions and situations. The British style requires courage and confidence with an internal focus because swimmers using this style swim alone with no assistance from their opponents.

The British style demands an extraordinarily high level of fitness and a well-developed navigational IQ that is best suited to endurance specialists who prefer to be the catalyst of action in a race as they swim to victory from the front.

## German Style of Racing

The German style is epitomized by multiple world champion and Olympic medalist Thomas Lurz. Lurz is known for taking advantage of the draft during the first part of a race; then gradually moving up toward the front in the lead pack until the last quarter of the race. When he senses an opportunity, he surges to the front and begins a relatively long sprint to the finish.

The German style is a hybrid strategy, using the Dutch style in the first half of the race, the Russian style in the middle of the race, and the British style in the late stages of a race. Swimmers who adopt this style are patient in the first half of the race, tactical in the middle portions of the race, and courageous leaders in the late stages of the race.

Once they make their move to the front, generally somewhere between 70 and 85 percent of the race distance, German style swimmers fully commit to leading the race until the finish. After forging to the front with a fast pace, they have no intention of backing off and are confident that their competitors will follow their course. They can navigate well and are able to push the pace from the front. Once in the lead, they enjoy clear water and can avoid the physical contact and mental stress that comes from swimming in the pack during the latter part of the race.

German style racers serve as the catalyst of the final sprint for the entire field. If they forge to the front with 2K to go, then it becomes a 2K sprint for the rest of the field. If they make a move with 3K to go, then it becomes a 3K sprint. By forcing the pace so far from the finish, they effectively make the race a two- or three-person race rather than a riskier, shorter sprint against a larger field where things can go wrong.

Physically, the German style requires a strong foundation of base training combined with frequent speed training and comprehensive race-specific training to cover all kinds of dynamic racing conditions and situations. The German style requires courage and confidence with a total commitment to finishing the race in first place once the person has forged into the lead.

The German style demands a balance between an extraordinarily high level of fitness and fast closing speed as well as a well-developed navigational IQ. It is best suited to tactical endurance specialists who prefer to be the catalysts of action in a race.

## YOUR OPTIMAL RACING STYLE

Depending on your goals and level of competition, train to reflect and perfect your chosen style. In the early part of your career or in the early season, experiment to find out what works best for you and what racing style fits your abilities and personality. You may prefer to swim in front of your competition, to swim near the leader, or to come from behind. All styles are exciting and enjoyable when they result in success. Table 7.1 on page 132 lists the characteristics, requirements, benefits, and disadvantages of each style and when to use them.

Your level of fitness, the configuration of the race course, and your competition dictate how you swim a race. If you are in good physical shape, but you cannot sprint as fast as your opponents, then push the pace so your quicker opponents cannot outsprint you. On the other hand, if you are confident in your ability to outsprint your opponents, or if the course has many turns, then hanging back for a fast-closing finish may suit the situation. You may also have to switch styles midrace as the competitive circumstances dictate.

The configuration of a race course is also a consideration when choosing a racing style. In a point-to-point lake course with few navigational landmarks or turn buoys, the front-leading British style may be a good choice. In these situations, the most physically fit swimmers can take it out fast and hang on. On the other hand, in an island circumnavigation or a loop course in a river, the hang-back-and-wait Dutch style may be your best choice. In these situations, swimmers with tactical smarts put themselves at an advantage.

## NUMBER OF RACES PER SEASON

Experienced middle-distance swimmers do several swims of various distances per year. Some require cross-country or overseas travel where recovery from jet lag must be figured into the equation.

As long as you have trained and recovered sufficiently, you can perform well in several competitive races per year. In fact, with each open water swim, you will learn more about your competitors and your own potential.

**Table 7.1** Comparison of Racing Styles

| Racing style | Athlete example | Characteristics | Requirements | Benefits | Disadvantages | When to use |
|---|---|---|---|---|---|---|
| British style | Olympic medalist and world champion Keri-Anne Payne | Lead the race from start to finish by swimming in the front. | Demands endurance and a high navigational IQ. | Saves energy because of little or no physical contact with competitors. Sets the pace and direction of the lead pack. | No drafting or navigational assistance. Competitors benefit by drafting and conserving more energy for a final sprint. | When the distance from the final buoy to the finish is a long straightaway and there is a lead escort. |
| Dutch style | Olympic gold medalist and world champion Maarten van der Weijden | Attack from the rear of the pack by forging to the front during the late stage of the race. | Demands great timing, patience, and excellent sprinting speed. | Conserves energy and reduces mental stress as a result of drafting off the lead pack while taking time to hydrate well. | Risky if one loses touch with the leaders. Sometimes, distance is too much to make up from behind. | Loop courses because the pack tends to bunch up around turn buoys. |
| Russian style | Olympic gold medalist and multiple world champion Larisa Ilchenko | Draft off leaders and overcome with a final short sprint. | Demands speed, awareness of competitors, and physical toughness. | Conserves energy and reduces navigational worries with close contact with the leader. Creates a two- or three-person race. | Constant need to protect one's position and maintain close contact with lead swimmers. | Useful under all conditions. |
| German style | Olympic medalist and multiple world champion Thomas Lurz | Draft within the pack and overcome with a long powerful finish. | Demands excellent endurance and closing speed. | Conserves energy for the majority of the race while eliminating a short sprint at the end. | Requires an ability to swim fast in the lead for the final 1-3K. | When the distance from the final buoy to the finish is a long straightaway without a lead escort. |

## WATER CONDITIONS

In ocean courses, the naturally changing environment can catch the entire field by surprise. When there are unexpected high waves or strong currents, you may be able to maximize your probability of success by swimming toward the front using the Russian or British style. On the other hand, if the weather and wind conditions are calm and the water is glassy, your strategy may be different.

## EXTREME WATER TEMPERATURES

If the water is either unseasonably cold or unexpectedly warm, you may not be able to sprint as well as you do under normal conditions. In these cases, because your ability to come from behind may be lowered, staying close to the leader throughout the race becomes paramount. Also, in either extreme temperature condition, hydrating and feeding more often can lead to a faster closing sprint.

## CHANGE OF SPEED

If you finish strongly, especially relative to your competition, then the fast-closing Dutch and Russian styles are your best bets. These styles require that you improve your sprinting ability so you can significantly pick up your pace at the end of the race. Your kick will help you make a powerful move, so incorporate frequent aerobically challenging kicking sets in practice. During your pool workouts, train long distances to build endurance, but keep in mind that your ability to quickly shift gears to another level of speed is also important.

For the Dutch and Russian styles to succeed, you need to be confident that you can outsprint your competition at all distances under 500 yards. With 200 yards to go, with 50 yards to go, and with 5 yards to go, develop the speed and confidence that you are the fastest competitor in the water. Learn how to shift gears in the water.

At the 2008 Olympic 10K Marathon Swim, the men averaged under 1:08 per 100 meters for the GPS-marked 10,000-meter course, but it was estimated that the medalists swam a 1:03-per-100-meter pace over the last 500 meters. The women averaged just under 1:12 per 100 meters for the same 10,000-meter course. They then shifted gears and finished with an estimated 1:08-per-100-meter pace toward the end of the two-hour race.

## NAVIGATIONAL BOATS

In the pre-race briefing, ask the race director how many and where the official boats, kayaks, Jet Skis, or paddlers will be on the course. Ask whether the fastest swimmers will be escorted by a lead boat. Do not be afraid to press for precise answers, especially when the athletes are assembled. Confirm whether the watercraft on the course will lead the swimmers on the best possible point-to-point course or whether the lead boat will simply position itself near the lead pack without consideration of the best possible line. This is an important, but subtle, difference. Of course, if your race allows personal kayakers, then your job is much easier because you can depend on your own escort.

If the top swimmers are aided navigationally by a lead boat or kayak, then the advantage goes to the lead swimmers because navigation is effectively eliminated as a key racing element. It is generally more difficult to catch those who are swimming with the assistance of a lead escort than it is to catch swimmers who must navigate the course by themselves.

If there are no lead escorts, then swimmers depend on their own navigational skills. This provides distinct advantages to those with a high navigational IQ or who know the course well. In an ocean course or a less well-marked course, swimmers tend to take slightly different courses to the finish, increasing the odds that navigation will play a part in the finish order.

Because there are innumerable bodies of water and racing conditions, it is impossible to make recommendations on every situation you may encounter. The permutations of any given race are too numerous to anticipate, but you can learn from each race and anticipate different situations as you become more experienced.

## PRE-RACE PREPARATIONS ON LAND

You will have plenty to do before you enter the water. The activities required on land must be factored into your pre-race preparations and time management. With all the activities that go on, you will probably stand and walk around more than you may expect.

Before the race, officials will write your race number on your arms, shoulder blades, and the back of your hands before the race. The numbers are used to monitor your progress, to announce your position to the crowd, and to inform you if you are committing a rule infraction during the race.

The length of your fingernails and toenails are checked at major competitions because many athletes have been scratched and cut. If officials judge that your fingernails or toenails are too long, you will be required to cut them to an acceptable length. Jewelry and watches are not permitted at major competitions. On the other hand, jewelry and nail length are rarely monitored at amateur races.

You may also be given transponders to attach to your wrists or ankles at check-in. Because transponders can come off or flap while swimming, tape the strap of the transponder down firmly to avoid these problems.

You may be required to attend a pre-race briefing. The briefing area may be crowded and full of commotion, hot and humid, or cold and breezy depending on the conditions. The pre-race instructions are important, especially if they address changes to the course due to weather or unforeseen logistical problems. Listen very carefully and ask questions if anything is unclear.

The start positions of the athletes at most races are random; some races, however, assign athletes start positions based on time, gender, or other parameters. Know which competitors go out fast, which are physically aggressive, and what pace may be sustained depending on the water temperature and conditions.

Officials tend to become more stressed out as the race gets closer to the start time, but one or two hours ahead of the race, you can probably approach them easily and privately. Knowing who the referees are is one part of your tactical knowledge. Ask them about the water temperature and confirm the number and placement of the turn buoys. Look for officials and lifeguards who help set the turn buoys and are visibly involved in the race operations. These people are usually local residents who are often involved in open water swimming or marine sports. Most will know a great deal about the local conditions and will be genuinely happy to share their knowledge of the course and water conditions.

If the swim is in the ocean, walk along the shore or up on a nearby pier or jetty to observe the surf conditions and currents from various vantage points. Once you have a good sense of the conditions, begin your warm-up, paying particular attention to the sight lines between the various elements of the course (i.e., start, turn buoys, and finish).

The length and time of your warm-up varies depending on how you feel and the placement of the buoys, especially the last few. In addition to getting physically warmed up, you should also make mental notes of everything you see and sense in the water. Answer for yourself the following questions and incorporate the information in your racing strategy:

- Where is the first buoy in relation to the start?
- Where is the last buoy in relation to the finish?
- Are there intermediate buoys?
- How many turn buoys are there?
- Are the turn buoys numbered?
- Do the intermediate buoys serve as optional guide buoys or do they officially mark the course?
- Are the intermediate buoys colored differently than the turn buoys?
- What are the angles of the turns: 45, 90, or 180 degrees?
- Are there obvious landmarks to aim for in the water?
- Is the water shallow at any point?
- Are there faster currents in the course along a seawall, jetty, pier, or deeper channel in a river? Does any sandbar or coral reef affect the water flow?
- If so, where is the best current?

- What direction is the wind blowing?
- Is there marine life? If so, what kind?
- How high is the touch pad at the finish?
- What other variables are there in the race?

The positions of the final few turn buoys and the finish are important. Some races longer than 5K have in-the-water finishes so there is no need to worry about dolphining or dealing with the gradient of the ocean bottom at the finish. Some finishes include elaborate timing systems set on floating pontoons, whereas others involve two people holding a rope. If the ocean waves are large or the wind is significant, the finish may move slightly, especially if a large pack comes into the finish chute together.

If there is a finish chute, confirm with the race director whether you must swim within the finish chute or are free to swim outside it as long as you properly cross the finish line.

## HYDRATION AND FUELING

Pre-race hydration is very important. Before any race, your urine should be clear or only slightly yellow, which indicates that you are properly hydrated.

The proper amount and most effective types of hydration depend on the person and take time and experimentation to determine. Decide what works best for you by experimenting with fluid intake during your longer pool and open water workouts.

Before the race, make sure you are well hydrated and eat a good meal, but do not overly hydrate or eat until you feel stuffed. Before your first middle-distance swim, you may feel unusually nervous. As a result, you may not feel like eating

**TRAINING TIPS**

### ALTITUDE TRAINING

The purpose of training at high altitudes is to induce physiological changes in your body to improve your aerobic capacity at sea level. These changes will include an increase of your oxygen-carrying capacity and a higher tolerance of oxygen deficit.

The optimal altitude for training is between 6,500 and 8,200 feet (1,981 and 2,500 m) above sea level. The duration of altitude training should be at least five days with an optimal length of three or four weeks. Studies have shown that the effects of altitude training vary among athletes with effects lasting up to five weeks in some athletes. Other studies have shown that the ideal time between the end of high-altitude training and competition is between one and two weeks.

(much) on race-day morning. At the very least, consume fruit or energy bars so your body has something to use other than the previous night's meal.

## INSOMNIA

Up to 50 percent of people are affected by insomnia. Insomnia is also very real issue in the open water swimming world, especially the night before any competition.

Although most endurance athletes sleep well during their hard-core training cycles, many report that they have problems sleeping both before and after their solo swims and races. Sleep, a key requirement for properly recovering from heavy-volume training, is relished in the busy daily lives of athletes whether they are students, working adults, or parents. Many swimmers who do morning workouts or long weekend swims often feel the need for naps throughout the day or after eating.

On the day before a race, a swimmer's nerves of steel can become a pile of nerves. A global survey of experienced middle-distance and marathon swimmers from eight countries and of all ages—from teenagers to Half Century Club members (swimmers over the age of 50 who have completed major marathon swims around the world)—revealed a common experience of insomnia before major swims. It is overwhelmingly clear that most swimmers do not sleep well the night before an open water event. The solution is, of course, to sleep well during the week leading up to the race.

## STAYING COOL, CALM, AND COLLECTED

You can imagine all that can go wrong with your race—or all that can go right. If you have an inner strength built on years of training and the confidence that you have done everything possible to prepare yourself mentally and physically, then you will do well.

However, if you are new to the sport, a feeling of nervousness is natural the night before, and morning of, the race. Fortunately, your pre-race jitters will decrease over time as you gain experience.

You can deal with your nerves in various ways. If you are able, swim the course before race day at different times of the day. The course may look slightly different depending on the amount of sunlight and water conditions (and without turn buoys), and you want to be comfortable under all conditions. Additionally, you can rent a kayak or boat to study the course prior to race day. Walking or cycling the entire length of the course is also beneficial if you have the opportunity.

Think about all the variables of the race and visualize yourself finishing well and enjoying the challenge. Visualize running into something (another swimmer, a log, seaweed, jellyfish, or trash) and breathing deeply to calm down. You can build confidence through mental preparation.

## TAPERING FOR RACE DAY

A taper is the training period just before a major race when you reduce your daily swimming volume and intensity. The purpose of a taper is to rest after a long training season to maximize your performance. A taper differs for every athlete and can vary from one to two weeks.

During your taper, decrease your daily swimming volume and intensity; do more open water workouts (open water acclimatization); fine-tune your feeding, drafting, and sighting plans (skills training); and learn more about the course and your competition (tactical knowledge).

The taper period is also the ideal time to increase your carbohydrate and fluid intake leading up to race day. If your race is overseas or far away in another part of the country, buy extra fluids (preferably in powdered form) and gel packs to take with you. Do not assume that you can purchase your preferred products in the area where your race is taking place.

---

**TRAINING TIPS**

### PHYSIOLOGY OF MIDDLE-DISTANCE TRAINING

The less oxygen you consume to maintain a given pace, the more economical you will be. Because you are most economical at the speed at which you train the most, spend as much time training at race pace as possible to increase your economy at that pace. By training fast at race pace and combining it with bursts of increased velocities, you will improve your performance.

You will need to accelerate quickly during different parts of your races. Combining a high level of endurance with the ability to swim fast for short bursts is a challenge that you must constantly work on during your pool and open water training sessions.

---

## PRACTICING NAVIGATION

Before the race, gather as much information as possible from a variety of sources. Study course maps with the assumption that surface chop and whitecaps will make sighting and navigation difficult. During the race, you will constantly make judgment calls as to where you are and where you are heading based on your pre-race knowledge.

Sources of information include your knowledge of your natural tendency to swim to the right or left, the placement of official's boats along the course, any landmarks you can see in the distance, and the relative number of swimmers on your right and left.

Because navigation in the open water can be a best-guess situation, play the odds. For example, if approximately 20 people are swimming to your left, but more than 80 people are swimming to your right, the chances are high that the correct course is on your right. Similarly, based on your tactical knowledge, consider taking the same line as swimmers who have swum the course before.

# STARTING FAST

In most races, the start will be quick. There may or may not be a countdown by a start official. Without a countdown, it is easy to get caught off guard. You can prevent this by having your hips up near the surface of the water before an in-the-water start.

You can practice in-the-water starts by starting your sets in the middle of the pool instead of at the walls. For example, with a set of 10 × 100 at 1:30, start each 100 from the same spot in the middle of the pool. During your resting interval, tread water as active rest. You can also do sprints at the end of your workout by starting off the wall.

## DOCK, PONTOON, PIER, AND SHORE STARTS

If the race start is from a dock, a floating pontoon, or a pier, you may be preassigned a starting position, which is drawn at random. Because the starter does not want any false starts, the gun will go off quickly. Always be ready for a fast or unexpected start. Do not assume that a false start will result in swimmers being called back.

When 25 or more athletes dive off a floating pontoon at the same time, the pontoon can kick back from the force. Place your toes at the end of the pontoon so you can dive off easily, or place one foot back so you are stable if the pontoon lurches unexpectedly.

For onshore starts, be quick, but do not rush. Even if you are not immediately in the lead or are not in the position that you want to be in, there is always time to make up ground in a middle-distance race.

## AFTER A FAST START

After a fast start, packs will immediately form. Remain calm, but quickly position yourself to avoid a traffic jam around the first few turn buoys. After some period of time, and certainly after the first turn buoy, the pace will slow back down.

You can prepare for fast race starts by swimming fast on your first interval set during pool practices. For example, if you do 5 × 200 at 2:30, swim the first 200 very fast; settle into a pace for the second, third, and fourth 200; and finish the set with a fast 200.

## MIDRACE STRATEGY

Middle-distance races are grueling events. You may swim stroke for stroke and shoulder to shoulder in a pack (see figure 7.1), constantly battling for position mile after mile throughout the race. Physical contact is part of the sport. Competitors may constantly bump into you, tap on your feet, or veer into you—intentionally or inadvertently.

During the long straightaway legs of the course, if the pace picks up, swimmers toward the back of the pack tend to get strung out. It is easy to fall off the pace if you are not diligent in watching and matching the pace of the lead swimmers. Stick with the pack in front for as long as you can. It is frustrating to fall into the undesirable no-man's zone between the lead pack and the packs behind.

To simulate this situation in pool workouts, practice pushing the pace during the middle of a set. For example, if you are doing 10 × 200 with three other swimmers, you can do swims 1 through 5 at a certain interval (e.g., 2:45) and pace (e.g., 2:30 per 200). Then, do swims 6 through 8 at a faster interval (e.g., 2:30) and faster pace (e.g., 2:20 per 200) before finishing up with the last two 200s, but everyone in your lane can leave only one or two seconds behind the swimmer in front. This will replicate drafting in the open water.

Dr. Jim Miller

**Figure 7.1** Packs form immediately and can lead to physical contact throughout the race.

## WATCHING THE REFEREES ON THE COURSE

During races, you may be surrounded by escort boats, officials' boats, kayaks, and Jet Skis. You may breathe boat exhaust depending on the proximity of the boats and direction of the wind. After the lead boat, the most important watercraft is the one carrying the referee. Before the race, confirm who the referee is, what boat the referee will be on, and what the referee will be wearing so you can recognize who has the authority to make judgment calls during the race. Depending on the race, there may be a head referee and an assistant referee, each in his or her own boat, as well as turn judges and feeding station judges who are responsibility for the areas around their posts.

Some races have very few boats and perhaps only a handful of safety kayaks and roaming jetskis. In these cases, the officials tend to follow the lead pack. If you believe a race has too few boats, officials, or safety personnel on the course, express your concern to the race director and to the online swimming community afterward.

The referee's job is to maintain order; identify potential problems between athletes; and issue warnings, yellow cards, and red cards during the competition in addition to making sure the conditions are safe for the athletes. It is a high-stress, difficult responsibility. Like water polo referees, they have much activity to oversee and adjudicate, both above and below the water's surface.

The universal rule used at many local, national, and international races states, "If in the opinion of a Referee, an action of a swimmer or an escort safety craft, or a swimmer's approved representative is deemed to be 'unsporting' the referee shall disqualify the swimmer concerned immediately (FINA Handbook 2009-2013, OWS 6.3.2)."

## LISTENING TO WHISTLES

During the race, you may hear whistles blown by the referee. Some warnings are to get the swimmers' attention, indicate to swimmers that they should separate if they begin to initiate inappropriate contact, or warn a swimmer who is inadvertently impeding another swimmer.

When swimmers are racing aggressively, the referee can be proactive and warn swimmers to avoid further escalation of altercations. In these cases, warning whistles are used as a form of preventive officiating.

Whistles are also blown when contact has occurred between two or more swimmers, but fault could not be assigned to any one swimmer. The referee may whistle in order to signal the swimmers to give each other more room to avoid future unintentional contact.

If you do not understand why whistles were blown during the race, feel free to ask the referee to explain the situations after the race. To increase your tactical knowledge, know the rules, be familiar with referees' interpretations of those rules, and learn who the aggressive swimmers are.

# INCIDENTAL AND INTENTIONAL PHYSICAL CONTACT

When highly motivated open water athletes compete, there is always both incidental and intentional physical contact. Accept physicality as part of the sport—or swim out in front or to the side. Incidental contact occurs when athletes accidently bump or touch one another or arms get tangled. In a competitive race with crowded course conditions, you can expect to be hit, bumped, pulled, banged, elbowed, cut off, scratched, kicked, or jostled at some point during the race, which can be frustrating or, at the very least, surprising. To keep other swimmers from grabbing or pulling your arms and legs, put a light coat of petroleum jelly on your ankles, lower legs, and outer shoulders before the start.

Incidental contact becomes problematic when it becomes repeated or leads to someone's progress being impeded. The offending swimmer can be warned by a whistle or receive a yellow card. A yellow card can be given even if the action was unintended or done in an act of retaliation.

Although referees will ignore or miss some physical contact between swimmers including times when their view is blocked by a turn buoy or swimmers are at a distance, they will deal with intentional contact by issuing warnings, giving yellow cards or issuing red cards that will result in swimmers being immediately removed from the course.

You can simulate race contact by swimming shoulder to shoulder with two other teammates in one lane in a pool. Swim an entire two-hour workout three abreast to give you an idea of the amount of concentration you will need and the amount of stress you can expect as a result of swimming in such close proximity with other swimmers for a 10K race. Switch positions with your two teammates after each set within your workout.

If you believe that you are being impeded by another swimmer and no warning whistle is given, shout out to draw the referee's attention to the offending competitor.

## YELLOW CARDS AND RED CARDS

When the referee judges contact to be intentional and unsportsmanlike (see table 7.2), a yellow card is given to the offending swimmer and the swimmer's number is written on a whiteboard for everyone to see. The referee holds the whiteboard up for a reasonable time, giving fair opportunity for the swimmers to see which athlete received the yellow card. On the second infringement, the swimmer is automatically given a red card and is immediately disqualified.

Frankly, few races are supervised closely by experienced referees. In most cases, much contact is not seen by any referees. However, keep in mind that if you regularly initiate contact, you can expect it in return at some time.

**Table 7.2**   Infraction Signals

| Action by referee | Reason |
|---|---|
| Give warning whistle (preventive officiating) | Indicate unsafe conditions ahead<br>Swimming too closely to another swimmer<br>Swimming too closely to official boats<br>Bumping into another swimmer<br>Locking arms with another swimmer<br>Touching or tapping another swimmer's feet |
| Issue yellow card (caution) | Intentional contact that impedes another swimmer<br>Unintentional contact that impedes another swimmer<br>Intentional interference (cutting off or veering into a swimmer)<br>Swimming crookedly into another swimmer<br>Swimming over the legs or lower back of another swimmer<br>Intentionally drafting off an official boat |
| Issue red card (disqualification) | Unsporting conduct (e.g., punching, elbowing, kicking)<br>Walking on or jumping off the bottom<br>Pulling another swimmer's legs<br>Pushing another swimmer underwater<br>Intentional interference when swimmers are approaching the finish<br>Accumulation of two yellow flag infractions |

## CHEATING IN THE OPEN WATER

Cheating does occur in open water races, although most instances are due to swimmers inadvertently missing a buoy or drafting in races with no-drafting rules. If you witness an obvious cheating incident, report it to race officials immediately after the race. Although you may want to let it go or ignore the situation, bring the incident to the attention of race officials. Some officials will appreciate it, and others may simply brush it off. In either case, your information may help rectify the situation if more than one person witnessed the act of cheating.

Your input will also help improve the race for the future. Although the sport is remarkably clean, nonsupervised loop courses with few officials and a limited number of buoys generally lead to more reported instances of cheating. Cheating cannot be completely resolved without the help of the athletes themselves.

## TRANSPONDERS

At the Olympics and professional swims, swimmers strap on two lightweight transponders, one on each wrist. You can simulate wearing transponders by using two waterproof wristwatches during practice. Bring waterproof tape and scissors to races because you need to tape the transponder straps down so they will not flap during the race.

## TIMING SYSTEMS

Wrist transponders and floating timing systems are innovations from Omega Timing, which has managed the timekeeping at every Olympics since 1932. Omega Timing developed the first semiautomatic timing system used at the 1956 Melbourne Olympics and later developed the original touch pads used in the swim pools at the 1967 Pan American Games. Transponders were first used at an international competition in 2004. They have revolutionized the sport by more accurately timing races and their finishes (see figure 7.2). Several vendors now offer timing solutions, including split timing.

An analysis of split timing has shown that women tend to even split their races with relatively little difference in speeds between the first and last parts of their middle-distance races. Men, on the other hand, typically split their races with a tremendous second half that follows a slower first half pace.

Dr. Jim Miller

**Figure 7.2**   Timed finish at the 2010 World Open Water Swimming Championships.

## THINKING SEVERAL STEPS AHEAD

The more races you do, the more familiar and comfortable you will be with all the various situations that come up during races. Repetition breeds familiarity, and familiarity breeds confidence. But once the gun goes off, know that things rarely go according to plan. Your ability to stay flexible and adapt to the race situations is critical for your success and overall racing enjoyment.

If swimmers crowd you on both sides, do not get frustrated. Think calmly about the possibilities of when and where you can extricate yourself from being boxed in. Perhaps you can get to the inside after a turn buoy or during a feeding station stop. Maybe you can speed up for 200 to 400 yards and find a gap to swim between your competitors. Also, you can slow down for a few strokes and move quickly over your competitor's lower legs to escape from the middle of the scrum. Try to become skilled in rolling over competitors' lower legs by practicing corkscrew moves in a pool or open water.

Like a good chess player, you need to think several steps ahead in a race. Tactical knowledge of the race course and your competitors is invaluable. Advantages in pack swimming can sometimes be a game of inches and a matter of timing.

## Taking Advantage at the Turns

Turn buoys come in all kinds of sizes, shapes, and colors. Heading into and rounding turn buoys is always a vital part of racing (see figure 7.3). Like the fifth stroke in pool swimming (streamlined underwater butterfly kick off the wall), take advantage of the turns in the open water by preparing for an effective turn well in advance. Set up your turns at least 200 yards before you reach the buoys. Push the pace or move around your opponents to gain an optimal position as the pack swims around the buoy.

When dozens of swimmers go around the turn buoys, several changes in position can result. Tightly swim around the turn buoy while protecting your head. You can use a twisting move combining freestyle and backstroke arm strokes to quickly corkscrew yourself around the turn buoy.

**Figure 7.3** Rounding buoys at the 2008 World Open Water Swimming Championships.

You must know where you want to be after the turn buoy to properly position yourself before the turn. Many times you will want to be on the inside of your competitors, but sometimes you may want to be on the outside. (e.g., if a left-shoulder turn is followed by a right-shoulder turn—or vice versa—or the angle is greater than 120 degrees).

You can also employ an underwater turn if you are boxed in on the inside and have no place to swim. As you approach the buoy, dive under the water and go around the buoy rope underwater. It is illegal to pull or move any part of the course layout, including buoys and ropes, but you may be able to twist your body around the rope underwater. As the last resort, you can literally grab the rope tied to the anchor with the understanding that a referee who sees your maneuver may give you a yellow or red card. As you rise to the surface, you may be in a better position after the turn than before. At the very least, you may be able to avoid contact.

Practice this underwater move in the pool. With the permission of your coach and the cooperation of your teammates, swim down the length of the pool in one lane, dive under the lane line near the wall, and resurface in the adjoining lane. On the way back, you and your teammates can do the reverse.

## FOUR STEPS TO FAST FEEDING

To feed quickly from a pier or feeding pontoon, use the following four-step process. Practice this process with your coach as part of your race-specific training.

1. Seek and spot
2. Reach and roll
3. Gulp and go
4. Toss and turn

### SEEK AND SPOT

As you approach the feeding pontoon, lift your head to spot your coach. Take into account the surface chop or swells and your position relative to your competition and your coach.

You will see your coach more easily if he dresses in easily identifiable clothing and draws your attention by yelling or whistling. He should have your hydration and feeding needs ready for you as well as an extra pair of goggles and swim cap if necessary. An extra cup or bottle should also be prepared in advance in case the cup at the end of your feeding stick is upended.

If there are no swimmers around you, your coach can extend the feeding stick out over the water in advance of your arrival. International rules allow for a small flag to be placed at the end of the feeding stick to help you locate it.

If several swimmers are around you, your coach should extend the feeding stick out to you only during your last few strokes as you approach the feeding pontoon. Occasionally, a large pack of swimmers will inadvertently hit your feeding stick, causing your drink to spill. If your coach sets your drink down in position at the last moment, there is a reduced chance accidents happening.

## REACH AND ROLL

As you arrive at the feeding station, reach up and grab your cup from your feeding stick as you roll over on your back, kicking strongly. Keep moving forward at all times to maintain your momentum. Resist the temptation to go vertical and tread water.

Ask your coach to set the end of the feeding stick at water level to make it easy for you to reach for the cup and immediately roll over on your back.

If you use a bottle, stick it high enough out of the feeding stick container so you can grab the side of the bottle. If you use a cup, place the palm of your hand over the top of the cup and lift the cup out of the feeding stick container. Your palm over the cup will help keep much of the contents inside the cup.

## GULP AND GO

Tilt the lip of the cup toward your mouth and immediately gulp the contents as in figure 7.4. Do not worry if some of the drink misses your mouth. Your feeding can be deemed successful if you consume half of the contents of the cup. Continue kicking on your back while staying as horizontal as possible while you drink.

Dr. Jim Miller

**Figure 7.4**  Feeding takes only a few moments and requires coordination between coach and athlete.

After you lift your cup from the feeding stick, your coach should lift the feeding stick straight up from the water's surface so as not to interfere with another swimmer or feeding stick.

Your coach can mix in the contents of a gel pack or other preferred solid into your drink, so you can quickly consume everything using only one hand. Deluxe feeding sticks have gel pack clips and a second (differently colored) container where other foods or another cup can be placed if additional foods or drinks are desired on longer swims.

## TOSS AND TURN

After you have finished consuming the contents of the cup or gel pack, immediately drop it in the water and turn over onto your abdomen to start swimming again. There is no need to throw it back to your coach. Your coach, race volunteers or officials will remove the discarded trash from the race course.

If you use gel packs, ask your coach to open them before placing them on the feeding stick. You or your coach should precut the opening slit of the gel packs so you can quickly consume the gel in the water. Gel packs will not leak much, and a larger opening will help. This will avoid you having to struggle in the water to open the gel pack. You may be tired, out of breath, or cold, which will make the pack difficult to open.

Practice these four steps in the pool and during open water workouts so the timing and coordination with your coach is perfect. The process should take no more than five seconds from the time you reach for the cup to resuming swimming.

# CARRYING GEL PACKS

You may want to carry gel packs in your swimsuit so you can consume them at your convenience or if you miss a feeding during the race. Place them anywhere in your swimsuit that is convenient.

Because gels are most effective when followed by 4 to 6 ounces (120 to 180 ml) of water, you can mix your gels with water. But even without a water chaser, the gel will provide the fuel you need. Another alternative is to consume the gel before you arrive at the feeding station and then have your coach provide you with water or your preferred.

In the second half of races, the competitive situation around feeding stations can be hectic. Time will either be made up or lost. If you stick gel packs in your swimsuit, you can consume them anywhere along the course and bypass the confusion at the feeding stations.

Practice grabbing and squeezing gel packs with either hand. Hold the pack in your palm and place the opening in your mouth. Then close your mouth and squeeze hard. Do not squeeze the gel pack like a tube of toothpaste. Rather, engulf the gel pack in your hand and "pop" the contents so the gel shoots quickly into the rear of your mouth.

Your coach must communicate quickly and effectively to you at the feeding stations. "You're in third," "25 meters ahead," or "Looking good!" are examples of briefly communicating useful information. If your coach asks open-ended questions such as, "How do you feel?" or "What do you want?", you will have little time to answer. On the other hand, if your coach senses any medical emergency such as an uncharacteristic lack of a response or other visual clues due to extreme cold or heat, then your coach must seriously and immediately consider pulling you from the competition.

# Effective Drafting

Open water swimmers know very well how effective drafting is, especially when they swim behind the feet of a swimmer ahead of them. The velocity of elite open water swimmers in various drafting positions was tested with SwiMetrics. The data led to an unsurprising conclusion. As with geese that migrate in formation, the optimal drafting position in swimming is close alongside the lead swimmer with the head of the drafting swimmer between the lead swimmer's hips and knees, especially if the lead swimmer is swimming fast with a strong kick.

Additionally, the faster the lead swimmer is, the greater the benefit of the draft.

## Rear Drafting Versus Side Drafting

Because the SwiMetrics research on drafting was conducted in a pool, the conclusions are primarily relevant in flat-water, non-current conditions on a straight course. Although the benefits of rear drafting (behind the feet of a lead swimmer) are undeniable, the rear-drafting position has its disadvantages.

One disadvantage of rear drafting has to do with head and body position. Your optimal head position is looking straight down, but the rear drafting position requires you to look up at an angle to sight off the lead swimmer. This leads to a suboptimal head and body position.

Another disadvantage of rear drafting is increased head lift. If the water conditions are rough, the water clarity is poor, or the course is not straight, you will lift your head more frequently to follow the lead swimmer. This is suboptimal because it causes your hips to drop and compromises your streamlined position.

A side drafting position has its benefits, especially in a well-marked or easy-to-navigate course (e.g., in a rowing basin or a race with a lead escort). Firstly, it results in less need to lift your head up and forward to sight. This will save you valuable energy that you can better use in the latter half of the race. Secondly, with side drafting you can navigate by sighting off the lead swimmer on each breath.

With rear drafting, you will occasionally bump into the feet or touch the toes of the lead swimmer, which can lead to retaliation. With side drafting, bumping into the lead swimmer is less frequent and easily avoided.

In really rough conditions due to strong winds or whitecaps, the optimal position may be on the protected side of the lead swimmer rather than directly behind. That is, if the waves are coming in from the right, it is often easier to swim on the left side of the lead swimmer.

When there are turns in the course, especially 180-degree turns, rear drafting generally results in a greater distance between swimmers after the turns, especially as you get farther back in the pack from the leader.

You can more easily see the lead swimmer begin a surge or a final sprint when you are side drafting than when you are rear drafting. With rear drafting, you can lose touch with the lead swimmer; even if this happens only momentarily, it can make a big difference in a race.

Psychologically, it is generally easier to overtake a swimmer you are side drafting. Overtaking a swimmer who is directly ahead of you is a bit more difficult, especially when the water is murky or surface chop is significant.

Another advantage of side drafting is that you can pick the optimal side to draft. This is beneficial when you approach a turn buoy or are swimming to the finish. If necessary, you can protect a more advantageous position by drafting off to the side versus drafting directly behind. Finally, you have less distance to make up in side drafting than in rear drafting.

You can practice drafting in various positions behind two or three training partners when you swim at various speeds, in both pool and open water workouts. You can also do paceline swims with three to five other swimmers at various speeds with everyone swimming in a straight line right behind one another. The first swimmer initially pulls the pack before peeling off and falling to the back of the pack.

---

## THE ILCHENKO

Throughout sport history, great athletes have created signature athletic moves. Track-and-field has the Fosbury Flop, gymnastics has the Thomas Flair, boxing has the rope-a-dope, and wrestling has the Karelin Lift.

Open water swimming has the Ilchenko, named after Olympic gold medalist Larisa Ilchenko, whose drafting strategy and closing kick enabled her to win the world championships in 2004, 2005, 2006, 2007, and 2008.

At the 2008 Olympics, Ilchenko characteristically drafted off the lead swimmers for the majority of the race, aggressively protecting her position in the pack right on the feet of the lead swimmer. This is difficult to do throughout a two-hour 10K race. Around the last turn buoy, she set up the Ilchenko. With the finish approaching and less than 100 meters to go, Ilchenko tremendously increased her stroke tempo and kick. She swept past her competition on the opposite side to which her opponent breathed.

Ilchenko's tactical knowledge included knowing what side her competitors favored during the main part of the race and the final sprint.

## Navigational and Positioning Drills

One easy drill to do to learn whether you naturally swim to the right or to the left in the open water is to swim 50 to 100 arm strokes with your eyes closed. Start from the shoreline and swim to a fixed point. After you have swum 50 to 100 strokes at different speeds (slow, medium, fast), see if you have veered left or right. Repeat the experiment several times so you understand how you tend to swim in the open water.

Practice swimming around turn buoys with teammates. Protect your inside position if you are on the inside and try to gain an advantageous position from various angles if you are on the outside. If you do not have access to bodies of water before race day, POW training is a useful alternative (refer to Chapter 6). When you are the lead swimmer in these drills, try to prevent the drafting swimmers from overtaking you. Conversely, when you are drafting in these drills, attempt to shoot the gap between the swimmers in front of you to replicate what may happen during races.

To replicate race conditions, ask teammates to purposefully pull on your ankles, feet, and arms during practice. Ask them to try to veer you in different directions, so these situations on race day do not surprise you.

## Increasing Your Ability to Concentrate in the Open Water

An excellent way to prepare for a middle-distance race is to stay mentally alert during your pool and open water practices. Instead of swimming mindlessly, think about your stroke, pace, and splits in workouts. Swim sets that require mental focus are a great preparation for open water races.

For example, try to complete an 800-yard swim in a certain amount of time (e.g., 10 minutes). Then, divide your 800-yard time by 2 and swim faster for the 400-yard swim (i.e., faster than 5 minutes). Then, divide your 400-yard time by 2 and swim faster for the 200-yard swim. Repeat this sequence down to a 25-yard swim.

## Training by Prime Numbers

Intense concentration is absolutely required at the highest levels of the sport of open water swimming. If you swim well for two hours but lose focus for a critical 30 seconds, your competition can drop you. To prepare mentally for one to two hours of intense concentration in a dynamic environment in which you are swimming fast against aggressive competition, try doing pool swimming sets based on prime numbers.

Instead of doing a typical 10 × 100 at 1:30, practice sets that entirely consist of prime numbers. For example, swim 13 × 100 at 1:23 as you swim the third, seventh, and eleventh 100s fast. Instead of repeats on 45 seconds or 1 minute, swim on intervals that cause you to think, calculate, remember, and focus (e.g., on 37.5 or 42.5 seconds per 50).

---

**FLEXIBILITY DRILLS**

There are many different dry-land exercise and flexibility programs available that may be appropriate for your body type, age and personal goals. Your shoulders, lower back, and ankles should be the focus of an aggressive flexibility program. Stretch your shoulders and arms before and after every workout to increase your range of motion. For your lower back, lie on the ground and move your straightened legs over your head as you remain on your back. Try to touch your feet to the ground. For your ankles, sit on the floor on top of your feet that are folded under your buttocks. Lean back as far as you can with a straight back with the top of your feet remaining flat on the floor. Try to bring your back flat against the floor.

---

You will find that prime number sets require intense concentration and will take some time to get used to. But after a few months of practice, your ability to focus while swimming hard will be enhanced—which is exactly what you want to achieve in middle-distance swims.

# PERFECTING YOUR FINISH

Open water finishes are frequently close. Occasionally, 10 swimmers finish within 10 seconds of one another. For this reason, officials use video cameras to record the finish and confirm the results. Every second, every stroke, and every inch counts.

If a finish is in the water, take a straight line to the nearest point. On a vertical touch pad on the floating finish pontoon, firmly touch or slap the touch pad to ensure that your finish is officially recorded (see figure 7.5). Crossing the plane of the finish line does not trigger an official finish in major competitions.

Some races have colored lane lines that serve as a funnel to direct you to the finish chute. Try to time your finish so your leading hand touches the touch pad well before your body crosses the plane of the finish structure.

Before the race begins, repeatedly practice your finish into the touch pad. Learn to reach up and over the water to hit the touch pad just right. Your timing on the last stroke could be crucial.

## Finish Drills

Practicing with a competitive group of swimmers can enhance your closing speed and improve your stroke turnover. Race against teammates to the finish from various positions, angles, and distances (25, 50, 100, 200 and 400 yards) to replicate real-world race conditions.

Ask your coach to video-record your race so you can study it later. Watch the video and pay attention to your strengths, weaknesses, moves, and mistakes—and those of your competitors—to increase your tactical knowledge and confidence.

**Figure 7.5**   Practice your finish tap before the race so you don't swim past the finish structure.

## COOLING DOWN

Cooling down after the race is highly recommended. A cool-down swim, doing both the freestyle and backstroke, will help you recover more quickly, especially if you have another race soon. If you are not accustomed to doing races over 5K, also consider taking a coated aspirin after the race to relieve the pain of inflammation.

The competitiveness of open water swimmers and the competitive strategies used are increasing at all levels worldwide. What used to be the domain of a handful of distance specialists is now attracting a much wider group of talented and focused athletes, along with an ever-expanding group of coaches. These athletes and coaches are collectively raising the bar for the entire sport and helping enthusiasts rethink what is physically possible, regardless of age, background, or ability.

Erica Rose

# PREPARING FOR MARATHON SWIMS

With over 70 percent of the world covered in water, and stunningly gorgeous lakes, seashores, channels, rivers, and islands dotting the earth, it is not surprising that people eventually took to marathon swimming. The catalyst of marathon swimming was when Captain Matthew Webb became the first person to successfully swim nonstop from England to France in 1875. His exploit dramatically enabled endurance athletes to think the impossible was within their reach.

At its most fundamental level, marathon swimming is a daring personal challenge in which swimmers pit themselves against the elements and experience a wide range of emotions that fluctuates between despair and relief. Marathon swimmers vividly remember their final stroke in the water after swimming for hours and hours on end. Their first step back on terra firma after struggling in relentlessly difficult conditions is the point when exhaustion turns to exhilaration. This love–hate relationship with the open water—strange as it may sound—creates the allure that draws endurance athletes to the waterways of the world.

# THE MARATHON SWIMMER

Marathon swimmers tend to be doggedly persistent people who are also successful in other aspects of their lives. They ply their trade far away from the media attention in arenas where there are usually no fans. They often achieve their greatest success on a barren shoreline where only their support crew can witness their victory. But their sense of accomplishment runs deep; their inner satisfaction is empowering and uplifting – and will remain with them throughout their lives.

Among the world's marathon swims, the most iconic and well-known waterway is the English Channel. Thousands of people have attempted the 21-mile (33.8K) swim since the first documented attempt in 1872. Yet the number of successful English Channel swimmers remains fewer than half of the number of people who have climbed Mount Everest since it was first scaled in 1953.

Of the 1,189 people who have crossed the English Channel through 2010, 33 percent have been women and 67 percent have been men, although the relative percentage of women who cross the English Channel has increased over time (41 percent during the 1990s).

The average one-way time is 13 hours and 31 minutes, and times range from the world record of 6 hours and 57 minutes to a patiently plodding 26 hours and 50 minutes.

The English Channel swimmers are a global mix, hailing from 63 countries. The average age of the successful channel swimmer is 31, but their ages range from 11 to 70 years, including 50 people who crossed it after their 50th birthday and are members of the Half Century Club. With a growing number of members in the Half Century Club around the world (25 in the Catalina Channel, 32 in the Strait of Gibraltar, 175 in the Rottnest Channel, and 51 in the Manhattan Island Marathon Swim), age seems to be no impediment nowadays in the marathon swimming world.

Marathon swimming requires discipline of the highest order, demanding long hours spent training often alone and under harsh conditions. But it is also a sport where the concept of team is paramount due to the essential roles played by the escort pilot, coach and support crew and where camaraderie and collegiality exist in abundance.

Marathon swimmers experience nature in the most tactile way possible: enveloped in water, surrounded by marine life, and interacting with a dynamically changing environment in nothing but swimwear and goggles. It is no wonder that marathon swimmers across borders and cultures often form profound friendships; they share experiences that are often difficult to endure and difficult to explain.

Marathon swimmers experience nervousness before a swim and a sense of accomplishment afterward. They know the sting of a jellyfish and of cold water. They understand problems with leaking goggles, removing lanolin, and breathing boat exhaust. They appreciate the feeling of swimming powerfully in calm, clear water in daylight hours and of being uncomfortably disoriented in rough water at night.

The collegial atmosphere in the marathon swimming world is a function of these shared experiences. As the athletes come out of the water exhausted beyond comprehension, punished into submission by the elements, some barely able to stand and some nearly unable to talk, they share smiles, looks, nods, winks, hugs, and handshakes that speak volumes about their mutual respect for each other and their escort boat crews.

## PAST AND FUTURE OF MARATHON SWIMMING

Marathon swimming became part of the sport landscape when Matthew Webb first crossed the English Channel in 1875. But his exploit went unmatched for 36 years. In the 1920s, the sport came to the fore again when Gertrude Ederle, an Olympic medalist, became the first woman to match Webb's feat. Gertrude was treated to a ticker-tape parade upon her return to New York City.

The sport went into a hiatus during the Great Depression and World War II until Sir Billy Butlin raised the profile of marathon swimming in the 1950s with the advent of professional races across the English Channel.

In the 1960s to the 1980s, Michael Read, Lynne Cox, Kevin Murphy, and other pioneers traversed the world in search of new places to realize their dreams and showcase their talents. Their exploits generated media attention and drew other athletes to the sport. To this day, swimmers continue to find locations in which to do unprecedented swims. Fortunately, the world remains relatively unexplored from the perspective of the marathon swimmer.

John Kinsella, an NCAA champion and Olympic gold medalist, and Dr. Penny Dean, a diminutive dynamo and collegiate All-American, pushed the boundaries of what was thought possible in the 1970s. They trained hard and swam relentlessly for over 20 miles (32K) to usher in the modern era of competitive marathon swimming.

In the 1990s, drafting was first allowed in competition, and pack swimming at the elite level became *de rigueur*. Racing in a peloton for hours on end suddenly changed the game at the highest levels. The Europeans excelled in international competitions when drafting, positioning, physical contact, and tactics became a major part of the sport.

During the early part of the 21st century, aquatics' most extreme discipline blossomed with thousands of swimmers plying their trade in every region of the world. The Triple Crown of Open Water Swimming—an exclusive club of swimmers who completed the English Channel, Catalina Channel, and Manhattan Island Marathon Swim—is gaining new members every year and is now up to 41 swimmers from six countries.

# OCEAN'S SEVEN

The Ocean's Seven (refer to chapter 3) is swimming's version of the Seven Summits, the highest mountains in each of the seven continents. Nearly 200 climbers have scaled the Seven Summits, but no one has yet completed the Ocean's Seven Races (see table 8.1).

Achieving the Ocean's Seven requires an ability to swim in both very cold and very warm waters. It demands that swimmers be physically and mentally prepared to overcome all kinds of conditions throughout the world. Like its mountaineering cousin, the Ocean's Seven requires a great amount of planning, time, financial resources, and physical prowess as well as support teams of knowledgeable local experts.

**Table 8.1** The Ocean's Seven Races

| Ocean's Seven | Obstacles | Location or window | History |
|---|---|---|---|
| English Channel (21.8 miles) | International waterway with cold water (60°F), strong winds, strong tidal flows, whitecaps, strong currents and variable weather. | Between England and France in June - September | First crossed in 1875 with over 1,600 successful crossings to date. |
| North (Irish) Channel (21 miles) | Rough seas, cold water (54°F), strong currents, normally overcast days, thunderstorms, large pods of jellyfish (if conditions are calm) and difficulty in accurately predicting weather and water conditions. | Between Ireland and Scotland in July - September | First crossed in 1947, but only 15 successful solo swims and 5 relays out of 73 attempts to date. |
| Catalina Channel (20 miles) | Deep-water channel with cold water (62°F) near the coast, strong currents, strong winds, marine life (whales, dolphins, sharks). | Between Catalina Island and mainland California in June - September | First crossed in 1927 with 199 successful crossings to date. |
| Strait of Gibraltar (10 miles) | Heavy boat traffic, logistical barriers, high winds, surface chop and extraordinarily strong tides and currents. | Between Spain and Morocco in June - October | First crossed in 1928 with 297 successful one-way crossings to date. |
| Molokai Channel (26 miles) | Deep-water (701 meters) channel with extraordinarily strong currents, large ocean swells, strong winds, whitecaps, heat, warm salty water and plentiful marine life in the middle of the Pacific Ocean. | Between Molokai Island and Oahu Island in Hawaii year round | First crossed in 1961 with 15 successful crossings to date. |

| Ocean's Seven | Obstacles | Location or window | History |
|---|---|---|---|
| Cook Strait (16 miles) | Immense tidal flows, cold water (57-66°F), strong winds, heavy surface chop, jellyfish, 1 in 6 swimmers encounter sharks (although no one has been attacked), start and finish have rock cliffs. | Between North Island and South Island in New Zealand in November - May | First crossed in 1962 with 77 successful crossings by 67 individuals to date. |
| Tsugaru Channel (12 miles) | Rough, windy waterway in the northern Pacific Ocean with extremely strong currents, large swells, cool water (62-68°F) and abundant marine life ranging from sharks to blooms of squid. | Between Hokkaido and Honshu Island in Japan in July - September | First crossed in 1989 with 3 successful swimmers and several relays to date. |

# WHY SWIM A MARATHON?

In the sport of marathon swimming, in which extreme distances, extreme temperatures, and extreme conditions (large ocean swells, strong currents, and marine life) are expected, individuals come from all walks of life. Their physical abilities to push themselves hour after hour are augmented by their tremendous mental focus and strength of character.

Marathon swimmers are generally an introspective group with plenty of opportunities to reflect upon their motivations while swimming. Some swim to achieve a personal goal. Others strive to set records or to gain some level of fame. Some raise money for charity. Others endeavor to promote a cause. But they all have an unwavering passion to achieve their goal.

## DEEPLY HELD PASSION

Without passion, a marathon swimmer cannot do the training necessary for success. They genuinely enjoy their time in the water and the challenges they inevitably face.

Training can be harsh and is always conducted without fanfare. Swimmers face the solitary walk to the shoreline, countless hours swimming alone, and shivering and muscle soreness afterward. Their ability to persevere is what defines them at their very core. They possess the uncommon ability to focus on the positive, ignore the discomforts they face, and readily accept sacrifices.

Passion helps push marathon swimmers past the pain, boredom, and difficulties. The immense joy and satisfaction of touching the ground and finishing by walking—or crawling—onto shore is a feeling they cherish for the rest of their lives.

## UNCOMMON COMMITMENT

The commitment shown by marathon swimmers takes many forms: physical, emotional, financial, and logistical. Physical endurance and strength of character are not enough. The financial means to support one's passion and the ability to assemble a knowledgeable support team cannot be underestimated.

The physical commitment has to do with the requirement to swim for hours. This commitment frequently requires the adjustment of work schedules, family obligations, nutritional habits, and sleep schedules.

The emotional commitment speaks to the marathon's swimmers sustained mental focus over time. Fatigue, boredom, nervousness, and discomfort are significantly more powerful forces in the open water than on land. When the conditions in the open water become difficult, it is tempting to stop, get out of the water, and look forward to another day. Marathon swimmers understand that the strength of their mental efforts and their control over their emotions enable their bodies to follow.

The financial commitment to marathon swimming is high because escort boats, support crews, hotel stays, meals, and travel must be arranged. The total cost, including a qualifying swim, travel for the swim itself, governing body fees, food, training time, and equipment, can easily run over $10,000 depending on the location of the swim.

The logistical commitment includes arranging for an escort pilot and support team. It also includes organizing all the travel, feeding, and equipment as well as completing documentation, visas and medical release forms in a timely manner. Pre-swim promotions, interviews, and a post-swim party or follow-up with one's chosen charity are just a few of the details swimmers manage before and after their marathon swim.

# CLARIFYING YOUR PURPOSE

The best way to achieve your goals is to clearly set them, not only for yourself, but also for others. Define your goals in writing and then create a detailed plan of action for achieving them.

Step 1 in setting a marathon swim goal is to research the possible swims and various bodies of water that may interest you. Ask other swimmers and join online swimming forums. Conduct an exhaustive search online to learn about water temperatures, best times to swim, weather conditions, and why people succeed or fail at a variety of locations. Study marine charts and read stories about previous swims, both in print and online. Talk to experts and those who have done these swims before.

Some questions to answer for yourself include: Do you want to do a solo swim well-established in the marathon swimming world or do you want to participate

---
**SETTING A MARATHON SWIM GOAL**

1. Research the possibilities.
2. Assess your abilities.
3. Assess your potential.
4. Make a plan.
5. Inform others.
---

in a marathon race? Do you want to do something that has never been done before, or do you want to take part in a marathon relay?

Step 2 to setting your marathon goal is to assess your abilities. Decide whether you can do a cold water swim or a warm water swim, a domestic or a foreign race, a lake swim in calm water or a tropical adventure at sea. Determine your level of commitment and the time you have available to train. If you want to complete the English Channel, do you have the time and opportunity to acclimate to cold water?

Step 3 is to objectively assess your potential. This is the most important step for any endurance athlete. How far are you willing to push yourself? You may be surprised at how far and how well you can swim when you are committed to reaching your goal. If you can swim 5 miles now, you can swim 20 miles with proper preparation. If you are comfortable swimming in 68 °F (20 °C) water, you can get acclimated to 60 °F (15.5 °C) with enough time to prepare. If you have only swum in glassy lakes, you can swim in the turbulent deep ocean with practice. Tap into your potential to achieve what you may currently believe is impossible.

After you have selected a location or race, make a plan of action (step 4). Decide who will be your pilot, what role your coach will play, and where you will train and with whom. Write a checklist of equipment and note what needs to get done, by whom and by when.

After you have made your plan, inform others (step 5). Do not be shy about sharing your goals, especially with others in the marathon swimming community. Join online social networks populated by marathon swimmers. Create your own blog or website. Tell people of your plans, worries, and expectations. Marathon swimmers will support you and make you feel part of their global community. They are willing to share their know-how, impressions and experiences. They know the requisite steps for success and will remind you of the milestones you must reach.

# CHOOSING YOUR EVENT

Like an artist, the canvas you paint in the marathon swimming world is entirely up to your creativity. You can aim to complete an unprecedented swim, a swim that has never been attempted or completed in the world. While others may be faster, you can be the first. You can also create a charity swim where others can benefit from your exploits.

With only a few exceptions (e.g., English Channel, Cook Strait, Manhattan Island Marathon Swim, Strait of Gibraltar, Catalina Channel, North Channel), you can do any marathon swim you want without the approval of the established governing body, if you obtain the permission of the local authorities. Outside of a relatively few number of marathon swimming organizations, you are free to do what you want in the marathon world. You can do a multi-day stage race where you start at a point where you finished the day before; you can wear a wetsuit, or do it as a relay under traditional rules or the rules that you determine. The choice is yours.

What is important for historical purposes is to carefully document your swim by noting GPS coordinates and the conditions of your solo swim or relay (with or without wetsuits, in-the-water start or finish, use of a shark cage or how many relay members and the length of each leg).

Set your goal, do your research, and begin your training.

## CHARITY MARATHON SWIMS

Charity swims are a great way to help others while achieving your own goals. A charity swim can also provide some powerful motivation. Plenty of free online tools are available to help you solicit donations in an automatic, responsible, and transparent manner.

## COMPETITIVE MARATHON RACES

Some of the longest races in the world listed in table 8.2 have qualification standards. These races include professional marathon races where you must demonstrate your ability to swim at a fairly fast pace. The amateur races have less stringent standards, but still require you to demonstrate your ability to finish the race.

**Table 8.2**   World's Longest Marathon Races

| Race | Location | Distance |
|---|---|---|
| Maratón Internacional Hernandarias – Paraná | Argentina | 88K (54.6 miles) |
| India National Open Long Distance Swimming Championship | West Bengal, India | 81K (50.3) |
| Santa Fe-Coronda Marathon Swim | Argentina | 57K (35.4 miles) |
| Maratona del Golfo Capri-Napoli | Italy | 36K (22.3 miles) |

| Race | Location | Distance |
|------|----------|----------|
| Traversée internationale du lac Memphrémagog | Quebec, Canada | 34K (21.2 miles) |
| Traversée internationale du lac St-Jean | Quebec, Canada | 32K (19.8 miles) |
| Ohrid Swimming Marathon | Macedonia | 30K (18.6 miles) |
| International Self-Transcendence Marathon | Lake Zürich, Switzerland | 26.5K (16.4 miles) |
| Manhattan Island Marathon Swim | New York | 45.8K (28.5 miles) |
| Tarnpa Bay Marathon Swim | Tampa Bay, Florida | 38.6K (24 miles) |
| British Long Distance Swimming Association Two-way Windermere | Lake Windermere, England | 33.7K (21 miles) |
| All India Sea Swimming Competition | West Bengal, India | 30.5K (19 miles) |
| International Swimming Marathon of Messiniakos Gulf | Greece | 30K (18.6 miles) |
| Ederle Swim | New York to New Jersey | 28.1K (17.5 miles) |
| U.S. Masters Swimming 25K National Championships | Indiana | 25K (15.5 miles) |
| Cruce del Puerto Rosario | Argentina | 25K (15.5 miles) |
| St. Vincent's Foundation Swim Across the Sound | Connecticut to New York | 25K (15.5 miles) |
| Villa Urquiza – Paraná | Argentina | 25K (15.5 miles) |
| St. Petersburg to Kotlin Island | Russia | 24K (14.9 miles) |
| Ijseelmeerzwem Marathon | Netherlands | 22K (13.6 miles) |
| Toroneos Gulf Crossing | Nikiti, Greece | 22K (16.1 miles) |
| International Marathon Swimming Beltquerung | Denmark to Germany | 21K (13 miles) |
| Travesia En Aguas Abiertas Por la Ruta de Olaya | Lima, Peru | 21K (13 miles) |
| Distance Swim Challenge | Santa Monica, California | 20.2K (12.6 miles) |
| Swim Around Key West | Key West, Florida | 20.1K (12.5 miles) |
| Rottnest Channel Swim (Rotto Solo) | Perth, Australia | 19.7K (12.2 miles) |
| Jarak-Šabac Marathon Swim | Serbia | 19K (11.8 miles) |
| Fiji Swims | Beachcomber Island, Fiji | 18K (11.1 miles) |
| La Jolla Cove Swim Club 10-miler | La Jolla, California | 16.2K (10 miles) |
| Kingdom Swim | Lake Memphremagog, Vermont | 16.2K (10 miles) |
| Deer Creek Lake Swim | Charleston, Utah | 16.2K (10 miles) |
| Swim the Suck | Tennessee River, Tennessee | 16.2K (10 miles) |
| Faros Marathon Swim | Croatia | 16K (9.9 miles) |
| Lake Trichonida Crossing | Greece | 16K (9.9 miles) |
| Swimming Peace Marathon | Greece to Turkey | 16K (9.9 miles) |

## STAGE SWIMS AND RELAYS

Stage solo swims and relays with any number of swimmers can be of any distance and are conducted over two or more days. You are responsible for decisions on the course, rules and logistics of these swims as well as the financing, promotion and safety. These swims can be down rivers, along coastlines, or across lakes and are limited only by your creativity in mapping out an interesting, safe, and challenging course.

## UNPRECEDENTED SWIMS

There are literally hundreds of thousands of locations where you can do unprecedented marathon swims. Marathon swimming has entered the Age of Discovery, in which modern-day adventurers challenge themselves in ever longer, colder and more remote waterways.

Solo swims and relays can be done in many open bodies of water. Many people are making their own mark on the marathon swimming world by being the first. Over 200 solo marathon swimmers and thousands of swims are documented in the archives of the International Marathon Swimming Hall of Fame (www. imshof.org), with several new swims certified each year. To certify your own swim, arrange for an independent observer to record your swim and complete an official Observer's Report (see www.openwatersource.com).

Because first-time swims have no history, the level of risk is higher. There is no body of information on unprecedented swims that require a truly pioneering spirit. If you are confident that you can swim the distance and handle the conditions, then focus on logistics with one major proviso: because anything can happen in a body of water that has never been swum before, it is wise to increase your safety net by organizing more than one escort boat, especially if the swim starts or finishes at night.

# TIMING YOUR TRAINING

Preparing for a major marathon swim requires a 12-month training program. Build up your volume and intensity each month, culminating in your last few training swims, which should be at least 60 percent of the total distance of your marathon swim.

For swims such as the English Channel, you must complete a six-hour mandatory qualification swim in water 61 °F (16 °C) or lower. For races such as the Manhattan Island Marathon Swim, you have to prepare documentation well in advance to position yourself to be one of the chosen athletes. For swims such as the 26K Self-Transcendence Marathon Swim in Lake Zürich, Switzerland, you must submit your application in a timely manner. The demand to swim in these races is very high and increasing over time, so timeliness is always rewarded.

The seven elements of the Pyramid of Open Water Success training philosophy (refer to chapter 6) are important in marathon swimming training, but a heavier focus on base training, distance tolerance, and open water acclimatization is needed. If you want to swim 25K and you have never swum farther than 5K, one possible 12-month training plan can look like the one in table 8.3. You can modify the intensity and mileage according to your goals.

**Table 8.3** Twelve-Month Sample Training Program for a 25K Marathon Swim

| Phase | Period | Focus of training | Swimming volume | | Water temperature range |
|---|---|---|---|---|---|
| | | | Daily average volume (yards) | Longest continuous swim in open water (yards) | |
| 1 | November | Base training Feeding experiments | 3,000 | 500 | 52-56 °F (11-13.3 °C) |
| 2 | December | Base training Feeding experiments | 3,000 | 1,000 | 52-56 °F (11-13.3 °C) |
| 3 | January | Base training Feeding experiments | 4,000 | 1,000 | 50-54 °F (10-12.2 °C) |
| 4 | February | Base training open water acclimatization | 4,000 | 2,000 | 50-54 °F (10-12.2 °C) |
| 5 | March | Speed training Open water acclimatization | 5,000 | 3,000 | 54-58 °F (12.2-14.4 °C) |
| 6 | April | Base training Speed training | 5,000 | 5,000 | 54-58 °F (12.2-14.4 °C) |
| 7 | May | Distance tolerance Skills training | 6,000 | 8,000 | 58-60 °F (14.4-15.5 °C) |
| 8 | June 1–15 | Distance tolerance Skills training | 6,000 | 10,000 | 58-60 °F (14.4-15.5 °C) |
| 9 | June 16–30 | Distance tolerance Race-specific training | 7,000 | 15,000 | 60-64 °F (15.5-17.8 °C) |
| 10 | July 1–15 | Distance tolerance Race-specific training | 6,000 | 15,000 | 60-64 °F (15.5-17.8 °C) |
| 11 | July 15–27 | Taper Tactical knowledge | 5,000 | 10,000 | 66-68 °F (18.9-20 °C) |
| 12 | July 28– August 1 | Taper Tactical knowledge | 1,000 | 1,500 | 66-68 °F (18.9-20 °C) |
| 25K swim on August 1 | | | | | 66-70 °F (18.9-21 °C) |

## DRYLAND EXERCISES

A comprehensive dryland exercise program can augment your swimming program. However, as you spend more time in the water, you will have less time and energy to continue a dryland program unless you have the luxury of being a full-time professional marathon swimmer, on sabbatical, or otherwise free to entirely commit yourself to the sport.

For most individuals with limited time, focus on two things: (1) core strength and (2) flexibility, especially that of your shoulders and ankles. Strengthening your core muscles will help you maintain a more streamlined position in the open water, which is very helpful, especially during the latter half of your marathon swim or when the conditions are rough. A strong core also helps to reduce lower back pain that some swimmers feel.

The exercises can be similar to the exercises described in chapter 7, although the frequency can be greater.

## TRAINING IN THE OPEN WATER

Ideally, you always train with a partner. However, if a swim buddy is not available, swim back and forth parallel and close to the shoreline during your open water workouts. Alternatively, ask a friend to join you on a kayak or a paddle board. In lieu of an escort, recruit someone to walk along the beach as you swim parallel to the shoreline.

Set up a training course between two points (e.g., a pier and jetty or two lifeguard towers) and regularly time yourself between these two landmarks so you can quantifiably measure your improvement. Buy a waterproof watch with a built-in thermometer so you can time yourself and keep track of the water temperature.

To break up the monotony and guarantee an increase in your heart rate, do an occasional in-and-out in which you run out of the water, up on the beach, and then back in. At the end of solo marathon swims, you have to stand up and clear the water's edge, so doing a few in-and-outs will help replicate this type of finish. If you do not want to get out of the water, you can pick up your pace every certain distance or a pre-determined amount of time.

Experiment with various foods and drinks to see what works best for you. Try lots of different combinations and concentrations. Your taste buds will be impacted by the hours in the water and what a drink tastes like will change the longer you stay in the water. Although marathon swimmers may give you advice on what works, you ultimately know your body best and have to make those decisions for yourself.

Open water acclimatization is critical, especially if the water conditions are expected to be very cold or very warm. If the expected water temperature is 65 °F (18.3 °C), then start training in water that is 55 °F (12.8 °C) in the months leading up to your swim. Although it is not necessary to be able to swim far in water that is 55 °F (12.8 °C), the fact that you can withstand it will help you prepare for a much longer swim at 65 °F (18.3 °C). As a rule of thumb, if you start training at a temperature 10 °F (5.5 °C) lower than the expected water temperature, you should be properly prepared.

## ADVANTAGE OF OVERTRAINING

Overtraining is undesirable in most sports, but can be defined a bit differently in marathon swimming. If your goal marathon swim is 25K, then you should train for 30K. The extra work you put in will be useful if the conditions get rough, the water gets colder than expected, or you are interrupted by marine life (e.g., jellyfish stings). Prepare yourself to swim a bit farther than your goal distance. You need to be prepared for anything.

Success requires that you put in the time and effort day after day, week after week, month after month. You may feel as though you spend all your time swimming, eating, sleeping, and heading to your next practice with bouts of work or school mixed in. However, this ceaseless dedication will pay off. Conversely, if you put off doing the hard work and hope something magical will occur during your swim, your hopes are likely to be dashed.

At times you will be cold, miserable, and frustrated during your training. You will feel the desire to get out of the water and call it a day. You will be totally exhausted, wondering how you can possibly go another 100 yards. But this feeling of being battered and beaten by the elements is exactly what you need to experience during your training.

The day-to-day grind of training is where you learn to overcome these obstacles. Every time you go beyond what you previously thought possible, you will get stronger both mentally and physically and you will be better prepared. When you are cold and tired in the middle of your marathon swim, your coach can remind you (and you can remind yourself ) of those days spent in training when you made it through to the end.

## TAPERING TOWARD THE BIG DAY

Similar to pool swimmers, a taper period and ample rest are critical before a marathon swim. As you decrease your swimming volume during your taper, simultaneously decrease your level of intensity. The taper period gives you time to complete logistical planning and enjoy sufficient rest for your marathon swim. Your longest and most difficult training swim should ideally be done two to four weeks before your marathon swim, giving you plenty of time to recover for your big day.

If you are attempting to swim one of the Ocean's Seven or another waterway whose conditions change frequently, your swim date will depend on the weather and the availability of an escort boat pilot. Your window of opportunity may range from a few days to a few weeks (or months in the case of the North Channel). If you are swimming in waterways that are less variable, such as a lake, you can pinpoint one ideal date with one or two days as alternative dates in case of unfavorable weather.

## Number of Marathon Swims per Year

Some top professionals do as many as 10 marathon swims per year, but most swimmers have neither the luxury of time nor the resources to spend so much time swimming. If you plan to do more than one marathon swim per year, your body's tolerance of the rigors of marathon swimming will increase after every swim. If you put in the training and have the financial resources and time, by all means attempt multiple marathon swims during any given 12-month period.

## Swimming Straight With Escorts

Swimming straight is relatively easy with the assistance of an escort team. Swim parallel to your escort boat and have complete trust in your pilot and support crew. If you have both a boat and a kayaker assisting you, position yourself between them, usually in eye contact with the pilot about midship. Your kayaker can transport your feedings to you from the boat and should stay in eye contact with you.

Swimming straight in a marathon race can be easier than in a solo swim, especially when everyone is assigned an escort boat. Of course, a larger number of boats means an increased probability of breathing boat fumes, which can make you cough or cause an upset stomach. If you start to breathe fumes, immediately tell your pilot and reposition yourself or have the pilot move the boat.

To maintain a straight course and good stroke mechanics, you must remain mentally alert hour after hour, especially if you are doing part of your swim at night or if the ocean swells loom large. Under rough conditions, the pilot of a large boat will have more difficulty keeping the boat on a straight course when traveling at your swim speed. If you constantly drift left or right, your crew will have to maneuver the boat to bring you back along the optimal navigational course. A capable pilot will maintain a straight and steady course for you to follow, but you are also responsible for keeping yourself in constant alignment with your escort boat.

## Swimming in Rough Water

Swimming well in rough water requires experience, patience, and persistence. In a marathon swim, expect to face surface chop at some point. When you do, try to remain balanced. Use your legs as ballast if you must, but do not let them drop to create additional resistance. When small surface waves batter your arms, maintain high elbows and a streamlined body position.

Sometimes the waves will come from behind you, sometimes they will batter you from the sides, and sometimes they will hit you head on. If you are able to breathe on either side, this ability to bilateral breathe and breathe farther back in your stroke will help you avoid swallowing water.

## Swimming Fast

During a marathon swim, you may hit currents or have to swim into large ocean swells. In these cases, you may have to swim faster to avoid a tidal change or have the opportunity to kick down the swells and utilize the power of the ocean to push you forward. Although endurance is the fundamental component of marathon swimming, speed and the ability to time your kick to essentially bodysurf along mid-ocean swells can also play a role in your success.

You can maintain or improve your speed by doing interval work in the pool. Instead of simply swimming for distance, keep your heart rate up during pool workouts by doing aerobically challenging sets. For example, instead of a straight 2,000-meter swim, swim $10 \times 200$ on a quick interval or $10 \times 200 + 50$ fast, in which you do a fast 50 after each 200 at your normal pace.

Alternate between slow, medium, and fast swims to break up your training sessions in the open water. Even in the ocean or a lake, combine some speed work with your endurance training. For example, divide your workouts into equal distances (1K slow + 2K medium + 3K fast) or time (repeating 5 minutes slow + 10 minutes medium + 20 minutes fast). During the medium- and fast-paced swims, increase your stroke tempo and kick so your heart rate increases.

You can get cold, especially if you do not kick in the open water. Kicking sets to strengthen your legs are important in both your pool and open water workouts. Kicking for propulsion, rhythm, balance, and warmth is much better than simply letting your legs drag behind you, creating needless resistance.

As you develop your aerobic conditioning, always focus on your stroke efficiency and do not get into bad habits. If you can slightly improve your stroke technique and efficiency, significant energy and time savings will follow. If you take 70 strokes per minute and swim the English Channel in an average time of 13 hours and 31 minutes, you will take approximately 56,770 arm strokes. Even a small improvement in stroke efficiency, multiplied over 56,770 strokes, will lead to a significantly faster time.

## Limiting Head Lifting

You do not have to lift your head to navigate during a marathon swim. You have the luxury of breathing normally to the side and navigating off your escort boat or kayak. Over long distances, frequently sighting only results in disappointment and frustration. Your finish will not come any sooner with frequent sighting.

Just put your head down and swim straight while trusting in your pilot and crew who will inform you of your position and progress.

## COUNTING STROKES

If you do not use a GPS unit that provides you with precise distance and time data, it is difficult to confirm how fast you are swimming in the open water. But your pace can be estimated by counting your strokes per minute (SPM). Fast swimmers can sustain up to 85 SPM for hours, whereas older swimmers are usually more comfortable swimming at a 55 to 65 SPM pace.

If your stroke tempo falls more than 10 SPM from your average during your marathon swim, your coach and crew should know you are getting tired or something is ailing you from hypothermia to a shoulder injury. Most well-trained marathon swimmers of any age can usually stay within 5 or 10 SPM of their average. That is, if 75 is your normal SPM, then train yourself to maintain at least a 65 SPM pace through the end of your swim.

## KEEPING A STEADY PACE

Pacing is important in a long-distance swim. Hold a steady pace that is based on your swimming abilities and the conditions you may encounter. Your coach can confirm your SPM and then communicate this pace to you every 15 or 30 minutes via a whiteboard. If your support crew provides accurate distance and time data (e.g., 6 miles in 3 hours), you can estimate your finish time and decide how best to pace yourself.

# COORDINATING YOUR SUPPORT TEAM

Whether you do a marathon swim under established rules, such as the English Channel, or one that falls outside any established governing body, you will work with several people, each with distinct roles and responsibilities: a coach, a pilot, an official observer, and a support team. It is important that you take the lead and decide how decisions will be made and who makes the final ones. Misunderstandings about who has decision-making authority can lead to problems.

Predetermine what happens in extreme cases. How far are you willing to push yourself? Who makes the call if your personal safety is at stake? What happens if a shark is seen? What happens if you start to vomit? What happens if you miss the tide? What happens if a relay member gets sick or injured?

Many minor decisions must also be made. Who prepares your drinks? How often should you stop to hydrate? What side of the escort boat will you swim on? Are you willing to change swimming from one side of the boat to the other if the water conditions change? Who will maintain the log of your swim? Table 8.4 shows a sample decision matrix.

**Table 8.4**   Decision Matrix

| | Swimmer | Pilot | Coach | Observer | Support crew |
|---|---|---|---|---|---|
| Swim date | √ | √ | | | |
| Start time | | √ | | | |
| Feeding schedule | √ | | √ | | |
| Feeding choice | √ | | | | |
| Feeding preparation | √ | | √ | | √ |
| Swimwear and swim cap approval | | | | √ | |
| Lanolin preparation | | | √ | | √ |
| Documentation check | | √ | | | |
| Marine life observation | | √ | | | √ |
| Medical approval | | √ | √ | | |
| Course navigation | | √ | | | |
| Support swimmer | | | | | √ |
| Kayaking rotation | | | √ | | √ |
| Kayak preparation | | | √ | | √ |
| Pacing | √ | | √ | | |
| Stroke count | | | √ | √ | |
| Official timing | | | | √ | |
| Record-keeping | | | √ | √ | |
| Document submission to International Marathon Swimming Hall of Fame | √ | | | √ | |
| Camera or video-recording | | | √ | √ | √ |
| Writing on whiteboard | | | √ | | |
| Cheering | | √ | √ | √ | √ |
| Emergency procedures, including SOS | | √ | | | |
| Engine problems | | √ | | | √ |
| Pulling from the water (involuntary or voluntary) | √ | √ | √ | | |
| Finish or landing | | √ | √ | | √ |
| Post-swim rewarming | | | √ | | √ |
| Media coordination | √ | | √ | | |

## Responsibilities of a Marathon Swim Observer

If you swim under the auspices of an established governing body, an official observer will be responsible for confirming that all rules are strictly followed. The observer will complete a written report that becomes your swim's official record. The report documents any incidents, your swim progress, the tidal conditions, water and weather conditions, feeding schedule, and start and finish times.

If your swim is unprecedented or is not governed by any established body, recruit a fair-minded, detailed-oriented person who can serve as your observer and document your swim in writing and with photographs and videos. A pair of individuals acting as an observer's team is ideal because they can trade off in two to four hour increments. If your team has Internet or mobile phone access during the swim, they can post frequent updates to your blog or online social networks (e.g., Facebook or Twitter) so your family and friends can follow your progress online or on their mobile phones.

After your swim, this documentation can be officially accepted and registered by the International Marathon Swimming Hall of Fame, the World Open Water Swimming Association, or the Guinness Book of World Records. The International Marathon Swimming Hall of Fame maintains a global archive of marathon swims attempted around the world (both successful and not). Documentation of unsuccessful swims is helpful because it adds to the cumulative marathon swimming information known about the waterways of the world.

## Choosing an Escort Pilot

Choose your escort pilot based on recommendations from other swimmers and feelings of good personal chemistry between you and the pilot. Your pilot must be skilled and knowledgeable with years of experience as both a licensed captain and seasoned escort pilot. He must know the currents, tides, and particularities of the waterway where you will push yourself, and how to safely position the boat alongside you in rough conditions at night on a straight path while traveling anywhere from 1 to 3 miles per hour (1.6 to 4.8K per hour) for hours on end. This ability requires excellent boating skills, extreme patience, uninterrupted concentration, and most important, a passion to help you achieve your goals. This combination is difficult to find, so your search for a good match is critical to your success.

If you are doing a competitive swim such as the Manhattan Island Marathon Swim, experienced pilots are provided. With the increasing popularity of the Ocean's Seven swims, you have to book your pilots early, sometimes years in advance. Conversely, if you are doing an unprecedented swim or a stage swim, finding a competent pilot may be more difficult. Ask for leads at local marinas, fishing ports, and yacht clubs or online. Talk to several candidates. The time and effort you spend to select your pilot will be invaluable.

Dr. Jim Miller

Proper marathon training requires time, focus, commitment and a dedicated support crew.

## SELECTING A SUPPORT CREW

Choose your support crew well. Your boat may be relatively small, and you may only be able to accommodate those with a specific role. If a friend or volunteer really wants to be involved, but there is no room on the boat, you can always assign that person a role on land (e.g., helping at the finish, preparing a post-swim party, working with the media, or providing real-time updates on a website, blog, or online social network).

Your support crew should include at least one person who is properly trained in first aid. The entire team should be comfortable with sitting in a very slow-moving boat for hours, which amplifies every wave and ocean swell. Because some members will get seasick, offer everyone seasickness medication before your swim begins unless they are restricted because of other medications. Anyone who gets seasick during your swim becomes either a distraction or unable to help you.

Decide the actions of your support crew during your swim. Do you mind if they eat or sleep en route? If they eat, can they do it within your view? If they sleep, make sure you have enough eyes on you when the conditions are rough, at night, or near the end of your swim. A crew member who gets seasick should have the courtesy to move out of your view.

In all cases, ask and expect your team to be visible and supportive. As they mold into a team over the course of your swim, they can cheer, watch for flotsam or jetsam, prepare your feedings, and share kayaking duties.

When you stop to feed, your coach should exclusively have the floor and be the first person to speak to you. You want to be able to clearly hear your coach's advice. After your coach finishes speaking, your support team can then provide encouragement. It is important to have a positive crew onboard who enjoys the ambience and challenge of marathon swims.

When you are physically exhausted and frustrated with your progress, you need people who can help you reach your potential rather than people who will sympathize with your plight and suggest that you get out.

If you see or run into marine life during your swim (e.g., sharks, turtles, Portuguese man-o-wars, jellyfish, dolphins, schools of fish, sea snakes, or manta rays), immediately tell your crew. They may not see what you can under the water. If necessary, your pilot can gun the boat engine to scare away the marine life. Swim closer to the escort boat and your kayaker if any marine life scares you. Increasing your proximity to other humans always feels better when you are nervous in the ocean or at night on a lake.

At night, your support team must be especially vigilant. Attach glow sticks or disc lights on your swimsuit or goggle strap so you are visible to your support team. Your pilot can also line the boat with glow sticks so it is easier for you to see if you do not want bright lights beaming from the boat that may hurt your eyes or attract marine life at night. Your kayakers can also clip glow sticks to their clothes and line the kayak with glow sticks to make it more visible to you and everyone on the boat. Your coach and kayakers should have whistles to use in case of an emergency.

Your designated coach should be the one to assess your situation when you are considering quitting, helping you to rethink your situation and your goals before you finally decide to climb aboard the boat. Once you touch someone or your escort boat, your swim is officially and immediately over. For this reason, family members are not always the best choice to be your coach. Sometimes their love blinds them to your goals. When they see you suffering in cold water or rough conditions, it is natural for them to want you to get out. At such times, you may be better served by the gentle prodding and watchful eye of your coach.

Of course, when your pilot or coach believe an unsafe condition exists (e.g., you are hypothermic or there are sharks lurking around), he has the ultimate call. His ability to act quickly, calmly, and decisively is invaluable. This is the primary reason your pilot, together with your coach, kayaker, and crew, must be prepared to act on a moment's notice throughout your marathon swim.

## COMMUNICATING YOUR MARATHON SWIM GOALS

You will be escorted by a support crew of your choosing on a solo marathon swim or relay. In contrast, during a race you may be assigned a crew by the event organizer. In either case, discuss your goals, background, worries, logistics, pace, breathing pattern, course strategy, racing tactics, feeding schedule

> ## EXAMPLE OF A SWIM GOAL FOR A SUPPORT TEAM
>
> Michael Miller, 56-year-old Triple Crown swimmer from Honolulu, Hawaii, had the following goals when swimming the 17.5-mile (28K) Ederle Swim from New York to New Jersey:
>
> 1. *Goal:* To finish under 6 hours
> 2. *Background:* I was a competitive swimmer in college and have completed the Molokai Channel, English Channel, Catalina Channel, and Manhattan Island Marathon Swim.
> 3. *Worries:* Water temperatures below 56 °F (13.3 °C) worry me. I train year-round in Hawaii.
> 4. *Logistics:* I will arrive in July and will stay in a rented apartment near the finish.
> 5. *Pace:* I have an average stroke-per-minute tempo of 60. I may slow if I get cold, but my stroke-per-minute pace should not decrease to less than 56 unless my shoulders start to hurt.
> 6. *Breathing:* I primarily breathe to my left, but I can bilateral breathe if necessary. I would like the escort boat to be on my left and my kayaker on my right with constant eye contact and no more than 15 yards away. I want to swim near the middle of the boat.
> 7. *Feeding:* I plan to stop every 30 minutes during the first 2 hours; then every 20 minutes until the end. I will drink warm electrolyte drink for the first six feeds and then defizzed Pepsi toward the end. All my feeds are labeled in the boat. I do not want to stop for more than 30 seconds on each feeding.
> 8. *Strategy:* I plan to hold a steady pace and do not get disturbed by winds or surface chop. There should not be much fluctuation in my hourly progress.
> 9. *Coach:* My coach is responsible for my feedings, stroke count, and navigational decisions.
> 10. *Emergencies:* If I ask to get out, please give me the opportunity to reassess. Pull the boat away and let my coach talk to me. But if there are any signs of hypothermia, immediately pull me out and begin the re-warming process.
> 11. *Others:* My coach will take plenty of photographs and video. The race website will track my progress throughout the race.

and preferences, and emergency procedures in advance with your support team. Explain in person and present this information in writing to them in advance to avoid any misunderstandings.

If your pilot does not speak your language, then communication of your goals is especially important. Send your goals via e-mail in advance and prepare hard copies to hand to your support team before your swim. Prepare both in English and in the pilot's native language using an automatic online translation tool, if necessary. Although online translations are not perfect, a passable translation is better than none at all.

Before you start your swim, relay or race, laminate your detailed instructions and give them to your support crew in a binder. This provides them with waterproof documentation of your wishes in an easy-to-reach, easy-to-remember format.

## A Coach's Value

Your coach is a special person who wears many hats. Ideally, your coach is a masterful motivator who also watches out for your personal safety, possesses the knowledge to analyze and refine your swimming technique, and assists in the creation of a training and logistics plan.

Your coach must be flexible in adapting to the inevitable situations that occur—both during training (e.g., injuries) and the swim itself (e.g., jellyfish stings). Your coach must understand your strengths and weaknesses as well as your capabilities and breaking point – and all aspects of open water swimming safety.

One of your coach's greatest values is helping you develop the confidence to succeed and maintain a hunger for and excitement about the sport. A good coach serves as a sounding board and will help you get back on the right track with positive feedback and useful advice when boredom, frustration, and despondency bubble to the surface.

An experienced coach will be honest with you at all times. If your training is not sufficient to achieve your goal, your coach will give you a fair assessment of your efforts and the difficulty of your chosen goal.

A good coach will motivate you during the long months of training, prepare your feedings to your liking, and know your average and maximum SPM. When the going gets tough during a marathon swim, the mutual confidence and trust you share with your coach will often mean the difference between success and failure.

During your swim, ask your coach to communicate with you frequently via hand signals and written messages on a whiteboard. Information can include your SPM pace, the time to your next feeding, the water temperature (if you want that information), the estimated distance to the finish, or some motivational messages.

If you do not have a personal coach, work with an advisor. This person can be someone with experience in marathon swimming or someone who is knowledgeable about the waterway in which you will do your swim. Advisors can keep you honest about your training and long-term goals while also reviewing your training schedule, logistics, planning, and feeding schedule based on their own marathon swimming experience. They can describe what to look for in an escort pilot and what kind of training is required.

**FACT**

According to the Channel Swimming & Piloting Federation, a swimmer may be accompanied in the water by one pace swimmer during solo swims, but not until the fourth hour. The pace swimmer can be in the water for a maximum of one hour, but cannot repeat until at least two hours have passed after the previous swim. The pace swimmer may swim alongside, but not in front of, the solo swimmer. In the Catalina Channel, a pace swimmer can be in the water for up to three hours.

On marathon swims, it can be comforting to have others get in the water to swim with you. Your coach can decide when it is a good time for your pace swimmer to get in the water with you, if you have one at all. If you are uncomfortable swimming at night, this is a good time for you to use your pace swimmer.

## PSYCHOLOGICAL FACTORS

Cyclists and runners have innumerable visual and audio clues on land, whereas marathon swimmers effectively swim blind, often out of sight of land, guided entirely by their support team, many times at night. In this environment, the mind of the swimmer becomes the powerful engine that drives the body.

Your mental state during a marathon swim or during training can vary from daydreaming to intense concentration on every element around you. Some athletes daydream, some sing, some fantasize, some count strokes, some pray, some go in a trance, and others do many of these things throughout the swim. These things are all ways to help you become calmer, stronger, more energetic, more focused, and can help draw your attention away from immediate issues such as rough conditions, cold water, or the temptation to quit or slow down.

You may wish to focus on your stroke or think about nothing—or everything. You will have plenty of time while you enjoy the tactile feel of the water and sights below. Swimming in the open water provides a unique opportunity to be focused and unfocused at the same time. You can be very cognizant of what is happening internally and oblivious of what is happening externally—or vice versa.

Changes in tides, currents, or surface chop can become frustrating, especially if you start off in calm water. After hours in the water, you can become depressed and discouraged as you increasingly struggle against the elements. Prepare for this challenge in practice—repeatedly. If you get tired and frustrated in practice and you stay in the water, it is unlikely that you will prematurely quit during a swim.

Talk to other marathon swimmers about their experiences and how they overcome their own difficulties. Read about the heroics that have been demonstrated by others in books and online.

# PHYSIOLOGICAL FACTORS

Unlike other endurance athletes, marathon swimmers have to deal with being totally immersed in the water for hours on end. This immersion can lead to unique problems due to the salinity of the water.

If the water is saltier than you are prepared for, you may face problems of swelling of your gums, tongue, and mouth. If this happens, periodically wash out your mouth during feeding stops with a mixture of freshwater and mouthwash.

Repeated swallowing of water, especially saltwater, can result in vomiting, which can lead to dehydration. Train in rough water where possible, especially when the winds are strong. Learn to breathe farther back in your stroke, under your armpits, to keep water from going into your mouth when you breathe.

## FIGHTING AGAINST CURRENTS

Swimming long distances is one issue, but it becomes even tougher when currents are added to the equation. Your best strategy when faced with currents is to accept the elements for what they are. Do not stress out. Use your energy to maintain a good body position and an efficient stroke. Frustrating as it can be, focus on making progress, however little that can be at the time. Positive thoughts lead to positive progress, even if that means merely holding your own against an oncoming tidal flow.

In river swims, your escort pilot may direct you to shallower parts of the river to fight against oncoming currents because water generally tends to flow faster in deeper water. In ocean, sea, or bay swims, your coach and pilot may direct you to swim diagonally against a current to blunt the total force of it. In a competitive race, when the entire field or the swimmers around you are fighting against a current, relax and draft behind other swimmers in the pack.

## HYPOTHERMIA

Hypothermia is a serious condition that may occur as a result of continuous exposure to cold water, cold air, or both. The probability of hypothermia increases as the water temperature drops and the length of your swim increases. Fatigue, chilly winds, and a relatively low body fat percentage also increase the chances of hypothermia.

Hypothermia occurs when your core body temperature drops below 95 °F (35 °C). It is a serious medical condition that must be understood and identified by your coach and boat pilot (see table 8.5).

**Table 8.5**   Signs and Stages of Hypothermia

| Stages of hypothermia | Signs and symptoms | Basic treatments |
| --- | --- | --- |
| **Mild hypothermia** | | |
| Core body temperature of 96-99 °F (35.5-37.2 °C) | Shivering and an impaired ability to swim. | Rewarm with blankets and warm clothing. Protect from exposure to wind. Give warm liquids. |
| Core body temperature of 91-95 °F (32.8-35 °C) | Shaking, shivering, impaired thinking, and slurred speech. | Same treatment, but rewarming may take more time. Consider a warm shower and watch closely. |
| **Moderate hypothermia** | | |
| Core body temperature of 86-90 °F (30-32.2 °C) | Shivering slows down and stops as mental function slows and the swimmer becomes confused and moves with jerky motions. | Prevent further heat loss by rewarming with blankets, towels, and warm clothing. Seek medical assistance. |
| **Severe hypothermia** | | |
| Core body temperature lower than 86 °F (30 °C) | Decreasing blood pressure, life-threatening cardiac irregularities. | Protect from losing heat during a rapid evacuation to a medical facility. |

Signs of mild hypothermia include shivering, an erratic stroke, or a significantly reduced stroke count. Severe hypothermia results in altered cognition, unusual behavior, slurred speech, or apathy. Your pilot, in addition to your coach or observer, has the authority and responsibility to pull you immediately from the water if you are exhibiting any signs of hypothermia. Although you may be fully committed to your swim, it is not worth putting your life in danger. This means pulling you out even when you are very close to your finish.

If you exhibit signs of hypothermia, you should be immediately dried and wrapped in warm clothes with a warm hat and placed out of the wind or near heaters if possible. If you are pulled out of the water far from shore and medical attention is still far off, your coach can jump in a sleeping bag with you to share body warmth. Warm, not hot, drinks can be given, and you may need to drink with a straw if you are shivering. In severe cases, warm baths, advanced warming techniques, and medical assistance are required because the medical issues are complex.

Prevention, of course, is the best option. Acclimatization to cold water is best achieved through diligent training over the course of months. The use of neoprene or double swim caps is restricted by several governing bodies, but earplugs are acceptable everywhere. Safety must be your first priority.

**FACT**

While contemporary marathon swimmers struggle with cold water acclimatization, the incredibly hardy Yahgan people who once occupied Tierra del Fuego in southern Chile along the shores of the Beagle Channel and the islands of Cape Horn existed in inhospitable conditions without the use of clothes.

The Yahgan covered themselves in animal grease and evolved significantly higher metabolisms than average humans while living in temperatures that were cold most of the time.

The Yahgan men hunted sea lions on boats while the Yahgan women often dove in icy waters in all kinds of weather to catch the shellfish and fish located in the thick kelp beds that thrive in the cold waters around the tip of South America. The Yahgan believed that women ruled the sea and the sea was the key to their survival. In times of disagreement, their word ruled.

## FREQUENCY AND TYPES OF FEEDING

For maximum performance, take quick feedings every 15 to 20 minutes. The feeding sequence is the same as described in chapter 7 for middle-distance swims. Be quick and disciplined in your feedings. Do not extend them too long. Feeding stops as shown in figure 8.1 are for consuming drinks or fuels and briefly listening to information from your coach that cannot be relayed in writing on a whiteboard.

Ask your support crew to refrain from asking you questions or initiating a conversation with you during your feedings. Every minute you spend conversing with your support team is another minute tacked on to the duration of your swim. If you need to stretch, then stretch as necessary. If you need a few moments to relax, then relax. But, do not carry on conversations without a purpose. If you want a different flavor or a special food on your next feed, tell your coach during your feeding stop.

Experiment with feeding patterns, types, and amounts in training to determine how best to keep your body fueled during your marathon swim. Practice your feeds, even in a pool. Get used to feeding every 15 to 20 minutes. Your body needs to learn to accept a variety of food and fluids while you are swimming for long distances. Try everything within reason: energy drinks, bananas, sliced peaches, chocolate, and cookies. Most—but not all—swimmers prefer flavored drinks to water. Test your feeds in the pool, in freshwater, and in saltwater. What works for another swimmer may not necessarily work for you.

**Figure 8.1**   Volunteers and coaches use feeding sticks during races.

Bottled water is usually available in most locations where you will swim, but specialty nutrition drinks and gel packs generally are not. To avoid issues with foreign language labels and regulations, plan ahead and bring your own.

Your overall eating habits will also affect how well you can train, recover and perform on marathon day. There are not any particular secrets in eating well. Follow these tips for healthful eating:

- Eat a variety of foods every day.
- Eat colorful fruits and vegetables and not mostly plain-colored foods.
- Eat often enough to avoid being hungry.
- Drink enough fluids to stay hydrated to avoid becoming thirsty.
- Eat enough to maintain your muscle mass.
- Eat within the first two hours after practice.

## Feed Temperature

When the water and air are cold, you may prefer warm liquids. When the water and air are warm, you may prefer chilled liquids. Changing the temperature of your feedings can help stabilize your core body temperature. To warm a gel pack, place it in an insulated bottle of hot water. Conversely, to provide a cool feed, refrigerate or chill your drinks, but do not put ice in them; you do not want to choke on an ice cube in the open water.

## Pre-Race Breakfast and Snacks

Even if you normally do not eat breakfast, you may want to eat something nutritious before your swim. If you depend only on the dinner you had the day before, you may not perform to your full potential. If you normally eat breakfast, then eat as you normally do unless you feel you want some extra water, juice, tea, or coffee.

If you normally have coffee with breakfast, do not change your pre-swim menu on race day. But if you do not drink much coffee, do not feel compelled to start drinking coffee on the morning of your swim. Stick with what you normally eat and drink. Fluids during the last 90 minutes leading up to race time should be limited to water and any preferred specialty drink.

## RELIEVING YOURSELF IN THE WATER

After hours and hours of swimming, it is natural to feel the need to relieve yourself in the open water. It may be difficult at first for some swimmers, but you can urinate as you swim with practice as you reduce your kick while you simultaneously push and relax your pelvic muscles. You may be able to urinate without any problems or significant changes in your stroke. You may need to concentrate while you drop your hips and let your legs drag and lower body relax. You may have to completely stop and go vertical to urinate. You might not be able to go at all because of the cold water or your proximity of a mixed-gender support crew.

Your bladder can hold up to 500 milliliters of urine. Generally, you feel the need to urinate after your bladder reaches the 200- to 250-milliliter range. However, if you are in the early stages of hypothermia, you may have problems urinating because your bladder and kidney have started to shut down. Urination in cold water often requires more concentration.

Conversely, you will find it much easier to urinate during warm water swims. Swimming with a full bladder can be uncomfortable and take away from your enjoyment or speed, especially as your swim increases in length. If your bladder is full, you may not be able to eat or drink much more, which is not beneficial on a marathon swim, so feel free to go.

Marathon swimming is one of modern society's most challenging adventures. Like the explorers of previous centuries, you can venture into the unknown to swim in exotic locations. In oceans and lakes, you learn how far you can push yourself physiologically and psychologically. For many, a marathon swim is among the most stressful, profound, and memorable accomplishments of their lives. It is a complex activity that requires the teamwork of many others, but it also depends entirely on your day-to-day level of commitment, and the ability to dig deeper than you have ever done before. Relish the journey.

CHAPTER

9

# RACING TACTICS FOR EVERY EVENT

Beyond the human versus nature aspect of open water swimming, a competitive atmosphere is clearly evident at local, national, and international races. Some people want to merely finish; others want to win. Most competitors are somewhere in the middle. Olympians, professional marathon swimmers, and competitive triathletes have arsenals that contain a variety of racing tactics that they deploy when they compete for medals, money, and pride.

## CHALLENGE OF THE OPEN WATER

During land-based endurance sports, athletes benefit from a variety of visual and auditory information that helps them understand where they are, how fast they are going, and where they are relative to their competition. In contrast, you have far fewer and far less accurate sensory clues to help you make real-time tactical and navigational decisions in the open water. You may desire navigational clues (e.g., what is the best course?), relative positioning information (e.g., who is in first?), and pace data (e.g., what is my speed per mile?), but this information is usually nonexistent, imperfect, or misleading.

Because you will rarely have access to precise information during open water races, consider a three-pronged strategic approach to counterbalance the lack of perfect information:

- Follow the two Golden Rules of Open Water Swimming.
- Understand human nature.
- Conduct a performance review.

## Two Golden Rules of Open Water Swimming

The unexpected happens a lot in open water races, especially in swims with several turns and fields of hundreds—or thousands—of competitors. Goggles get knocked off. Hands get smeared with petroleum jelly. Errant elbows are caught. Turn buoys move unexpectedly.

Those who take part in, appreciate, and enjoy the sport follow two Golden Rules of Open Water Swimming:

1. Expect the unexpected.
2. Remain flexible.

If you expect the unexpected, you will remain unflappable during your races. You will retain a mental edge over your competition. Before the start, remain relaxed but confident that you are ready after months of hard training and strategic planning. After the race starts, many things can—and will—go wrong. Getting stung by jellyfish, stepping on a rock, and swimming into a buoy are just a few examples of unplanned mishaps. These occurrences are frustrating for anyone and can temporarily shatter your focus or self-confidence.

Racing in the open water can be a constant series of unexpected events that can disrupt your focus, rhythm, and confidence. When these happen, maintain good stroke mechanics, continue to eyeball your competition or support crew, and focus on your positioning and navigation. Above all, enjoy yourself and accept the challenges as they come.

If you prepare emotionally to expect the unexpected, you will be able to adapt to nearly every situation due to weather, human error, or course layout changes.

In particular, changes in water temperature and weather conditions can result in frustration in the open water. For example, the water temperature can suddenly drop several degrees overnight. Swimmers who follow the Golden Rules understand the possibility of water temperature fluctuations and mentally prepare themselves to swim in a wide range of conditions and temperatures. Some athletes bring different swimwear to their races to handle every possible condition; others simply bring the "expect the unexpected" mind-set. They remain unworried instead of allowing stress to affect their performance.

Sometimes, unexpected weather or operational problems lead to unscheduled or unannounced changes to the course layout. Rain and fog can reduce visibility, and buoys can lose their moorings. Timing systems, and their backup systems, occasionally fail. If you accept these challenges, you can gain an upper hand relative to your competition.

# Understanding Human Nature

Human nature does not change past the shoreline. In fact, it becomes even more predictable in the open water.

Most swimmers find it easier and less risky to simply follow the swimmers in front of them in the open water. Like a school of fish, swimmers have a natural instinct to act collectively. Swimmers significantly influence one another in the open water without using words or the body language clues and directions commonly used on land (e.g., pointing, nodding, or smiling).

Use your knowledge of human nature on land to gain advantage in the open water. Concepts such as the self-fulfilling prophecy, role models, and unintended consequences are important to understand and will give you strong hints as to what to expect in the open water.

## Self-Fulfilling Prophecies in the Open Water

A self-fulfilling prophecy is a belief or expectation that affects the outcome of a situation or the way a person or a group behaves. For example, if a majority of swimmers believe the currents in an ocean race run in a particular direction, this collective belief will affect the direction of the field. Likewise, if swimmers anticipate a fast pace at the start, their collective intention will ultimately result in a fast starting pace.

If you want to directly affect the collective thinking of the field, share your insights and findings with every swimmer you meet before the race start. If you are so inclined, talk with many other swimmers at the check-in table, during the warm-up, and before the start. For example, tell them that the currents run north to south and that you heard that the pace will be fast. Make comments and give suggestions such as, "The lifeguards said the currents get stronger by the buoys. What do you think?" or "Last year, the winners hugged the shoreline. Looks like the way to go, but I am not sure." By making suggestions or passing along information to several key competitors, you can partly influence the field whether your information is right or not. You can present the information not as your own advice, but as tips that you are passing along.

## Role Models in the Open Water

The concept of a role model is part of our vernacular. In the sport of open water swimming, its linguistic equivalent is *lead swimmer*. Like a role model whose behavior is imitated by others, the lead swimmer significantly affects the pace and navigational direction of the entire field.

Being able to anticipate what the lead swimmer will do in a race can be useful. Before the race, ask what the best swimmers will do during the race and what course they are likely to take. With good information, you can plan appropriately and prepare alternative strategies that may exploit your strengths. For example, if you know the defending champion will swim close to the pier at the finish, then this is probably the best strategy to follow.

## UNINTENDED CONSEQUENCES IN THE OPEN WATER

Unintended consequences frequently occur in open water races. For example, a swimmer who is in second place coming into the finish may get ahead by bodysurfing a large wave or be able to exploit a navigational error by the lead swimmer caused by the lead boat. Either situation may result in the second-place swimmer winning the race from behind as a result of something that no one had intended or expected. Following are examples of unintended consequences:

- The course has multiple currents, and you benefit from a different navigational choice than your competition.
- You accidently bump into another swimmer and he retaliates and is given a yellow card (warning) or red card (disqualification).
- You are first into the feeding station, but are boxed in by the competitors who come up behind you.

Unintended consequences in the open water are caused by a number of factors, including the following:

- Inaccurate or imperfect information
- Lack of experience, understanding, reason, or sense
- Self-deception (e.g., swimmers believe they are going in the right direction, but in fact are not)
- Failure to account for human nature in the open water

The chaotic nature of open water swims makes the sport exciting for some swimmers. On a given day, any number of people might win a particular swim, depending on the situation, which is often unpredictable. Chaos can be seen at the start of the race (e.g., swimmers start running into the water before the official start), in the middle of the race (e.g., a turn buoy moves after being separated from its anchor), or at the finish (e.g., a large pack comes into the finish together after swimming through the surf break).

Following are some of the causes of unanticipated consequences and ways to mitigate them:

- *Ignorance*: Because it is impossible to anticipate everything in the open water, swimmers sometimes use incomplete information that results in poor decisions. To offset this, be aware of what is going on around you—both behind and in front—throughout the race; constantly process this information.

- *Error*: Incorrect analyses of the water conditions, poor positioning in a pack, or following tactics that may have worked in the past but do not apply to the current situation may result in you or your competitors making bad decisions. To reduce this possibility, ask a friend to video-record your swim and conduct a postrace review to increase your understanding of what can go on in a race.

- *Immediate interest*: During a competitive situation, short-term needs may override long-term interests. For example, you may choose not to feed in the middle of the race because you believe you will lose ground. Ultimately, however, this decision may result in an inability to sprint well at the end of the race. The solution is to balance the immediate situation with what might occur later in the race.

- *Self-defeating prophecy:* Fear of consequences drives some people to seek solutions before problems actually occur. For example, if you are worried about the end of the race, you may slow down at the surf break. But the waves may disappear when you swim through the surf zone. To avoid this, make a commitment not to anticipate problems, but rather, to immediately seize opportunities throughout the race as situations develop. In the case of surf at the finish, go with your instincts and make a quick decision. If you see there is a lull in the surf, sprint in. Later, you can analyze what you did and learn from the consequences of your decisions.

## Conduct a Performance Review

Ask a friend to video-record the start, the finish and as much of your race as possible. The camera should focus on you (perhaps from a pier or other vantage point) so you can review your performance after the end of the race. There is a comprehensive set of questions that you can ask yourself as part of a post-race performance review in chapter 10. By watching videos of yourself and conducting an honest assessment of your performance, you can quickly learn your strengths and weaknesses and how best you can improve.

# RECOMMENDATIONS FOR NOVICES

If you are a newcomer to the sport or less able to compete with the fastest athletes, certain tactics can make your swim more enjoyable and successful. The recommendations in this section can help you achieve success.

## Starting

Parts of open water races that are problematic or stressful for some people may be exciting for you—and vice versa. However, the starts of open water races, especially large mass participation races, are usually stressful for nearly everyone.

- If you are nervous about losing your goggles during a race, relieve some anxiety by placing your goggle straps underneath your swim cap, or wear two swim caps and place your goggle straps over the first cap and under the second cap.

- Before you wear a new swimsuit or wetsuit on race day, make sure you have done several practices with it before race day. Different swimsuits and wetsuits chafe in different places.

- If you are nervous at the race start, strike up a conversation with your fellow competitors. Ask them about the course, the rules, and the competition. Most swimmers are flattered to be asked and happy to share their tactical knowledge. If an athlete is ultra-competitive and tight-lipped, ask swimmers of another gender or in different age groups or divisions who may not view you as competition.

- Whether it is an onshore or in-the-water start, position yourself at the sides or rear of the field. There is no need to be in the middle of hundreds of experienced swimmers and get pummeled in the crush at the start and smashed among the chaos around the first turn buoy.

- Delay slightly at the start to let the field thin out. You will enjoy yourself more with fewer people around.

- If there are waves at the start of an ocean swim and you are not experienced in rough water, take your time going through the surf. As you head out, swim with your head up. Take a deep breath and dive under the water for a few seconds as the wave breaks over you. After you feel the power of the wave surge past you, come up quickly and look for the next wave as you proceed through the surf zone. Continue swimming, diving under and checking for the next wave until you get in deeper water where the waves are not breaking.

- As you run out into the water at the start, keep your knees above the water by high-stepping and swinging your feet wide over the shallow water for as long as you can. When the water is about mid-thigh deep, dive in the water and start swimming or dolphining. Dolphining starts by placing your hands above your head and diving forward. When you reach the bottom, grab or hold it with your hands and pull your legs up under you; then push forward at an angle off the bottom. As you break the surface of the water, take a breath and judge whether you can repeat another dolphin. If the water is still shallow, keep dolphining until the water is deep enough to swim at your normal pace.

- As you get farther from the shore, you may encounter sizable ocean swells. Swim through the swells by piercing the top of the wave with your lead hand. You do not have to dive deeply under each of the rolling swells.

## NAVIGATING

Some swimmers are naturally gifted in the open water; they feel comfortable in most conditions and relish rough conditions. Others have to work hard on their navigational IQ and enter the water with trepidation.

- If you are confused or off-course in the middle of the race, switch to breast-stroke, swim several strokes with your head up, or stop, tread water and look around. Take your time to regain your bearings. Survey the race course and the

## OPEN WATER SWIMMING LESSONS FROM NATURE

Geese flying in formation provide hints about the benefits of drafting in the open water. When geese migrate, they fly in a V formation for several reasons:

- Flying in a V formation is 71 percent more efficient than flying solo.
- When a goose temporarily drops from the V formation, the bird feels a greater air resistance and quickly comes back to the formation.
- When the lead goose gets tired of leading the formation, the bird goes to the end of the V formation and another goose takes the lead.
- When the geese fly in a V formation, they honk to encourage the lead bird, enabling the entire flock to continue flying at the same speed.
- When a goose gets tired, injured, or sick and leaves the V formation, other birds also leave the formation and fly with the slower bird to help and protect it until the slower bird recovers or dies.

field of swimmers, both ahead and behind you. Look for safety personnel ahead of you. Select the course taken by the greatest number of swimmers.

- If there are swimmers on your left and on your right as well as swimmers in front and behind you, then you are swimming in the right direction. Enjoy the experience and go with the flow.
- If you are worried that you are too far left or too far right, look ahead and angle toward the middle of the field ahead of you. Group intelligence amounts to the collective decision-making of a large number of swimmers coming up with the same conclusion. Most swimmers in most races swim in the right direction, so you are usually well-positioned to follow the herd.
- If you are really worried that you are heading in the wrong direction, stop and wave your arms to signal a race official or safety personnel. When they come over in a boat, kayak, or paddle board, ask them where the next buoy is or in what direction you should swim. After you have asked for advice, responsible officials will keep an eye out for you.
- Do a little breaststroke or backstroke if you get tired. Breathe deeply, relax, and take your time. Whether the water is too cold or too warm, these alternative strokes can help you catch your breath, relax, and assess the situation.

## DRAFTING

Swimming in large packs is comfortable for some people, especially in courses that you are unfamiliar with. Other prefer to swim alone or away from the main pack. If you are in the first group, drafting will come into play in most races.

- If you feel uncomfortable drafting behind a swimmer because you are hitting his feet, swim a bit off to his side or farther behind. If someone is swimming

---

### DRAFTING ETIQUETTE

• As in car racing and cycling, drafting is an acceptable tactic and a requisite skill of open water swimmers. Seriously competitive swimmers have a healthy respect for those who are able to outmaneuver and outsprint them at the finish because of their strategic drafting abilities. But there is an etiquette about drafting.

• Tapping on feet and constantly bumping into swimmers is certainly in poor taste at the non-competitive level. Those who enjoy the collegial atmosphere of open water swimming and the camaraderie with fellow swimmers can view drafting behind and then sprinting ahead to win as poor etiquette. Impeding—in any way intentional or unintentional—another swimmer's progress is definitely considered poor sporting behavior.

---

crookedly in front of you or changing his pace too often, give yourself more room and swim clear of him. Effective drafting can make swimming easier, but it is also more stressful for the uninitiated. Drafting is also less effective behind a slow swimmer than it is behind a faster swimmer. If you free yourself from worrying about drafting, you will have an easier time focusing on your own stroke at your own pace and on your own navigational line.

• If you are boxed in between swimmers and feel claustrophobic, speed up or swim slowly on purpose. If you speed ahead, you may either swim into some clear water—or will run into packs ahead. Swimmers behind you will get impatient and swim around you. As swimmers pass you, angle towards the outside of the pack—and the entire field—to give yourself more clear water.

• If you are bothered by someone behind you tapping on your feet, swim diagonally or laterally—even for a few meters or strokes. The problem usually resolves itself. Alternatively, you can use an easy backstroke or breaststroke until the offender has passed you and you can swim unencumbered in clear water. If drafting swimmers follow you and continue to tap your feet, kick hard for several leg beats to indicate your displeasure—or simply stop and give them space to move around you and let them swim past.

## BUOY TURNS

If you prefer not to get bumped or kicked around the buoy turns, swim wide of the buoy to avoid the crowd. However, if you are already stuck in a crowd, then swim around the turn buoy with your head up (see figure 9.1). Swimmers occasionally do some scissor kicking around the turn buoy and unintentionally kick others. If your head is above the water, you can avoid being kicked.

After you swim around the turn buoy, look up and assess your direction. Take time to regain your bearings so you have confidence in your direction.

**Figure 9.1**   Look ahead, like the center swimmer, when swimming around a turn buoy.

## FEEDING

If you foresee swimming for more than an hour, put a gel pack in your swimsuit if you are comfortable swimming with one. Stick the gel pack somewhere on your back with the end of the package sticking out of your swimsuit. The elastic around the edges of your swimsuit will hold the gel pack in place. If you take a feeding along the way, the fuel will work wonders and give you a second wind.

Experienced swimmers know to expect the unexpected. Things will happen in the open water and you want to make the best of the unexpected situations.

## EQUIPMENT MALFUNCTIONS

• If your goggles come off during a race, stop immediately and look around. Do not panic; your goggles are most likely floating somewhere near you. Slowly survey your area by treading water and doing a 360-degree revolution. Your goggles may be under the surface of the water as a result of the thrashing and commotion caused by many swimmers.

• If your goggles are lost, then close your eyes when your eyes are underwater and open your eyes when you breathe. For millennia, people swam without goggles. You can do so too for a short distance, although it might be uncomfortable or you may swim with contact lenses.

• When you find your goggles, take time to put them on. Do not rush and start swimming again with your goggles filled with water. Before you participate in your first open water swim, practice putting on your goggles in the deep end of a pool while you tread water.

- If your swim cap is lost, swim on. The best you can do the next time is to anticipate the situation and use hair clips. With hair clips, at least your hair will be a manageable clump instead of a wild mess. A swim cap will stay on better if you do not use shampoo or conditioner in your hair a few days before your race.

## MARINE LIFE

In the open water, we are the visitors, so do not be surprised by what you may see or run into in the marine environment. You may be startled if you run into seaweed or see marine animals. Try to keep calm and breathe slowly. If you start to panic or hyperventilate, stop and tread water until you can catch your breath. Wave to the safety personnel if you are scared. Talking with other people out in the open water can help calm you.

If you get stung by a Portuguese man-o-war or jellyfish, the venom is going to hurt for a while. There is nothing to do but hang tough until you reach shore. Focus on another part of your body and know that other swimmers are also probably getting stung. When you finish the race, apply white vinegar or a commercial product such as StingMate to your wound. If you are allergic to jellyfish, then forewarn the race officials so they are prepared to come to your assistance immediately.

When the end is near, many swimmers feel an adrenaline rush or, at the very least, feel relieved. But it isn't over until you are firmly back on terra firma.

## FINISHING

- If there are waves near the finish and you are uncomfortable bodysurfing, take your time. Frequently lift your head to check for oncoming waves from both sides. If you are intimidated by the size of a wave, stop or let it pass as you duck underwater. If you are really scared, stop, wave your arms, and wait for the lifeguards or safety personnel to help guide you through the surf.

- When the surf is large at the finish, constantly watch for waves that you can bodysurf or avoid, if you are uncomfortable. These are the best opportunities for you to pass people who are faster than you.

- Practice bodysurfing at all your open water workouts if there are waves. If the surf is large, carefully watch how the waves break before the race and practice a few rides during your warm-up.

- If there is an onshore finish, your heart rate may increase when you stand up and start to run through the shallow water and up the shore. As you approach the shore, slow down so your heart rate decreases in preparation for the short run up the beach. There is no need to run unless you are competitive and want to finish quickly.

- As you stand up and start to walk, jog, or run, remove your goggles from your eyes so you can see better—unless you wear prescription or optical goggles. Solidly plant your feet on every step. Look down for holes in the sand, rocks and shells to avoid. Falling down in front of cheering crowds at the finish can be embarrassing, but the last thing you want to do is injure yourself.

## CULTIVATING A SENSE OF ADVENTURE

If you are in the middle of your first race, things may be more difficult—or enjoyable—than you imagined. Your heart may pump faster than you expect. The race may be more crowded than you prefer. The distance may feel longer than you anticipated. This is why endurance sports are alluring to many people. How tough are you? How far can you push yourself? How do you deal with unexpected situations? Open water swimming gives you opportunities to dig deep, presenting an honest challenge that pits you against the elements. Enjoy the adventure and know that many others have encountered and overcome similar obstacles.

If you are nervous about your first open water swim, get comfortable by going to a beach or lake without any intention of working out. Just have fun. Enjoy the sea air or the tranquility of the lake. Watch children play in the water and imagine how you will enjoy the same environment on race day with like-minded athletes.

# RECOMMENDATIONS FOR INTERMEDIATE AND ADVANCED SWIMMERS

Even if you are experienced, pre-race preparation involves a number of logistical issues, equipment checks and a good physical warm-up.

## WARMING UP

• If a pool is available, even if it is a hotel pool, you may want to use if before heading down to the race venue.

• If the water is cold and you are not completely acclimated to the temperature, change your normal warm-up. Stretch more or go for a short jog. Drink warm fluids and stay warm until the start. You can use the first part of the race as a warm-up.

• If the water is colder than expected, enter it slowly to adjust to the temperature difference between the air and water. Splash water on your upper body, face, and head. Focus on your warm core and not on your cold extremities. Bob up and down in the shallow water or splash yourself until you are comfortable enough to start swimming in the cold water. Some people just like to jump in and deal with the sudden cold.

• If the water is warm and overheating is a concern, shorten your normal warm-up. It is easier and quicker to get prepared under warm conditions. After you finish your warm-up, hydrate and stay comfortable in the shade. Alternatively, drink an iced drink, put on wet socks, place ice on your head under your swim cap or hat, or put your hands in ice water to temporarily decrease your core body temperature.

- Get to the venue early. At popular swims, parking can be a hassle. You also want to have time to decide where to set your belongings before other competitors arrive. Give yourself time to walk casually along the shore or pier to observe the water conditions.

- Race officials and volunteers are stressed as the race gets closer to the start. However, you can easily approach friendly race officials and volunteers privately one or two hours before the start. In a more relaxed setting, ask them about the water temperature and water conditions.

- During your warm-up, check the relative position of the first few turn buoys and the last turn buoy into the finish. Check for holes, rocks, and the gradient of the shore if the race has an onshore start and finish. Swim to the first few buoys and confirm convenient landmarks that can help you.

- Confirm whether there are any currents by floating on your back for 30 seconds and seeing where or how the currents cause you to drift. Alternatively, take off your goggles, place them on the surface of the water, and check the direction and speed in which they float away.

- Ask competitors who did the race before whether the conditions were similar to the past and what their times were to give you an idea of how long you will be in the water.

## Equipment

- If swim caps are mandatory, confirm with the race director whether you must finish with your swim cap. If it is a warm water swim and you have short hair, you can loosely place your swim cap on your head. Once you start swimming, your cap will either naturally come off or you can purposefully nudge it off. If you are worried about littering, take your swim cap off and stick it in your swimsuit.

- Apply a thin layer of petroleum jelly on your lower calves, upper shoulders, and upper arms. The petroleum jelly will discourage your competitors from repeatedly grabbing your ankles, pulling on your legs, or bumping into you.

- Wear silicone earplugs to minimize heat loss if the water is cold.

- In some competitions, race officials will check the length of your fingernails and toenails and will not allow jewelry or watches. Be prepared to cut your nails to a reasonable length.

- Invest in a pair of prescription or optical goggles if you do not have good eyesight. Prescription goggles are more expensive than the off-the-shelf optical goggles, but either will help minimize your disorientation in the water. Most athletes would not run or cycle without their contact lenses or eyeglasses on land, so it makes sense to use corrective goggles in the water.

• Use clear goggles for foggy and overcast race days and tinted goggles for sunny days. With at least two pairs of race-ready goggles in both light and dark colors, you are prepared for every possible climatic condition. Alternate goggles in practice during the last few weeks before race day, so you are confident that all pairs of goggles are ready to go.

• Keep your goggles over your eyes throughout your entire pool swimming workout. Many swimmers regularly place their goggles lenses on their forehead between sets during pool workouts. Instead, keep your goggles on and learn to adjust your goggles by minutely moving your facial muscles while you are swimming. Alternatively, learn to adjust your goggles when you quickly roll on your side or on your back without losing much momentum. If you are constantly taking off and adjusting your goggles during pool workouts, you will not learn how to adjust them on the fly during an open water race.

## STARTS

As the countdown begins, the tension among the swimmers naturally builds. The nervousness of the field is palpable. Hundreds (or thousands) of athletes will be swinging their arms, stretching, fidgeting, and shifting into position at the start. Take care to avoid accidently smearing petroleum jelly, sunscreen, or lanolin on your goggles or hands in the final minutes. Prepare for a worst-case scenario by carrying a small hand towel or tissue paper to remove any ointments, sunscreens, creams, or lanolin that get smudged on your goggles or smeared on your hands by yourself or your competitors.

### IN-THE-WATER STARTS

• In-the-water starts often use a rope along the water's surface that all athletes must touch. The rope is usually not straight because the swimmers tread forward while they hold the rope with one hand, trying to gain a small advantage. In these situations, the referee will ask athletes to refrain from creating an unfair start, but it is frankly difficult to do so. Even if the start rope is not straight and there are some slight advantages for some athletes, the start will go off. In this situation, referees very rarely call back the field or disqualify swimmers who get a slight edge at the start.

• Position yourself anywhere to take advantage of currents along the starting line. Expect some jostling among the field, even in the water. Move away from the most aggressive swimmers if you want to avoid this physicality.

### ONSHORE STARTS

• Starts from the lakeshore or a sandy beach are the most popular in the open water swimming world (see figure 9.2 on page 196). They range from soft sand beaches to flat, hard-packed lakeshore edges.

Michael Zoetmulder

**Figure 9.2** Typical onshore beach start with multiple participants.

• As you run into the water, high-step through the shallow water as long as you can, dolphin for as long as you can, and then start swimming when you are in deeper water. Running and good dolphining are always faster than swimming.

• If there are currents, position yourself where you can take advantage of them. However, you also need to consider the size of field, the level of competition, the amount of surf, and the distance to the first turn buoy.

• Some overzealous competitors view everyone as an obstacle in their way. These types of competitors—both male and female—are aggressive and inconsiderate. They do not apologize for swimming over you, pulling you back or getting tangled with you. Avoid them by starting off to the side or fall in line behind them. It is better to draft behind them or simply let them go ahead of you. If you focus on retaliation, your enjoyment of the race and ability to think clearly about more important tactical moves will suffer.

• If you do not mind starting at the front of the pack, start off to the side of or behind the non-smiling, non-verbal swimmers who constantly scan the course and jostle for position at the start line. Start behind these open water warriors. They do not let anyone get in their way so you can draft behind them around the first turn buoy. The chaotic situation will be more bearable if you swim after them.

• If there are heats that start before you, note where and how the swimmers in the earlier heats start and swim around the first few turn buoys.

• Depending on your skills and experience, the worst position to be in at the start is the middle of a large pack with swimmers all around you. If possible, avoid being boxed in before you even enter the water.

## Dealing With Ocean Swells, Surf, Whitecaps, and Surface Chop

• Once you are past the surf zone, quickly get into your rhythm. If there are swells, whitecaps, or surface chop, do not forgot your proper stroke mechanics. Even with surface chop, try to stay as streamlined as possible to minimize the resistive forces against you. Use your legs as ballast, but keep your hips high and feet pointed, swimming in as narrow a cylinder as possible.

• The best way to prepare for an open water race is to practice in the open water or do POW workouts (see chapter 6). Find a swim buddy and practice in the open water on windy afternoons.

• Take advantage of any opportunity during a race in which you feel the swells, whitecaps, or surface chop moving with you. Pick up your kick and lengthen your stroke to take advantage of the power of the waves. Breathe farther back under your armpit to avoid swallowing water.

## Drafting and Positioning

• If competitors of your similar speed swim straight and have high navigational IQ, draft to their side and significantly reduce the number of times you have to sight as shown in figure 9.3. Breathe normally to the side, follow their navigational line and save your energy for the finish.

• Sight forward, to the sides, and diagonally to broaden your visual field. Always be aware of your position relative to your competition.

• If your competition is drafting off you, you are in control of the race and the direction of the pack. Steer the pack in a direction that positions you closer to a turn buoy or puts you in the best position to take advantage of the waves. If you are drafting behind a swimmer who primarily breathes to one side, position yourself on the non-breathing side so you can make a tactical move without being seen.

**Figure 9.3** Drafting, either behind or at the side of a competitor, is an essential open water swimming skill.

Ivan Torres

• Draft right off the hips, knees, or feet of experienced swimmers to give you the advantage of their draft and to minimize the number of times you must lift your head. Draft and navigate off your competitors while you position yourself to overtake them as you approach the finish or swim–bike transition.

• Even if you are not a regular bilateral breather, occasionally breathe on both sides to be aware of what is going on to your right and left. The ability to breathe on both sides enables you to breathe away from the sun, waves, surface chop, or exhaust from escort boats at any time.

• Bilateral breathing is useful in an ocean swim when there is sizable surf. As you approach the surf, look for waves on your left and right. Look farther behind than usual as part of your normal breathing cycle.

• If you see a wave coming, time it so you can bodysurf to the finish. If the wave passes you before you can catch it, kick hard as the wave passes over you to gain some momentum. If necessary, kick faster and pick up your stroke pace to catch a wave. Conversely, if you need to slow down a bit to catch a wave, it will be worth it. But do not slow down and then completely miss catching the wave. The experience you gain from practicing bodysurfing before race day will come in handy in these situations.

## FINISHING

• To swim faster, most people either have to swim more efficiently or pick up their tempo. Increasing your efficiency in the middle of a race in the open water is much more difficult than kicking faster to picking up your tempo. Kicking faster will also help you prepare your legs for an onshore finish.

• Swim until your hand touches the bottom. Then stand up and begin dolphining toward the shore the same way you dolphined out at the start. As you reach the shallow water, high-step and swing your legs over the surface of the shallow water (see figure 9.4) rather than simply plowing through the water.

• If you catch a wave toward the finish, bodysurf it for as long as you can. Kick hard and continue to ride the wave until you are in very shallow

Michael Zoetmulder

**Figure 9.4**  Start running for an onshore finish when the water approaches knee level.

water where you can run faster than you can bodysurf. Even if you are body surfing at an angle away from the finish line, stay in the wave. Landing away from the beach finish is acceptable because you run more quickly on land than your competitors swim.

• Training for a fast finish requires practice, preferably in the open water. But, if you do not have access to an open water venue, do an occasional deck-up set at the pool.

## POSITIONING VIS-À-VIS RIP CURRENTS

Rip currents are strong, narrow currents that generally flow perpendicular from the shorelines through the surf and then offshore. They are caused by an accumulation of water near the shore as a result of wave action. Although rip currents can be dangerous, strong swimmers with ocean experience and a competitive zeal can use them to their benefit, both at the start and finish.

Before the start of an ocean race, especially when there is sizable surf, observe the waves and water flows near the start and finish. Carefully check for sandbars, breaking waves, smooth water, and whitewater. Rip currents flow in deeper water next to piers and sandbars or in shallower water where the waves are breaking. Look for rip currents where no waves breaking and a visible flow of water is flowing away from the shore. Use the power and speed of the rip current in these areas to gain an advantage over your competitors at the start of the race. For fast starts, take advantage of the rip currents *out* to the first buoy.

Conversely, on your way back to the finish, use the reverse strategy. Avoid swimming *into* a rip current and avoid deeper water channels, if they are apparent. Swim toward the shallower water or in areas where you can catch a wave.

## COMPETITION AT THE HIGHEST LEVELS

Even the fastest and most experienced veterans do not always make the most optimal choices during a race. Open water swimming is conducted in dynamic environments in which the elements and the competition are in a constant state of flux. This usually results in lead changes, navigational errors, and a variety of tactical maneuvers throughout the race. Fortunately, recovery from tactical errors is usually possible, except in the last part of races.

The cost of making tactical errors increases as the race progresses. Mistakes in the first half of the race certainly cost you some time and energy, but mistakes in the latter stages of the race will cost you victory.

You may encounter waves, currents, poor or minimal course designs, surface chop, boat exhaust, physical contact, marine life, or a mass of churning competitors who are making constant changes both intentionally and not. The environment can be intimidating, confusing, and frustrating, but success demands that you remain analytical and calm throughout the race.

Race tactics in open water swimming are as varied and subtle as the race tactics used by cyclists and marathon runners with the following important differences:

- Swimmers move more slowly than land-based athletes do.
- Tactics in the open water are significantly influenced by the elements.
- Moves and maneuvers executed in the open water are more difficult to see than those on land.
- Even a small lead in the open water is difficult to overcome for athletes of equal ability.

Because of these differences, as an open water swimmer, you

- have more time to prepare for your competitors' tactics,
- can anticipate some tactics based on the water and weather conditions,
- have less time to respond to your competitors' moves, and
- have less opportunity to make up for your mistakes at the end of a race.

## MAKING A MOVE

Reaction time is very important in the open water. You must anticipate your competitors' moves and respond quickly. To do so, you must be constantly observing and adapting to everything and everyone around you. When you do make a move, swim decisively. Moves include changes of pace, changes of direction, and changes in position.

### CHANGE OF PACE

A change of pace is easy to detect. You can see your competitor's change of pace when he picks up his kick or stroke tempo. A quickening of your heart rate as you try to keep up and a separation between you and your competitors are other indications of a change of pace.

Observing a change of pace in the packs ahead of or behind you is more difficult. The following will help you detect a change of pace in those ahead of you:

- Keep in mind that an escort boat or kayak following a pack of swimmers will move at the same pace as the swimmers. Sight off the escort because it is easier to see. If the escort is moving slightly away from you, you can assume that the pack in front has picked up its pace.

- Instead of being at the back of your pack, position yourself up toward the middle and to the side of the pack. This will give you a better vantage point from which to observe any situation in front of you.

- Occasionally observe the last swimmer in the pack ahead of you. Watch for any sudden separation that occurs or the splash of their kick. Increased splashing is usually an indication that the pace is increasing.

If the pack you are in begins to fall behind a faster pack, you have a choice: stick with your current pace and stay with the slower pack, or sprint to latch yourself to the end of the faster pack.

## CHANGE OF DIRECTION

A change of direction can range from subtle to abrupt, but is relatively easy to detect if the water is calm and flat and is much harder to detect if the water is rough or there are ocean swells. Beware of both: A subtle change of direction will be slow and gradual, whereas an abrupt change of direction may catch you off guard.

Experienced and seriously competitive swimmers can be masters of the subtle change of direction. Competitors may move into your space ever so slightly as you swim stroke for stroke. They gradually work to move you slightly to your left or right, off the optimal straight-line path. They put you at a disadvantage without you even suspecting it—until it is too late. A bump here, a nudge there, and an off-kilter angle over a long straightaway is all it takes for another competitor to subtly move into a more optimal position at your expense.

Conversely, as you swim shoulder to shoulder over a long straightaway, you can move your competitor just slightly off the best line, and then suddenly angle 10 or 20 degrees toward the next turn buoy. Within one or two arm strokes, you can establish an advantage that you plotted 500 yards in advance. As a result, you can go around the turn buoy at a better angle and come out ahead by a body length.

You can also change direction when you bodysurf past a competitor. This is the most dramatic of all maneuvers in open water swimming.

## CHANGE OF POSITION

A change of position usually requires you to quickly shift gears in a pack. You may be boxed in by a pack of swimmers and want to dislodge yourself from this position. You may want to get on the right side of a competitor who primarily breathes to the left side. To make a change in position, slow down suddenly, but only for a stroke or two; then dart across the lower legs of your competitor before immediately kicking hard and shifting back in a higher gear to complete your maneuver.

If a competitor is in the lead but wants to give it up, they may slow down while looking back at you. You can either take the bait and the lead, or similarly slow down and maintain your relative position. Alternatively, you can blast confidently into the lead and increase your pace for 50 to 100 yards. The pack will follow—it is human nature. After the pack has correspondingly picked up its pace to keep up with you, slow down suddenly and watch your competitors unwittingly pass you as you resume your original drafting position behind the new leaders.

If the race is a loop with currents flowing in one direction, you will have numerous opportunities to make or react to a move. Generally, packs bunch up when the current or surface chop is against the field. Conversely, when swimmers benefit from currents, everyone swims faster and the field generally tends to get strung out.

When you swim against the current, being at the back of the pack is not a bad position because the number of body lengths from the front to the back of the pack tends to be small. Conversely, if you are in the back of the pack when the field is swimming with the current, the distance between you and the leaders is much greater and much more difficult to make up.

Following are general rules to keep in mind when there are currents, waves, whitecaps, or rough water:

- You should try to keep close to the leaders (mid-pack or closer) when swimming with the current.

- There is an opportunity to stretch out the field when swimming with the current.

- Being at the back of the pack is acceptable when swimming against the current.

- Do not push the pace when you are in the lead when swimming against the current.

- When there is a 180-degree change of direction around a turn buoy into an oncoming current, the field will soon converge. The lead of the top swimmers will shrink.

- When there is a 180-degree change of direction around a turn buoy into a positive favorable current, the field will spread out. The lead of the top swimmers will increase.

- When there is a 90-degree change of direction around a turn buoy into an oncoming current, the field will spread out laterally along the course as everyone seeks the best line.

Hundreds of scenarios and situations can occur during a race. Figure 9.5 lists 12 common scenarios in ocean races that you may face when you are swimming either with or against the current around various course configurations.

## TACTICS IN UNUSUAL OR ROUGH CONDITIONS

Many different types of situations in open water competitions may occur —from the presence of sharks and the crowding of escort boats to sudden thunderstorms and foggy conditions.

In the extreme conditions, such as the presence of sharks or thunderstorms, get out immediately. Bravado has little place under life-threatening conditions, not only for yourself, but also for the volunteers and event staff that are supporting the race or solo swim.

If escort boats get dangerously close to you, stop and yell your displeasure of the situation to the pilot and staff. If you breathe exhaust from an escort boat, inform the race officials of the situation. Yell, "Exhaust!" or "Move boats!" Most race officials will understand and comply with these requests.

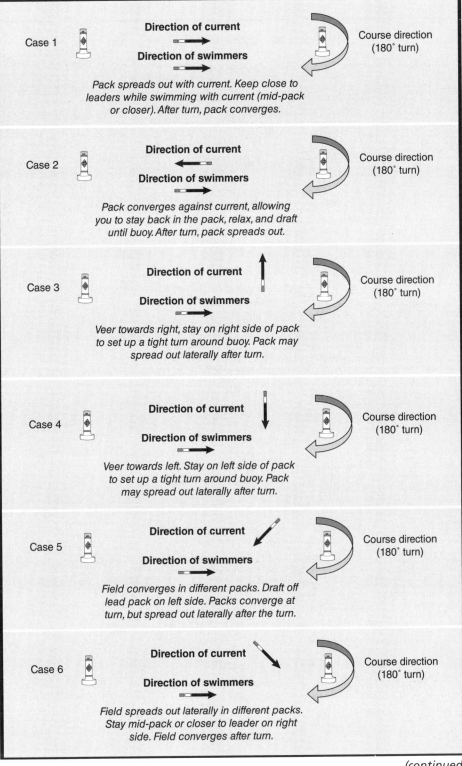

**Case 1**

**Direction of current**

**Direction of swimmers**

**Course direction** (180° turn)

*Pack spreads out with current. Keep close to leaders while swimming with current (mid-pack or closer). After turn, pack converges.*

**Case 2**

**Direction of current**

**Direction of swimmers**

**Course direction** (180° turn)

*Pack converges against current, allowing you to stay back in the pack, relax, and draft until buoy. After turn, pack spreads out.*

**Case 3**

**Direction of current**

**Direction of swimmers**

**Course direction** (180° turn)

*Veer towards right, stay on right side of pack to set up a tight turn around buoy. Pack may spread out laterally after turn.*

**Case 4**

**Direction of current**

**Direction of swimmers**

**Course direction** (180° turn)

*Veer towards left. Stay on left side of pack to set up a tight turn around buoy. Pack may spread out laterally after turn.*

**Case 5**

**Direction of current**

**Direction of swimmers**

**Course direction** (180° turn)

*Field converges in different packs. Draft off lead pack on left side. Packs converge at turn, but spread out laterally after the turn.*

**Case 6**

**Direction of current**

**Direction of swimmers**

**Course direction** (180° turn)

*Field spreads out laterally in different packs. Stay mid-pack or closer to leader on right side. Field converges after turn.*

*(continued)*

**Figure 9.5** Twelve common scenarios in ocean races.

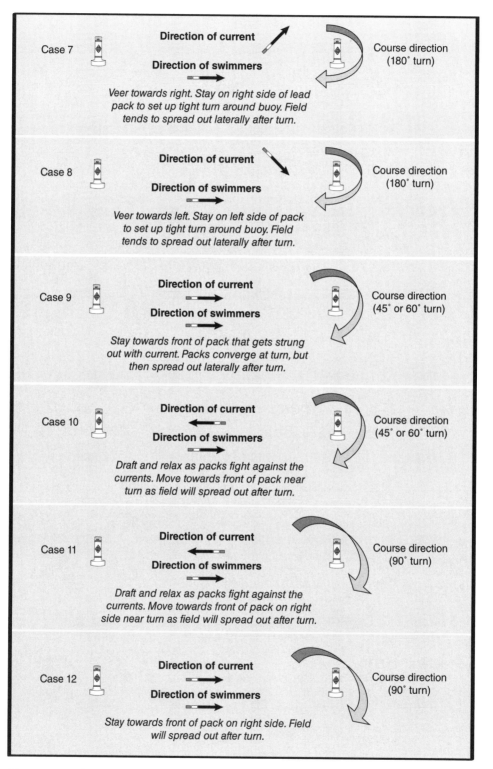

**Figure 9.5** *(continued).*

204

If your view of the turn buoys or finish in the distance is blocked by escort boats, inform the race officials by yelling out to the drivers. If you are swimming near a pier and there are still fishermen with their fishing lines in the water, immediately inform the race officials.

When weather and water conditions are particularly rough, there are two advantages to swimming toward the front. First, safety personnel and race officials will be on alert and will attempt to guide the lead pack on the best possible course. If you are up toward the front, you will gain this navigational assistance. Second, if the race is cancelled, the places of the swimmers are usually determined by the relative position of the athletes in the water at the time of cancellation.

## DISTANCE ORIENTATION

Like a professional golfer, a good open water swimmer should be able to judge distances at a glance. The ability to judge distances, whether you are swimming parallel to a shoreline or around a pier, is extremely helpful.

To best learn how to make these judgments, first research some empirical information. Before you go to a lake or ocean for practice, learn the distance of a pier or jetty or the distance between lifeguard stations. Use Google Earth or online marine charts or ask the lifeguards what the distances are.

If you know that a pier extends 400 yards from shore, then swim out to the end of the pier and create a mental picture for yourself of how far 400 yards looks, both from the water's surface and from the shore. If you know that the distance between lifeguard stations is 200 yards, then swim between the stations to create and reinforce a picture in your mind of how far 200 yards appears at water level. During a race, these etched mental images will help you.

Additionally, learn how many arm strokes you take in one minute in the open water, both while swimming at a comfortable pace and while swimming fast. Ask your coach or teammate to count your arm strokes in the open water, both when the water is flat and when it is rough.

## POSITION ORIENTATION

It is important to know where you are not only relative to your competition but also relative to the next turn buoy, feeding station and finish. Ask where the halfway mark is on a point-to-point course or the distance between turn buoys in a loop course. Ask the race director or the officials out on the course during warm-up to provide this information. If this information is not available, encourage the race director to name (or provide) a midway buoy for future races. The midway buoy can be a different size, shape, or color from the other buoys or numbered in a unique way. Successful race directors always appreciate valuable feedback from swimmers, so they will listen to your requests.

Use cables or coral visible underwater, intermediate buoys, or landmarks (e.g., trees, buildings, or bridges) to guide you. If the water is clear and you can see coral reefs, sea flora, or kelp beds underwater, observe the direction of the flora so you know the water flow and can optimally position yourself along the best line to the finish.

Separate packs always form during the course when different groups take different lines to the next turn buoy. As a general rule, packs tend to converge at the turn buoys and then spread out again between the buoys.

If you get disoriented or confused out in the open water, know that swimmers in a large field collectively navigate fairly well. Position yourself to keep an approximately equal number of swimmers on both your left and right. In an overwhelming majority of swims, this strategy will lead you to a reasonably good line along the course.

## DOLPHINING FAST AT THE START AND FINISH

Dolphining, or jumping off the ocean or lake bottom at the start and finish of the race, is an absolute must for the competitive open water swimmer. The speed in which you can move by running and dolphining is far faster than what you can do by swimming.

High-step through the shallow water and swing your feet over the surface of the water. Run into the water until the water level reaches about mid-thigh. Without hesitation, dive forward at a shallow angle with your arms in front of your head in a streamlined manner. As your body enters the water, kick butterfly or freestyle until your hands touch bottom. Grab onto the bottom as you quickly bring your legs under your body. Plant your feet and push off the bottom at a 45-degree angle. Remain streamlined as you kick toward the surface of the water. Dolphin until the water becomes deep enough to swim in.

Toward the end of the race, start to dolphin once your hands touch bottom. After your hand touches, bring your legs under your body and spring forward at a shallow angle, just slightly clearing the surface of the water. With both hands overlapped and stretched in front of you, remain in the streamlined position until you reach the bottom again. Grab the bottom, pull yourself forward, recoil your legs, and leap off the bottom again. Repeat until it becomes faster to run than to dolphin.

Because the depth of the water can change, there may be times where you alternate dolphining and swimming before you finally reach water shallow enough for you to run straight to the finish or the swim–bike transition area.

## USING BUOY TURNS TO YOUR ADVANTAGE

In open water swimming, you will need to make left- and right-shoulder buoy turns of varying degrees and in various situations (i.e., alone, in the company of a few swimmers, or in a large pack), including the following:

- 45- and 60-degree sharp turns
- 90-degree right-angle turns
- 120-degree wide-angle turns
- 180-degree hairpin turns

Use your legs to quickly execute 45-degree and 60-degree sharp turns and 180-degree hairpin turns. In a tightly bunched pack, do a scissors kick and strong crossover arm stroke to change directions and separate yourself from your competition.

In most situations, you can execute a 90-degree right-angle turn or a 120-degree wide-angle turn by simply twisting your body to change direction. A strong crossover stroke is necessary on a 90-degree turn, whereas a slight crossover stroke will suffice on a 120-degree turn.

The size of the turn buoys may also affect how you turn. There is less need to use a scissors kick and crossover stroke at large turn buoys. With larger buoys, it is often easier to simply swim and twist your body as necessary.

Because other swimmers may also use scissors kicks and crossover arm strokes to change directions at 45-, 60-, 90-, and 180-degree turns, there is a high possibility of tangling arms with your competitors and bumping hands, feet, heels, knees, and elbows. If you keep your head up around the turns, you will be less likely to get kicked in the head. If your arms get tangled with another swimmer's, immediately drop your shoulders and arms to untangle and restart your stroke. If you and your competitor struggle by trying to outmuscle each other, you will both get frustrated and lose valuable time, energy, and position.

## TYPES OF OPEN WATER TURNS

Following are some ways to get around turn buoys in a race:

- Twist in the direction you are swimming
- Scissors kick with a crossover stroke
- Corkscrew turn
- Underwater turn

A corkscrew turn is the most elegant and most difficult open water turn. To execute it properly, take your last freestyle stroke with the arm closest to the buoy, roll over onto your back using one backstroke stroke, and then continue rotating over onto your belly with another freestyle stroke as you twist your body around the turn buoy. Practice this turn many times in workouts before you execute it in a race. It is easy to get a bit disoriented in a corkscrew turn in competitive situations. With other swimmers around you, it is most important to come out of the corkscrew turn headed in the correct direction.

An underwater turn is another radical but less frequently used alternative. In a very close pack in a competitive race, especially when you are squeezed on the inside, you can take a big gulp of air and dive underwater underneath your competition. As you kick around the turn buoy, twist around the rope anchoring the turn buoy and resurface with authority on the other side, kicking strongly with a fast arm turnover. As you pop to the surface, this maneuver will enable you to squeeze into space among the tight pack. When you seemingly come out of nowhere (i.e., from below the surface of the water), your competitors tend to slow down and watch you resurface, giving you the opportunity to rejoin the pack in a more advantageous position. There are a multitude of turns and appropriate techniques depending on the angle and direction of the turn and whether or not you are in light traffic or a large pack. Table 9.1 lists the types of turns and the best technique you should use to navigate them.

## BODYSURFING INTO THE FINISH

Bodysurfing is an important part of competitive ocean racing. When you swim toward the finish and catch a wave to the shore, let it take you in the direction it is heading. Even if the waves are breaking at a slight angle to the finish, bodysurf the wave for the longest ride possible. Instead of going straight to shore, you might angle a bit left or right. Bodysurf away from the whitewater of the wave to get a longer ride.

Bodysurfing requires exquisite timing to catch the wave and a strong kick once you feel the surge of the wave. Pick up your pace as the wave starts to engulf you. After you are being pushed by the wave, turn a bit on your side with one hand in front of you, palm down to break the surface of the water. Do not let the wave completely engulf you; continue to kick hard to stay just slightly in front of the wave's surge. If the wave surrounds and starts to pass you, start to quickly pull with one arm while your other arm remains extended. Do what you can to stay in the wave. After the wave either dissipates or surges past you, continue swimming and look for the next wave, or dolphin to the finish if the water is shallow enough. Even if the wave pushes you slightly away from the finish line, it will enable you to get to shore more quickly.

If you are not an experienced bodysurfer or do not like the ocean waves, simply let the waves surge past you. As the whitewater engulfs you, extend both arms straight in front of you. Continue to kick and remain in a streamlined position. Let the power of the wave push you forward. After the wave passes, resume swimming and look backwards for the next wave.

**Table 9.1** How to Execute Turns With Authority

| Type of turn | Kick | Arm stroke | Breathing | Caution |
|---|---|---|---|---|
| 45- or 60-degree sharp turn | Use a strong scissors kick. | Use a strong crossover stroke. | Look up if necessary or do an underwater turn. | Possibility of tangled arms and errant feet with others. |
| 90-degree right-angle turn | Use a slight scissors kick. | Use a crossover stroke. | Normal, or do an underwater turn. | Possibility of tangled arms and errant feet with others. |
| 120-degree wide-angle turn | Continue a normal kick. | Use a corkscrew turn or twist the body with a slight crossover stroke. | Normal | Slight possibility of physical contact on the inside line. |
| 180-degree hairpin turn | Use a strong scissors kick. | Do a U-turn to change direction. | Look up if necessary or do an underwater turn. | High probability of physical contact in the pack. |
| Underwater turn | Use a streamlined freestyle or butterfly stroke. | Resurface with a rapid arm turnover. | None | Can resurface in the path of a competitor. |
| Left-shoulder turn | Push the right leg outward for a change of direction. | Cross the right arm over the centerline for a change of direction. | Normal | May want to keep head up to avoid contact. |
| Right-shoulder turn | Push the left leg outward for a change of direction. | Cross the left arm over the centerline for a change of direction. | Normal | May want to keep head up to avoid contact. |
| Solo turn | Kick normally. | Pull normally. | Normal | None |
| Turns in light traffic | Use a scissors kick if on the inside of the pack. Use a normal kick if on the outside of the pack. | Use a strong crossover stroke if on the inside of the pack. Use a slight crossover stroke if on the outside of the pack. | Normal | Slight possibility of catching an errant foot or elbow. |
| Turns in heavy traffic | Use a scissors kick or go underwater to gain an advantage. | Increase stroke tempo and/or go underwater to gain an advantage. | Either lift up head or dive underwater. | High probability of physical contact in the pack. |

# FIVE FUNDAMENTAL RACE SEGMENTS

Open water races have the following five fundamental segments, each of which sets you up for the subsequent one:

- Warm-up
- Start
- Middle segment
- Final positioning
- Finish

## WARM-UP

The warm-up is your best intelligence-gathering opportunity and the final opportunity for you to add to your tactical knowledge. Besides confirming the water temperature and currents, check the gradient of the bottom at the start and finish. Ask questions and obtain insights from the race officials who set the directional and turn buoys. Talk to people who have done the swim before, hydrate well, and apply lubrication on your chafing points and potential points of contact with other swimmers (e.g., ankles and outer shoulders). Formulate your race strategy and visualize how you are going to execute it.

## START

The warm-up sets the tone for the start. Based on your pre-race intelligence, position yourself either on the combative frontlines with the most aggressive swimmers, tactically at the sides to take advantage of any lateral currents, or toward the back of the pack for a comfortable, stress-free start.

As the countdown begins, expect your competitors to inch forward. The race officials will attempt to keep the field in line, but it is not always possible. Because the starting lines at many open water events are not perfectly straight (e.g., a shoreline, a rope in the water, or a line in the sand), a handful of swimmers always try to gain an advantage. When a few athletes move forward, the entire field correspondingly moves forward. If your competitors inch forward, do the same. If your competitors take off before the start, go with them.

Officials often start the race a few seconds early if they see the field moving forward too much, moving too fast, or ignoring their requests to move back. It is safer to start the race early than to attempt to call a false start, which rarely happens.

## THE GREATEST RACE TACTIC

In 1963, $15,000 was offered for first place in a 60-mile (97K) race in Lake Michigan. The greatest professional marathon swimmers of that generation showed up, including Abdel-Latif Abou-Heif of Egypt and Americans Greta Andersen and Ted Erikson. Intense tactics began almost immediately after the sound of the starting gun.

Three hours and 15 minutes into the race with Abou-Heif and Andersen sharing the lead, Andersen found herself between Abou-Heif and his escort boat. Abou-Heif took a 90-degree turn straight toward his boat, cutting right in front of Andersen and interrupting her stroke. Two minutes later, Andersen did the same, tit for tat, right back at Abou-Heif . . . with still more than 53 miles left in 66 °F (18.9 °C) water.

As the swim continued through the afternoon and into the evening, Andersen and Abou-Heif tried to surge and lose the other. Back and forth, their battles continued as they pulled far ahead of the rest of their competition. Thirteen hours and 50 minutes after the see-saw battle, Abou-Heif finally broke free and surged into the lead as night began to fall.

Meanwhile, Erikson and his crew hatched an audacious plan to make up Abou-Heif's 1-mile (1.6K) lead. Sensing an opportunity around 10 p.m., Erikson's escort boat turned off all its lights. Erikson decided to swim in total darkness hoping to catch Abou-Heif unawares.

For seven hours through the pitch-black summer night, Erikson swam dangerously close to his escort boat, quietly and steadily gaining on Abou-Heif, who was lulled into believing he remained far ahead of his competition. Stroke by stroke with the focused aid of his crew, Erikson swam like a man possessed.

With morning approaching, but still under the cloak of darkness, Erikson dramatically closed the gap to less than two city blocks when a rope accidently became entangled in his escort boat propeller. Disappointingly, valuable time was lost. At 4 a.m., race officials unexpectedly came across Erikson and informed his crew that they had to turn their lights on for safety reasons. The gig was up. Abou-Heif was suddenly alerted of Erikson's proximity and infuriated with his brilliant tactic.

Incensed and motivated, Abou-Heif gradually pulled away to win in 34 hours and 38 minutes, but Erikson's valiant and unheard-of efforts through the night on Lake Michigan showed the extent to which tactics have been used at the highest echelons of open water racing.

## Middle Segment

Your actions at the start set the tone for the middle segment. If you get off to a good start and are well positioned, the middle segment will most likely go well. With a good start behind you, your confidence will soar. Conversely, if you get off to a poor start, you may feel pressured to recover. In the worst-case scenario, you may have to exert significant energy to make up time or distance, but because the middle segment is the longest part of the race, you have ample opportunity to recover from any mistakes. Be patient and take small steps to recover.

Your success in the middle 75 percent of the race depends largely on three factors:

- An ability to draft well and conserve energy
- Good navigational IQ
- Aerobic capacity

If you are fit and can stick with the competition, tuck in right behind them and conserve your energy for the latter parts of the race. If you are more aerobically fit than your competition, push the pace without expending all your energy. You can push the pace by taking the lead or putting in repeated surges and then backing off the pace.

Good navigational IQ is partly a result of the intelligence you picked up during the warm-up and your overall race experience. Where are your competitors? Where are the next turn buoys? Is the pace too slow, just right, or too fast? Should you change position within your pack?

In the middle segment, you can either conserve energy for the final positioning or push the pace. When you conserve energy and the pace is comfortable, you are following a strategic pace + fast finish plan, in which the final times tend to be slower than average. Conversely, if you and the rest of the field push the pace, you are following a fast pace + strategic finish plan, in which fast times are more likely.

### Strategic Pace + Fast Finish

If the pace starts off slowly and continues to be comfortable, swimmers will gain confidence in their ability to perform well as the race progresses. Instead of getting tired as the race continues, the field will get anxious to increase the pace while a competitor may throw in a number of short surges. In a slower-paced swim, your competitors will throw in an increasing number of short surges.

If you are in a good drafting position near the lead of your pack, maintain this position. If you find yourself in a suboptimal position, work to make incremental changes in your position during each loop or mile. Move up and attack through a series of sequential moves throughout the race. Make these changes in your relative position, either around the turn buoys or when your competition lets down its guard. The slow-paced race will end in a fast-paced finish. You want to be up toward the front when the final sprint comes.

### FAST PACE + STRATEGIC FINISH

Conversely, you may find yourself in a long test of endurance in which all the athletes are swimming close to their aerobic limit. This type of race may feel long because your heart continues to pump fast, often near its maximum, and lactic acid builds as you fight to hang with your competition.

As the fast-paced race nears the finish, everyone is too exhausted to significantly increase their pace. The high price of setting a fast pace from the start is usually a number of changes toward the end of the race. In this kind of race, continue to draft and wait patiently for the inevitable changes that will take place during the final positioning.

## FINAL POSITIONING

Final positioning occurs in the last 25 percent of the race. Tactical mistakes become fatal here. Conversely, excellent tactical choices can lead to victory. Final positioning begins before the final turn buoy. On many courses, gaining the inside or first position around the final turn buoy greatly increases the chances of victory.

Final positioning begins when a swimmer attempts to make a decisive break during the latter stages of the race and sustains this pace until the finish. Although the swimmer who makes the first commitment to pick up the pace may not win, he serves as the catalyst of the final positioning, in which the race-savvy and aerobically fit swimmers separate themselves from the field.

If you are drafting behind swimmers during the middle segment, move up along their hips or shoulders during the final positioning. If you are leading the competition and the pack is following you, position yourself to react to any radical maneuver that may occur. If you are swimming stroke for stroke and shoulder to shoulder with competitors, you may want to veer them subtly off the best tangent to the finish.

In the final positioning, it is advantageous to have only one competitor on one side of you. If you are boxed in between swimmers, your options become limited. Not only will you be jostled when you come into the finish, but also you will have less ability to make a tactical maneuver.

## PROTECTING YOURSELF
## AGAINST PHYSICAL CONTACT

Some competitors unnecessarily hit and grab the feet, ankles, calves, arms, and shoulders of their opponents. In most amateur races, there are either no referees or few referees along the course and, therefore, rule infractions are not seen and aggressive swimming goes unreported. Even when witnessed, unsportsmanlike conduct may be difficult to assign fault because it happened so quickly and so far away with unconfirmed intent.

In major races where there are certified referees on the water in boats, the rules are more frequently and uniformly applied, but you can still expend significant energy protecting yourself. Following are some ways to discourage the most aggressive and unscrupulous swimmers whether or not their actions are intentional or unintentional:

- Swim with a wider-than-normal underwater stroke.
- Swim with a wide-arm recovery and rap the back of your competitor's head with your knuckles.
- Give a series of large, fast kicks that create a lot of turbulence and splash.
- Come to an immediate drop-dead stop that causes an offending swimmer behind you to run right into your feet. Keep your toes pointed downward so your competitor swims into the soles of your feet.
- Purposefully entangle or bump into your competitor's arms on their recovery in order to interrupt their stroke.
- Swim extremely close to—or even directly into—the offending swimmer.

These types of defensive maneuvers are not intended to hurt anyone, but only to protect your space from an overly aggressive competitor. Punches, pull-backs, hard elbows to the face or body, zipline pulls of a competitor's ankles or legs, kicks with the heel, and scratching are definitely off-limits, uncalled for, illegal and not encouraged under any circumstances. However, because rough stuff occasionally happens in competitive open water races, it is best to be prepared.

Swimmers, purposefully or unintentionally, veer others off course and jostle for any advantage within the rules, and occasionally outside the rules. If it is in line with your competitive spirit, do not shy away from this physicality. On the other hand, if physical contact is not your preference and retaliation is not in your nature, then simply swim slightly away from aggressive competitors, give them space, and enjoy the sport for its other inherent challenges.

## FINISH

The finish is usually frantic as you and your competitors give it your all. Your lungs scream for air. Your heart feels like it will burst. Lactic acid fills your muscles, and your stomach is in knots. Unlike in pool swimming, in which you simply put your head down and go for it, success in the open water demands that you keep thinking and strategizing right to the very end.

If you are coming into the finish through a surf zone, look backward and try to catch a wave, even if it requires that you slow down slightly. If you catch a wave, keep kicking and ride it as far as possible. If you are just a stroke or two behind your competition, keep swimming hard and dolphin quickly toward the finish, knowing that most people have not prepared themselves in training to quickly transition from the horizontal to vertical position.

In major international races, the finish can be a banner or touch pad elevated above the surface of the water. Your official time is recorded at the moment you touch the banner or pad. Even if your head or body passes the plane of the finish line, you are not officially finished until you have hit the touch pad with your hands. Because the finish is elevated above the water's surface, you have to reach up and out to finish. Touch or slap the pad with the palm of your hand and keep it on the pad for a few moments, especially in a close race.

## WORKING WITH A TEAMMATE

Unlike in cycling, in which visibility is not a problem, working with a teammate in an open water swim is quite difficult. With many other competitors and limited visibility, it is often difficult to find your teammate in the open water, even if you start together. If you do find your teammate, working together in the open water will give you a distinct advantage over any single competitor of equal ability.

If you choose to work with a teammate, first clearly decide your goals by deciding the following:

- Are you swimming together to share in the experience?
- Are you swimming together to enable either of you to win overall or in your age group?
- Are you swimming together to help either of you finish or set a best time?

Then decide on your contingency plans by deciding the following:

- What happens if you get separated?
- What happens if one teammate gets tired?
- What happens if one teammate starts to head in the wrong direction?

After these questions are answered, decide whether and how you will draft off one another. Consider these questions:

- How long will each of you lead?
- Will you draft behind or to the side?
- Will you alternate every two minutes, every ten minutes, or some other time period?
- How will you indicate to each other when to switch positions?
- What happens toward the end of the race?

Here are some tips that will help you and your teammate stay together during a race:

- Start at the sides or rear of the pack, where it is easier to stay together.
- Wear swim caps of the same color and design.
- Put brightly colored zinc oxide on your arms so you can see or find each other easily if you get separated.
- Swim side by side at the start and until the first turn buoy as the field starts to string out along the course, so it will be easier to swim together.

## MAKING A BREAK

To be able to make a break at any point in a race, you need to practice shifting gears. Practice suddenly increasing your pace in the open water before race day. Practice turning it on during pool workouts and open water training sessions. Pick up your kick and increase your stroke tempo to increase your speed.

If you sprint into and out of a turn in the open water, you may be surprised at how much distance you can pick up on your competitors. Great turns in, around, and out of the turn buoys can be dramatic game-changers in the open water.

Open water races require that you make a series of tactical decisions in a dynamic environment where your vision is limited and competitive situations are in constant flux. As the race proceeds, you may not know whether the decisions you make are right or wrong; you can only learn their impact vis-à-vis your positioning relative to your competition on the course. As you learn more, you will find that you will make fewer mistakes and better decisions, but the perfect tactical race will still be something to aim for.

Great North Swim, Dave Tyrell

# 10

# Triathlon Training and Finishing Fast

You do not need a passport to cross it, but the shoreline is a distinct border marking the beginning of the world of open water, where rules and expectations are significantly different from those of the terrestrial world. If you cannot see the bottom, the open water course is essentially unfathomable, leading to an experience that can be either captivating or overwhelming—and sometimes both.

Humans have walked and ran for millennia. You probably have been riding bikes since childhood. But the first leg of the triathlon causes great concern for many; in swimming, technique is more important than endurance, and being efficient is more beneficial than having a high $\dot{V}O_2$max. You may be able to endure discomfort while on the bike and running, but the advantage definitely goes to Mother Nature in the open water.

## FEAR OF THE OPEN WATER

Fear of the known and unknown elements of the open water is undeniable and a challenge for many people. In a global online poll conducted by the Daily News of Open Water Swimming (January 1, 2010, www.dailynewsofopenwaterswimming.com) swimmers and triathletes were asked to indicate their greatest fears about open water swimming. Athletes could select multiple choices which were reflective of reality (e.g., many were afraid of both sharks and jellyfish). Here are the results:

- Sharks: 39% of the total votes cast
- Jellyfish and stingrays: 27%
- Pollution: 24%
- Things that cannot be seen: 21%
- Cold water: 18%
- Waves, currents, and tides: 17%
- Going off course: 12%
- Not finishing: 12%
- Marine life other than sharks, jellyfish, and stingrays: 11%
- Nothing: 9%
- Goggles coming off: 8%
- Other: 7%
- Physical contact by competitors: 7%
- Not seeing the bottom: 4%
- Seaweed or kelp: 4%
- Everything: 2%
- Vaseline or lanolin getting on goggles: 1%

Although we are not physically shaped to swim in the same way marine animals are, we are buoyant. Even though we are not marine creatures, we have hands and feet that can generate propulsion and can build sufficient endurance to swim long distances. Nevertheless, many of us are uncomfortable in the offshore world. Whereas some see a world of beauty, others see a world of risks.

You can get comfortable in the open water in your own way and within your own time frame. Here are some options that may help you suppress your initial fears:

- Go in, swim to where you cannot touch bottom, and return to shore. Repeat.
- Swim parallel to shore in shallow water.
- Swim with friends on either side of you.
- Swim with fins.
- Swim while being escorted by friends in kayaks.
- Swim in a calm lake before tackling the rough seas.

If you are very nervous, swim only a short distance on your first attempt. Swim where you can stand. On your next outing, swim to a point where you cannot stand or see the bottom. On your third try, swim parallel to the shore. On each successive workout, swim farther realizing that you may always be apprehensive.

# IT TAKES A VILLAGE

Triathletes in the open water are rarely alone. Viewed from shore or from a boat, triathletes in the open water resemble a line of industrious ants or dancers in a conga line. They instinctively adjust their direction to match the course of the swimmer in front of them. At the start, triathletes run and dive in the open water, intent on reaching their potential. But immediately past the shoreline, they latch onto the competitors around them with an unseen, yet undeniable force of magnetic energy.

In addition to the large size of the field, this communal mind-set and collective energy is what helps make triathletes coalesce into large packs in the open water. All triathletes in the field do their individual best to keep up, and in line, with the ones in front of them. If the field veers left, they veer left. If the field goes right, they go right. The power of the single triathlete is multiplied, providing protection and inspiration to those who are less confident in their abilities. But there are outliers in this wetsuit-clad community—the alpha swimmers.

# ALPHA SWIMMERS

Alpha swimmers have total confidence in the open water. Their experience is palpable as they demonstrate mastery of open water techniques and skills. They understand the effects of the currents, waves, and wind and make split-second decisions like seasoned sailors. They know when and where to start dolphining in and out of the water. They have no problem settling on a good pace or heading off on their own navigational lines.

Like alligators, alpha swimmers cruise along the course, elegantly lifting their heads to sight and swimming confidently from start to the swim-bike transition. Like sharks, they analyze the situation and then attack the swim leg rather than cautiously moving forward. Once in the water, they are confident in themselves and their decisions.

## LEARNING FROM ALPHA SWIMMERS

If you are new to triathlons, find these alpha swimmers. Befriend them. Learn from them. Alpha swimmers are not just the fastest. They are focused, seriously minded athletes of various ages and speeds. They are visibly loose and relaxed at the start, the polar opposite of the newcomers and those less experienced in

Confidence, fitness, experience, and speed enable smooth transitions and onshore finishes.

the open water who exhibit a nervous energy. They calmly set out their equipment and methodically prepare their gear. They smoothly apply skin lubricants and sunscreen; their hands do not shake. They may not win, but they exude a quiet professionalism and stoic poise.

Alpha swimmers are focused, not distracted. They do not walk around aimlessly before race time, swiveling their heads with every distraction like a wind vane on a blustery day. Whether at a world-class or casual pace during the race, they are on a mission to get from point A to point B without alarm. Some are fast, some are slow, but they always exhibit pure confidence in their chosen path.

## Becoming an Alpha Swimmer

Unlike swimmers who focus on only one sport, triathletes spread their training time over three sports, with biking and running deservedly the priority. This priority of the land-based disciplines means that every hour spent swimming needs to serve a specific purpose. For this reason, strategically incorporating the Pyramid of Open Water Success into your overall triathlon training program is crucial (see chapter 6).

Although everyone comes into the sport of triathlon with different levels of experience, the following are the six steps to becoming an alpha swimmer:

1. Take basic swim lessons.
2. Join a competitive swimming program, usually a U.S. Masters Swimming program.
3. Find an open water swimming group.
4. Become comfortable in the open water.
5. Compete in an open water race.
6. Compete in a triathlon.

## BASIC SWIM LESSONS

Learn the fundamentals of stroke mechanics under the direction of an experienced swim coach. Watch videos, attend clinics, go to camps, and read books. Swimming in a controlled, balanced manner demands patience and time. Swimming well and confidently often requires years of practice. Achieving the proper body rotation, good hand acceleration, a straight pulling pathway, proper breathing technique, and an efficient sighting technique requires time and repeated effort. Every triathlete needs different periods of time to master these basic skills.

## COMPETITIVE SWIMMING PROGRAMS

Start practicing with an organized swimming program. The best-in-class for athletes over the age of 18 in the United States are registered U.S. Masters Swimming (USMS) programs that place an emphasis on triathletes and other multi-sport athletes and are headed by coaches with experience and interest in the open water (www.usms.org). The benefits of training under such programs will be immediate and ongoing.

USMS is a national organization that offers pool and open water competitions, clinics, and workshops for adults 18 years of age and older. The 692 USMS swim teams across the United States, with over 54,950 active members, welcome swimmers from every walk of life. The swim clubs offer structured workouts both in the pool and in open water, coaching excellence, and the camaraderie of like-minded adults, including triathletes and competitive, noncompetitive, and fitness swimmers. As you progress and improve, a good coach will continue to push you to faster intervals and raise your expectations. Outside the United States, similar masters swimming programs are organized and provide instruction and structure for improvement in the open water.

## OPEN WATER SWIMMING GROUPS

Triathlon clubs and masters swim teams often organize formal and informal open water swimming groups. Join one of these groups and head down to the shore with your teammates. If you are nervous, offer to escort other swimmers in a kayak for the first few times. You will reap great benefit in first escorting for

Join like-minded athletes to enjoy the open water and train together.

your teammates, then joining them in the water on your next workout. If you are not as fast as your new teammates, use fins. Fins will help you keep up with the faster swimmers, some of whom are alpha swimmers. Later, when you are more comfortable in the open water, swim without your fins. Use your wetsuit if you want, but as the water gets warmer and you gain more confidence, try doing an occasional open water practice without your wetsuit.

## BECOMING COMFORTABLE IN THE OPEN WATER

One way to increase your comfort level with open water swimming is to invite the alpha swimmers on your swim or triathlon team for coffee or lunch. Ask questions to learn about their training, their early experiences and their choice of equipment. Ask them for details on their past swims. Find out how they prepare for their competitions and how they conserve their legs on the swim—and how they kick just enough to remain streamlined and balanced to minimize their resistance in the open water.

Consider going to an open water swimming clinic or reaching out to one of the many experienced open water swimming coaches who offer their services online (www.openwatersource.com). If jumping straight into the open water swimming community is a bit too intimidating for you, reach out to experienced open water or triathlon coaches found online or attend one of the many triathlon clinics where you can feel comfortable with other newcomers. SlowTwitch (www.slowtwitch.com), Open Water Source (www.openwatersource.com), Team in Training (www.teamintraining.org) and Beginner Triathlete (www.beginner-triathlete.com) are a few websites that have a plethora of information on these introductory clinics and camps in which knowledgeable coaches can take you step by step through the process of becoming comfortable in the open water.

## COMPETING IN AN OPEN WATER RACE

Before you compete in your first triathlon, consider entering an open water race. With over 900 events throughout the United States and over 3,600 races worldwide, it is relatively easy to find a race somewhere near your home. At these open water competitions, go with a friend, preferably someone who is at your level or an alpha swimmer who will enjoy swimming alongside of you.

With a partner, you can focus on your swimming and more easily get over your nervous energy. Go early, observe, and absorb everything at the race. Try to get comfortable in the festive race day atmosphere. Lay out your gear, apply your sunscreen and skin lubrication, put on your wetsuit, and survey the race course. Be patient and enjoy the experience. Talk with people before and after the event. Learn as much as you can from your first experience before you tackle your first triathlon, which will require much more preparation.

## COMPETING IN A TRIATHLON

Before competing in a triathlon, set goals for yourself. Write them down and talk about them with your coach and teammates. Your goals should address the following three elements:

- *The outcome:* Finish, meet a certain goal time, beat a friend, or place in your age group.
- *Your performance:* Achieve fast transition times or maintain a certain stroke tempo or pace.
- *The process:* Keep your elbows high and a streamlined two-beat kick.

Set goals that are measurable, realistic, and challenging. Then, after the race, review your outcome, performance, and process. But on race day, enjoy the moment and relish the competition and excitement of the race.

# FUNDAMENTAL TIPS FOR THE SWIM LEG

At your first triathlon, you will experience sensory overload. Try to stay calm and remember all the little details that make up a successful swim leg, bike leg, run leg, and transitions. Remember the following before, during, and after the swim:

- *Lube up:* Liberally apply sunscreen early in the morning. Then reapply sunscreen and skin lubrication to all possible chafing points before the start, but not before getting numbered (black ink and petroleum jelly do mix).
- *Easy Wetsuit Removal:* Apply skin lubricant to your ankles and wrists so your wetsuit comes off more easily at the end.

- *Can't hear much*: Use silicone earplugs if the water is cold. These will also help you ignore the extraneous noise of the event and the crowd before the start.
- *Twosome*: Bring an extra pair of everything, but especially broken-in goggles. Number all of your equipment.
- *Feed off the crowd*: You may be nervous, but keep in mind that many, if not most, of the athletes around you feel the way you do. Enjoy the community, camaraderie, and challenge.
- *Start wisely*: If you are not fast or uber-competitive, start toward the sides or rear of the pack. If you are fast, leave nothing on the course.
- *Catch them on the bike*: If you want to finish the swim leg within the time limit, but with as much energy as possible, let the fast swimmers go. Follow the sprinting mob at the start and see where the leaders head.
- *Tackle the turns*: Be prepared for some bumping around the turn buoys. Swing wide and keep your head up if you prefer to face less commotion and thrashing from large, tightly bunched packs.
- *Follow the leader*: Follow other swimmers unless you know they are off-course or something they do not. If you get disoriented, stop, look up, and check out the situation.
- *Follow in their wake*: Swim behind or just off the hips of your competitors to take advantage of their draft. If you stick with others, you can conserve energy by not lifting up your head so much. Let others guide you around the course.
- *Wetsuit comfort*: Choose the right wetsuit for the water conditions. If your wetsuit is too thick, you may start overheating during the swim leg. If you anticipate swimming for over 45 minutes, stick a gel pack in your wetsuit and consume it during the swim leg.
- *Acclimatize*: Rarely is an open body of water as smooth as a pool. Get used to open water conditions before race day. Train at a beach or a lake on a windy day. If you feel seasick in rough conditions, lift up your head and look off in the distance to fixed objects onshore. Close your mouth and try not to swallow any water.
- *Murphy's Law rules*: Things will not always go according to plan. Anticipate problems and know how to address them in the middle of the swim leg. If you feel nervous, raise your hands and wave to the safety personnel. You do not have to quit; talk to them and try to get reassured before getting out.
- *Swell advantage*: If you feel the surge of waves around you, kick harder and lengthen your stroke to take advantage of the momentum of the waves. If you cannot bodysurf, then proceed cautiously through the surf or call over a lifeguard for help.

## PICKING THE RIGHT STROKE RATE

For your swim leg, your stroke rate (measured in strokes per minute) can be under 60 spm or whatever is most comfortable to you. You can swim comfortably with a wetsuit and a relatively slow heart rate. Save your legs for the bike and run and let your legs slowly move up and down at the same rate as your arms (one kick beat for every arm stroke). If you are more competitive, increase your stroke rate to over 70 strokes per minute, knowing your heart rate will correspondingly increase. Your kick, however, can remain a steady two-beat kick (2BK).

Before you start spinning your wheels with a rapid stroke rate, take it slowly and build a solid foundation. Aerobic conditioning is not as important as is your focus on and mastery of your stroke mechanics. As you gain more experience, increase your stroke rate in practice to learn how to sustain a faster pace. The ability to swim at various speeds is essential in the open water, just as it is when biking and running. Your ability to accelerate is helpful when you want to escape from being boxed in or respond to a move by competitors. Practice these variable speeds and stroke rates in a pool so they become second nature in a race.

## PREPARING FOR A GOOD SWIM-BIKE TRANSITION

The transition from the swim leg to the bike leg, called T1, involves much preparation. It involves preparing your equipment, memorizing the T1 transition area, and being able to move smoothly from the time your hand touches the ocean floor or lake bottom to the time you are cycling on the bike course.

Set out your equipment in a logical manner in the T1 transition. Experiment with the layout and combination of equipment to find what is best for you. Practice laying out your gear and removing your wetsuit and swim gear before changing into your bike gear; practice being patient. Over time, you will increase your transition speed, perhaps using some of the following tricks of the trade:

- Use a checklist the night before to make sure you do not forget anything.
- Spray skin lubricants around your joints before the race so you can easily and quickly remove your wetsuit in the T1 transition.
- Forget the physical contact that may have occurred during the swim leg. That leg is over once you are on land.
- Have water to wash off the sand, dirt, or pebbles from your feet, preferably in a pan.
- Leave your goggles in an area where they will not be run over or forgotten. Bring your protective case.
- Have a towel to dry off and for general use.

- Keep your gear in a well-organized, compact area so you are not reaching for anything.
- Do not push or block others in the transition area.
- Use a mat or a towel to avoid standing on hot pavement, gravel, or dirt after the swim.
- Buckle your bike helmet before getting on your bike.

## SWIMMING AT THE PROPER PACE

Most triathletes swim at a controlled, steady pace on their swim leg to minimize energy expenditure and generate as little lactic acid buildup as possible. Competitive triathletes, or those whose strength is in the water, may expend much more energy to gain an advantage during their swim leg. Your own personal goals will dictate your pace on the first leg.

Competitive triathletes have higher stroke rates, which are more readily seen in dedicated swimmers who understand that swimming faster in the open water requires increasing their stroke tempo. With a faster stroke turnover, you generate greater propulsion per minute. The greater propulsion allows you to overcome any corresponding increase in the amount of resistive forces. The negative forces of oncoming currents and surface chop will exist in relatively the same amount whether your arm turnover is slow or fast. But you can slightly reduce your arm stroke tempo and maintain a longer stroke length if you are effectively drafting within the wake of the swimmers ahead of you.

## FINISHING THE SWIM LEG

A good way to finish the swim leg of your triathlon is to generate confidence by overtaking some of your competitors. When you pass other athletes on your swim leg, you will feel a rush of adrenaline. Build on and utilize these positive feelings when you are on your bike leg. Stroke by stroke, as you pass others at the end of the swim, your confidence will build. As you swim pass others, you will feel as though your training and sacrifice has come together for a defined purpose.

Psychologically, most athletes have a stronger feeling of control being the chaser than they do when being chased. This is especially true in the open water where your field of vision is limited. Conversely, if you are passed by others, you may experience the opposite feelings, unless you have purposefully slowed down.

If you are being passed, you may think your technique is slipping or you may notice a muscle ache or the beats of your heart a little more. Negative thoughts may begin to impair your ability to stay focused and calm. Make critical decisions to draft off the swimmers overtaking you, pick up your pace, or maintain your steady pace and start transitioning mentally to your bike leg. Think about your pace and your strategy for the bike leg.

### JOHN FLANAGAN'S TRANSITION TO TRIATHLONS

John Flanagan, father of two and full-time swim coach from Honolulu, took up triathlons later in life. Like many in the sport, he believes he is hitting his stride as an athlete in his fourth decade of life.

After a stellar pool swimming career, in which he was a high school swimming champion in Hawaii and part of Auburn's 1997 NCAA championship team, 35-year-old Flanagan is stronger and faster than ever, constantly finding new ways to improve his strength and speed.

But his road to triathlons was not direct. Flanagan initially transitioned from competing in pools in the Southeastern Conference to oceans around the world. He represented the United States for four years in international open water competitions, peaking in a fourth-place finish at the 2001 World 10K Championships. After a five-year retirement, he attempted to make the 2008 Olympic team, only to fall frustratingly short. But the experience fired up his competitive juices when he found he could balance the demands of work, family, and a new sport.

In his first two Ironman World Championships, Flanagan posted two of history's top ten times on the 2.4-mile (3.9K) swim leg (47:02 in 2008 and 47:42 in 2009), but it is his time management skills and competitive zeal that he most closely shares with the multitudes of adult triathletes who share the starting line with him.

The alpha swimmers' advantage comes from their attitude. This same mindset is possible for you. Swimming speed is irrelevant. Even if you are not a fast swimmer, you can still be an alpha swimmer, competing at your own pace and in your own zone.

# POST-RACE ANALYSIS

After you finish your first triathlon, conduct a post-race analysis of your performance. Recall who you were standing with onshore, who you swam with, and your pace. Draw the shape of the pack you swam with on a piece of paper and your estimated navigational line in the swim leg. Analyze your pacing and positioning during the race. A detailed, honest post-race analysis will help you become a more seasoned performer in the water.

The following are questions to consider in your post-race analysis. Write down the answers in your training log or discuss them with your coach or teammates.

**Questions to Answer**

1. Did you use the proper amount of skin lubricants?
2. Did you chafe anywhere?

3. Did you miss or need any equipment?

4. Who was your competition?

5. How did they do?

6. How did you feel during your swim?

7. Did you achieve your goal on the swim and in the triathlon?

8. Where were you at the start?

9. Did you specifically choose that position, or did you pick a position by default?

10. What was the pace at the start?

11. How did you feel before you reached the first turn buoy?

12. Did you feel comfortable during the swim?

13. Would a faster pace have helped or harmed your bike leg or your overall time?

14. Where were you in the middle of the race?

15. Did you purposefully swim this course, or did you follow a pack?

16. Were you boxed in at any point?

17. Who was swimming in front of you, behind you, and to your left and right?

18. What was your approximate stroke tempo?

19. Did you speed up before or after the turn buoys?

20. Did you have the inside position around the turn buoys?

21. Did you run into anyone?

22. Did you know where you were going at all times?

23. Was it hard to see anything?

24. Did you take a good line to the finish?

25. Did you encounter any ocean swells or surface chop during the race?

26. How often were you lifting your head to sight? Was it hard to see the buoys or finish?

27. Did you see the lead boat or kayak?

28. Did you dolphin at the start and finish? Were you out of breath if you did?

# TRIATHLON'S GLOBAL SUCCESS: A BLUEPRINT FOR SUCCESS

The sport of triathlon, which was born in the 1980s, matured in the 1990s, and has blossomed after its introduction at the 2000 Sydney Olympics, has reached its tipping point. With millions of triathletes around the world and an increasing amount of media exposure and corporate sponsorship, the triathlon

## FACT

The Waikiki Roughwater Swim is a 2.4-mile (3.9K) race along the length of Waikiki Beach on Oahu. The race was started in 1970 by Jim Cotton, founder of the Waikiki Swim Club. The event grew in numbers and competitiveness over the decades, attracting some of the world's best pool and open water swimmers, including many Olympic medalists, to the annual Labor Day swim.

In 1977, members of the Waikiki Swim Club, members of the Mid-Pacific Road Runners Club, and U.S. Navy Commander John Collins agreed to settle their discussion on who was most fit (a swimmer, a runner, or a cyclist) by organizing and competing in a one-day race, now known as the Ironman Triathlon, which consisted of the Waikiki Roughwater Swim, the Around Oahu Bike Race, and the Honolulu Marathon.

The Ironman Triathlon was held on Oahu for the first three years of its history and was later moved to the Big Island of Hawaii as the swim distance of the Waikiki Roughwater Swim (2.4 miles) remains the standard full Ironman distance.

has achieved an enviable coolness factor and has blazed a trail of success for open water swimming.

## TRIATHLON'S EARLY YEARS

In the early years of the respective histories of the triathlon disciplines (ocean swimming, biking, and marathon running), only small numbers of hard-core enthusiasts practiced each sport. Quietly enjoying their sports in isolation, outside the scope of established governing bodies and the attention of the sporting media, these individuals enjoyed their chosen paths. Growing pockets of triathletes emerged in San Diego and Hawaii, while die-hard open water swimmers regularly gathered along shorelines from San Francisco to Boston.

## TRIATHLON'S CATALYST TO GROWTH

Awareness of triathlons exploded with Julie Moss's dramatic finish at the 1982 Hawaii Ironman. Her effort, captured on U.S. television, caught the public's attention. Almost overnight, multisport endurance racing ignited the imagination of many athletes and non-athletes while the media perked up in attention.

A similarly seminal event in open water swimming was the Olympic 10K Marathon Swim at the 2008 Beijing Olympics, which was broadcast live to much of the world (although its impact in the United States was significantly less than its impact in Europe). In Beijing, Maarten van der Weijden, a leukemia survivor from the Netherlands, dramatically won the men's gold medal, and South African Natalie du Toit, who had lost her left leg in an accident and had to relearn to swim, valiantly swam shoulder to shoulder with the world's best open water swimmers, only to fall short of medaling after two hours of hard swimming. With the Olympic 10K Marathon Swim and triathlon being showcased in Hyde Park in central London at the 2012 Olympics, the two sports will undoubtedly benefit from the worldwide exposure.

## STEADY EMERGENCE OF TRIATHLONS

The initial waves of triathlon pioneers of the 20th century were joined by an increasing number of enthusiasts. Some never considered themselves athletes before, but they were anxious to try something new, fun, and inspirational. With new media forms emerging, the ability to swim, cycle, and run for hours was widely discussed, celebrated, and reported online.

The underground buzz, enabled by an increasingly connected world via the Internet and mobile devices, led to communities that continued to fuel new levels of virtual and real-world interactions. Triathletes are effective at creating a distinct culture, a robust community, and a unique lifestyle. Newcomers from all walks of life began to wear their sacrifices for training and competition like badges of honor. Men with shaved legs walking in restaurants with bike cleats and tan marks from their goggle straps is only one example of the triathlon lifestyle. How far and hard people could swim or run became topics of discussion and generated a healthy respect among peers at work, at school, and in the greater community. To date, open water swimmers remain the more sedate cousins of triathletes in the endurance sport world. Open water swimming remains more decentralized and less organized with far fewer global standards for distance, rules and protocols than triathlons.

## THE TIPPING POINT

Athletes, race directors, sponsors, and administrators of both triathlon and open water swimming continue to meander through and experiment with rules, regulations, and equipment as they try to find a happy medium among the various opinions and new voices in their sports. Some ideas are well received; some require modification; others fall flat. Collectively and cumulatively, the sports emerge stronger and richer with each new initiative. Like triathlons, open water swimming is expanding with new forms of competition, additional regulations and innovative uses of technology.

Commercialism in triathlon has provided a tremendous helping hand. Triathlons have long outgrown the days when races were simply a labor of love of a few volunteers to a sport where corporate sponsorship, media exposure, equipment manufacturers, and professional athletes collectively push the sport to new heights. While open water swimming is still formulating its larger game plan in each country, triathlon's entrepreneurs have stepped up when the established brands slept. With the support of these entrepreneurial companies, the media and race organizers feed the public's demand for information and mass participatory events. On the backs of millions of enthusiasts, triathlon has clearly earned its place in the sporting lexicon and on the Olympic stage, while open water swimming is playing catch up in its own unique ways.

The commercial market and national publications gravitate toward experts and anoint gurus who are able to explain and define triathlons to the public clamoring for more information. Innovative race organizers and athletes take leadership roles in the sport, both in the public eye and in administrative roles. Magazines and websites continuously reinforce the image of top athletes, while average athletes and newcomers talk about the training and equipment of newly minted triathlon heroes and heroines.

Professional event managers have turned triathlons into emotionally and financially rewarding weekend spectacles. Open water swims are not quite at the same level, but the sport is on a similar fast-paced trajectory which triathlons began in the 1980s. Online and print media feed the public's demand for insightful opinions and entertaining perspectives as well as information on new events, insights, products, and heroes of every age and ability.

## FUTURE ISSUES AND OPPORTUNITIES

As both triathlon and open water swimming grow exponentially around the world in every type of venue and waterway, the road will not always be smooth. Issues will arise along the way, from drafting and drug testing to new regulations and ensuring the safety of athletes. But with the intense interest of so many passionate and talented people, the future remains extraordinarily bright. If the past is any indication of the future, race directors, athletes, and administrators will creatively and communally resolve the issues . . . nearly always for the better.

The time is now. Enjoy.

# RESOURCES

## INFORMATION SOURCES FOR THE OCEAN'S SEVEN

- 21-mile (33.8K) English Channel between England and France www.channelswimmingassociation.com (Channel Swimming Association) www.channelswimming.net (Channel Swimming & Piloting Federation)
- 21-mile (33.8K) Catalina Channel between Catalina Island and California www.swimcatalina.org (Catalina Channel Swimming Federation)
- 26-mile (41.8K) Molokai (Kaiwi) Channel between Oahu and Molokai Islands in Hawaii www.hawaiiswim.org/hawaiianChannel/kaiwiChannel.html
- 21-mile (33.8K) North (Irish) Channel between Ireland and Scotland www.bangorboat.com/page6.html
- 16-mile (25.7K) Cook Strait between the North and South Islands of New Zealand www.cookstraitswim.org.nz
- 12-mile (19.3K) Tsugaru Channel between Honshu and Hokkaido in Japan www.tsugaruchannelswimming.com
- 10-mile (16K) Strait of Gibraltar between Spain and Morocco www.acneg.com

## INTERESTING OPEN WATER SWIMMING WEBSITES

- America's Top 50 Open Water Swims: A list of 50 outstanding open water swims www.americastop50openwaterswims.com
- Cape Swim: Open water swimming in South Africa www.capeswim.com
- Daily News of Open Water Swimming: Daily news of open water swimming www.dailynewsofopenwaterswimming.com
- English Channel Swimmers: Information on English Channel swimming www.thechannelswimmers.com
- FINA: Information on the FINA World Cup and FINA Grand Prix professional circuits www.fina.org
- Great Swim: The largest swim series in the United Kingdom www.greatswim.org
- King of the Sea Challenge: Professional and amateur open water swimming races www.reidomarbrasil.com.br
- Traversée international du lac St-Jean: A bilingual French-English website of the famous Lac St-Jean pro swim www.traversee.qc.ca
- La Jolla Cove Swim Club: Open water swimming in La Jolla, California www.lajollacoveswimclub.org
- Lewis Gordon Pugh: British open water swimming pioneer and environmentalist www.lewispugh.com
- Maarten van der Weijden: Olympic 10K Marathon Swim gold medalist and leukemia survivor www.maartenvanderweijden.com
- Marcos Diaz: Dominican Republican open water swimming pioneer and ambassador www.marcosdiaz.net

- Midmar Mile: The world's largest open water swimming event www.midmarmile.co.za
- Natalie Du Toit: Incredible South African Olympian and Paralympian www.nataliedutoit.com
- New Zealand Ocean Swim Series: The largest open water swim series in New Zealand www.oceanswim.co.nz
- NYC Swim: Open water swimming in New York City www.nycswim.org
- Ocean Swims: Open water swimming in Australia www.oceanswims.com
- Open Water Source: A comprehensive source of open water swimming information www.openwatersource.com
- Open Water Swimming in Europe: Open water swimming in Europe www.openwaterswimming.eu
- Outdoor Swimming Society: Open water swimming in Great Britain www.outdoorswimmingsociety.co.uk
- Pacific Swims: Open water swimming in the South Pacific www.pacificswims.com
- RCP Tiburon Mile: The world's most competitive professional short-distance race www.rcptiburonmile.com
- Santa Barbara Channel Swimming Association: Open water swimming in Santa Barbara, California www.santabarbarachannelswim.org
- Swim Across America: Open water charity swims across America www.swimacrossamerica.org
- Swim Trek: Open water swimming holiday adventures www.swimtrek.com
- Triple Crown of Open Water Swimming: A list of members of the Triple Crown of Open Water Swimming club www.triplecrownofopenwaterswimming.com
- Water World Swim: Open water swimming in San Francisco Bay www.waterworldswim.com
- Wild Swimming: Open water swimming in Great Britain www.wildswimming.co.uk
- World's Top 100 Open Water Swims: A list of 100 outstanding open water swims www.worldstop100openwaterswims.com

# 25 Top Open Water Swims Around the World

**1.** Sun Moon Lake International Swimming Carnival

- Location: Sun Moon Lake (Jih Yueh Tan in Taiwanese), a beautiful tranquil lake at 2,493 feet (760 m) in central Taiwan.
- Course: 3K (1.9 mi) mass participation lake crossing with over 25,000 participants.
- Description: The world's largest mass participation open water swim with different start groups for people of all ages and abilities. Swimmers are required to swim with a red flotation buoy for safety purposes.

**2.** Midmar Mile

- Location: Midmar Damin Kwazulu Natal in South Africa, a one-hour drive from Durban.
- Course: 1-mile (1.6K) straight point-to-point swim across a flat-water dam.
- Description: The world's largest competitive open water swim that has attracted nearly 19,000 swimmers is the culmination a series of qualification swims through-out South Africa.

**3.** Vansbrosimningen

- Location: Vansbro in central Sweden.
- Course: 1K, 1.5K, and 3K (0.6, 0.9, and 1.9 mi) downstream river swim under the six bridges of Vansbro.
- Description: Founded in 1950, nearly 10,000 swimmers participate in Europe's largest multirace open water swimming event in which wetsuits are commonly used. Event includes a separate 1K race for women.

**4.** Great North Swim

- Location: Picturesque Lake Windermere, the largest lake in England.
- Course: 1-mile (1.6K) course in a flat, scenic, cold lake in the rural Lake District.
- Description: A very competitive race with a separate start for elite swimmers; it is the largest mass participation open water swim in Great Britain, and wetsuits are widely used.

**5.** Bosphorus International Swim

- Location: Istanbul Strait, which connects the Black Sea with the Sea of Marmara in Turkey.
- Course: 7.1K (4.4 mi) from Meis on the Asian continent to Kas on the European continent in the world's narrowest strait used for international navigation.
- Description: The race has grown to nearly 5,000 swimmers from dozens of countries.

**6.** Lorne Pier to Pub

- Location: Seaside community of Lorne, Australia, southwest of Melbourne.
- Course: Fast 1.2K (0.7 mi) pier-to-beach swim.
- Description: The first 4,300 swimmers with an average time of 22 minutes compete in one of the most popular charity swimming events in Australia.

7. Rottnest Channel Swim
   - Location: From Cottesloe Beach, near Perth, to Rottnest Island in Western Australia.
   - Course: A challenging and extremely popular 19.2K (12 mi) ocean swim with over 750 boats providing support.
   - Description: A solo and relay swim to an offshore island, where a maximum limit of 2,300 randomly selected swimmers face strong currents and abundant marine life. Solo swimmers receive an automatic entry.

8. King and Queen of the Sea Challenge (Rei do Mar Desafio in Portuguese)
   - Location: Copacabana Beach, Rio de Janeiro, Brazil.
   - Course: 2K (amateur) and 10K (professional) ocean course.
   - Description: Beach start and finish for over 2,000 swimmers in the 2K race and the invitational professional field in the 10K televised race. Pros run 150 meters on the soft sand after each 2K loop.

9. Navia's Downstream Swim (Descenso a Nado de la Ria de Navia in Spanish)
   - Location: Navia River in Asturias in northern Spain
   - Course: Downstream 1.1K, 1.7K, 3K, and 5K (0.7, 1, 1.9, and 3.1 mi) swim along a picturesque river.
   - Description: Formerly started in 1958, the multirace event offers multiple cultural events, a parade, and cash prizes. Also serves as an official leg of the LEN Open Water Swimming Cup, which attracts the top swimmers throughout Europe.

10. Acapulco 5K International Swim
    - Location: Acapulco Bay along the west coast of Mexico.
    - Course: 1K, 1.5K, and 5K (0.6, 0.9, and 3.1 mi) ocean swim in warm water across the flat bay of Acapulco.
    - Description: The race starts as the sun rises over the bay; swimmers race along the shore lined with resort hotels.

11. Bermuda Round the Sound Swim
    - Location: Harrington Sound in Bermuda, 650 miles (1,046K) east of North Carolina.
    - Course: Warm water 0.8K, 2K, 4K, 7.5K, and 10K (0.5, 1.2, 4.7, 6.2 mi) ocean swims within Palmetto Bay.
    - Description: Swimmers swim over pristine coral reefs amid beautiful marine life in crystal-clear warm waters along astoundingly beautiful coastline.

12. Round Christiansborg Swim
    - Location: Copenhagen, Denmark.
    - Course: 10K (6.2 mi) swim in Fredericksholm's Canal around the island that houses the palace of the Danish Parliament.
    - Description: A popular swim for amateurs to swim through the canals of Copenhagen.

13. Jarak-Šabac Swim Marathon
    - Location: Šabac, Serbia.
    - Course: A downstream 2K, 4.5K, and 18.7K (1.2, 2.8, and 11.6 mi) river along the Sava River.

• Description: Amateurs and professional swimmers compete in this multirace event with a 40-year history; children's races of 50 meters.

14. La Traversée internationale du lac Memphrémagog
   • Location: Lac Memphrémagog, Quebec, Canada.
   • Course: 0.5K, 1K, 2K, 5K, 10K, and 34K (0.3, 0.6, 1.2, 3.1, 6.2, and 21 mi) races in a large lake between Vermont, USA, and Quebec, Canada.
   • Description: The 34K race attracts many professional swimmers in an out-and-back course in a scenic, rustic lake where thousands of people come to support both the amateurs and the pros.

15. Clean Half Marathon Swimming Open Water Relay
   • Location: Hong Kong Bay, Hong Kong.
   • Course: 14.5K (9 mi) ocean course around the beautiful waters of Hong Kong's south side.
   • Description: Solo and five-person relay race in blue, clean waters in the back half of Hong Kong Island. Swells can get large with heavy surface chop depending on the wind. Relay swimmers can compete in the carbon-neutral division, in which swimmers use an outrigger canoe instead of a traditional motorized escort boat.

16. Fiji Swims
   • Location: Treasure Island and Beachcomber Island, Fiji.
   • Course: 1K, 2.7K, and 18K (0.6, 1.7, and 11 mi) races held in a tropical island paradise with crystal-clear waters, beautiful coral reefs, and abundant marine life.
   • Description: The 1K race is from a floating pontoon in the ocean to Beachcomber Island. The 2.7K swim starts on a sandbar. The 18K race can be done as a relay or solo swim. Numerous Olympic medalists participate annually.

17. Galata-Varna Swimming Marathon
   • Location: Varna on the west coast of the Black Sea in Bulgaria.
   • Course: 4.4K and 10K (2.7 and 6.2 mi) loop course with the start and finish at Varna's main beach.
   • Description: A warm water course with the start and finish having occasional large swells and heavy surface chop; the race has been held for nearly 70 years.

18. New Zealand Ocean Swim Series
   • Location: Throughout New Zealand, from Wellington to North Shore City.
   • Course: The six-part 0.7K and 2.8K (0.4 and 1.7 mi) series are held along stunning beaches and in major waterways.
   • Description: Includes the Harbour Crossing in Auckland, Capital Classic in Oriental Bay, Corsair Classic in Christchurch, Russell to Paihia in the Bay of Islands, Sand to Surf in Mt Maunganui, and the King of the Bays in North Shore City.

19. Flowers Sea Swim
   • Location: In the pristine waters of Seven-Mile Beach in the Cayman Islands.
   • Course: 1-mile (1.6K) point-to-point, in-the-water finish in shallow and incredibly clear waters.
   • Description: Described as the world's flattest and fastest ocean mile race with over $100,000 in randomly distributed prizes.

20. Sandycove Island Challenge Race
    - Location: Sandycove Island in Kinsale, Ireland.
    - Course: 2K (1.2 mi) counterclockwise circumnavigation in the clean water around Sandycove Island.
    - Description: Currents can present problems for slower swimmers; the race takes place in one of the prime training locations for open water swimmers and triathletes in Ireland with visible sunken reefs and kelp.

21. Lange Afstandzwemwedstrijd Sluis
    - Location: Canal Hoeke in the Netherlands.
    - Course: Out-and-back 2K, 2.5K, and 5K (1.2, 1.6, and 3.1 mi) in an old shipping canal with the turnaround point in Brugge in Belgium.
    - Description: The turning point is in Belgium. The 2.5K is a breaststroke-only swim.

22. Traversata dello Stretto
    - Location: Strait of Messina in Sicily, Italy.
    - Course: 1.8K to 5.2K (1.1 and 3.2 mi) courses between the eastern tip of Sicily and the Italian mainland.
    - Description: The Strait of Messina has strong currents and natural whirlpools that make for a challenging and enjoyable event to do and watch, especially on a clear day.

23. Gozo-Malta Open Water Channel Race
    - Location: From Ras il-Qala to Marfa in Malta.
    - Course: 5.5K and 11K (3.4 and 6.8 mi) race in the Mediterranean Sea, off the coast of Sicily in Italy.
    - Description: Swimmers swim between Malta's main islands.

24. The Bay Challenge
    - Location: Sandy Cove to Kitsilano Beach in Vancouver, Canada.
    - Course: 0.75K, 1.5K, 3K, and 6K (0.46, 0.9, 1.9, and 3.7 mi) solo and relay swims.
    - Description: Wetsuits are mandatory, and neoprene swim caps are strongly recommended for the cold water swim in 50 to 66 °F (10 to 19 °C) waters.

25. Balaton Átúszás
    - Location: Lake Balaton (known as the Hungarian Sea) in Hungary.
    - Course: 5.2K (3.2 mi) lake swim in calm water.
    - Description: Upwards of 10,000 swimmers participate in the largest lake in central Europe; Lake Balaton is the site of open water swims nearly every weekend during the summer.

# GLOSSARY

This glossary includes some common terms used in the open water swimming world. The entire Open Water Swimming Dictionary is posted at Open Water Source (www.openwatersource.com).

**acclimate**—To become accustomed to warmer or colder water temperatures, wind chop and waves, and various other conditions before an open water race or solo swim.

**beach finish**—A finish that is on land, requiring the swimmers to exit from the water and run up a beach to a finish line.

**bilateral breathing**—Breathing on both the right and left sides during freestyle swimming.

**boxed in**—Being caught between swimmers in the front and back or on the left and right sides to the extent that one is unable to swim in the desired direction, to swim at the desired pace, or to make a move within the pack. Synonyms: *sandwiched, squeezed.*

**breakaway**—To speed up or alter one's direction to separate from the rest of the field. Synonyms: *sprint ahead, swim faster, put on a spurt, pick up the pace, drop the hammer, increase the tempo, drop the field, make a move.*

**brood**—A group of jellyfish. Synonyms: *smack, smuth, smuck, fluther,* and (improperly) *school.*

**buoy**—A distinctively shaped or marked float, sometimes identified with signage or logos, anchored to mark a race course, channel, anchorage, or swimming hazard.

**carbon-neutral relay**—An open water relay that has a net zero carbon footprint. Carbon-neutral relays rely entirely on human power and thus do not use motorized escort boats; rather, they use outrigger canoes, kayaks, or canoes.

**chafing**—Irritation caused by repeated rubbing of the skin against swimsuits or other items (including other body parts) due to the swimming stroke and waves. Chafing is common around swimsuit straps; in armpits; and on the shoulders, upper thighs, neck, and chin.

**channel grease**—A combination of petroleum jelly and lanolin used by channel swimmers.

**channel swim**—A nonstop solo or relay swim that crosses a natural or man-made body of water, generally understood as an ocean strait, between two land bases or two larger navigable bodies of water, although it can also refer to a traverse across a river, slough, bay or between islands in an archipelago.

**charity swim**—A swim, relay, stage swim, or race with the goal of raising money for or media attention and awareness of a cause, individual, or nonprofit organization, especially among individuals and nontraditional donors.

**chop**—Wave action at the surface of the water caused by wind. Small, frequent waves can be irritating to open water swimmers because they can impede forward movement and reduce visibility. Synonym: surface chop.

**criterium race**—An open water race that requires swimmers to exit the water along the race course to run a short distance onshore before diving back into the water to finish. The onshore run, which can occur once or multiple times, can be anywhere along the course, which can be a loop course or a point-to-point course.

**crossover athlete**—An athlete who competes in both pool swimming and open water swimming events, or an athlete who competes in both open water swimming and triathlons or other endurance sports. Also, an athlete who competed in pool swimming, triathlons, or other endurance sports and now focuses exclusively on open water swimming, or vice versa.

**crossover move**—A move by one swimmer over the ankles, knees, upper legs, or lower back of another swimmer during a race in order to change direction or move to the other side of the swimmer. The move can be performed by swimming over the opponent using the normal freestyle stroke or by rolling over on one's back and doing a stroke or two of backstroke over the legs of the opponent. However, if the swimmer impedes the forward momentum of another swimmer while making the crossover move, a yellow card (warning) or red card (disqualification) may be called by the referee.

**dark swimming**—Swimming at night in natural or man-made bodies of open water.

**DQ**—Disqualified. To be ruled ineligible as a result of a violation of rules.

**draft**—To swim close behind, or slightly to the side of (usually somewhere between the hips and ankles) another swimmer (or swimmers) to take advantage of their slipstream, especially in a race.

**ebb tide**—The receding, or outgoing (seaward), flow of water that results in a lowering of the water level near the shore. The reverse flow is called a flood tide, in which an inflow of water results in rising water levels near shore.

**eco-swim**—An open water swim, relay, stage swim, race, or charity swim that (1) aims to protect, conserve, or call attention to the environment or ecology; (2) aims to improve or protect the welfare of marine life or the local area; (3) is conducted in an ecologically sustainable or environmentally friendly manner; (4) is held in areas that are under environmental protection or that protect marine life; (5) raises money or provides direct financial benefits for conservation, marine life or environmental protection, research, and education; (6) lobbies local governments or officials for access to, protection of, or a clean-up of a waterway; or (7) minimizes the human impact on the environment.

**expedition swimming**—Swimming in natural or man-made bodies of open water including oceans, lakes, rivers, bays, and reservoirs, together with teammates or swim buddies, usually as part of a guided tour with or without escorts.

**feeding**—Eating or drinking during a race, relay, or solo swim.

**feeding station**—A boat or other temporary or fixed floating structure, such as a dock, pier, or pontoon, used by coaches to provide fuel (i.e., food) or hydration (i.e., drink) to swimmers in a race.

**feeding stick**—A long, slender mechanical implement with a cup or bottle holder at the end that coaches use to hand fuel (e.g., gel packs, food, chocolate) or hydration (e.g., water, Gatorade, tea) to their swimmers during races or solo swims.

**finish cameras**—Video cameras set up in fixed locations onshore or on docks, piers, or other locations to record the finishes for official review after a race.

**finish chute**—A series of lane lines, buoys, or other such markings that indicate the finish area and help direct the swimmers to the final finish line or touch pads.

**fish**—The colloquial term occasionally used by marathon swimmers and their support crew for the type of fish with a cartilaginous skeleton and a highly streamlined body with a tough, usually dull gray skin, commonly known as a shark. Synonyms: *shark, the man in the gray suit, mack, old toothy, garbage can of the sea, the landlord.* (Some scholars believe that the word *shark* is derived from the German word schurke, meaning "villain.")

**flood tide**—The inflow of water (from the sea) that results in rising water levels near shore. The reverse flow is called the ebb tide, in which a receding, or outgoing (seaward), flow of water results in a lowering of the water level near the shore.

**freestyle relay**—An open water swimming relay in which each swimmer can swim any distance or for any amount of time he or she wishes. Unlike the traditional English Channel relays in which each swimmer swims for one hour, staying in the same rotation, swimmers have freedom in deciding their own distances and times in freestyle relays.

**grease up**—To apply a lubricant, ointment, spray, or petroleum-based jelly at the friction points on the body to prevent chafing and irritation (e.g., arms, chin, neck, inner thighs, under swimsuit straps).

**guide buoy**—A distinctively marked or colored float in the water along the race course, anchored to provide navigational guidance for swimmers. Guide buoys may be passed on either side.

**Half Century Club**—A club for people who have completed any marathon swim (e.g., English Channel, Catalina Channel, Strait of Gibraltar, Cook Strait, Manhattan Island Marathon Swim, Rottnest Channel) after their 50th birthdays.

**impede**—To obstruct, interfere, or retard movement or progress by cutting off; swimming into; blocking; or pulling on the legs, ankles, arms, or shoulders of other swimmers during a race. Impeding may result in a warning, yellow card, or red card disqualification.

**intermediate buoys**—Buoys placed between required turn buoys or markers that may be passed on either side without penalty.

**knot**—A unit of speed equal to 1 nautical mile or about 1.15 statute miles per hour or 1.852 km per hour.

**lanolin**—A greasy, fatty substance, insoluble in water, that is extracted from wool-bearing animals and used to coat the skin of open water swimmers, especially at friction points (e.g., under the arms, inside the thighs, on the chin and neck) to prevent chafing or reduce the impact of cold water.

**lap**—One complete round, length, or circuit around a race course.

**left- (or right-) shoulder turn**—The required turn direction when swimming around a turn buoy. A left-shoulder turn means that the swimmer must keep the turn buoys on the left side while swimming counterclockwise around the turn buoys.

**loop**—One complete round, length, or circuit around a race course, especially one that is circular.

**mass participation swim**—A non-timed, non-competitive swimming event in which communal enjoyment of an open water swim and post-event entertainment and fraternization with like-minded athletes are the goals.

**naked division**—A race category for those who swim without wetsuits.

**navigational IQ**—The ability to swim the straightest and fastest path in the open water, especially in a race.

**neap tide**—A tide that occurs twice a month, in the first and third quarters of the moon, when the difference between high and low tide is lowest.

**Ocean's Seven**—Marathon swimming's equivalent of mountaineering's Seven Summits. The seven swims, which have yet to be all conquered by the same individual, include the

North (Irish) Channel between Scotland and Ireland, the Cook Strait in New Zealand, the Molokai Channel in Hawaii, the English Channel, the Catalina Channel in California, the Tsugaru Channel in Japan, and the Strait of Gibraltar between Spain and Morocco.

**OTL (over time limit)**—The official designation when an athlete does not finish the race within the specified time given by the race organizer. The specified time can be a predetermined time or certain number of hours or minutes after the start or the maximum amount of time allowed for swimmers to remain in the water after the first swimmer finishes the race.

**positioning**—A place relative to that of other competitors, often strategic and intentional, but occasionally unintentional or accidental, in which swimmers find themselves during an open water race.

**red card**—A red penalty card that indicates the immediate disqualification of a swimmer because of poor sportsmanlike conduct or a serious infraction of the rules during an open water race.

**riptide**—A strong flow of water away from the shoreline, typically near a pier or jetty or through the surf.

**sandbar**—A long mass or low ridge of submerged or partially exposed sand built up in the water along a shore, river, or beach, or between or near islands, that is caused the action of waves, tides, or currents.

**seeded start**—When swimmers are divided by specific abilities or times at the start (as opposed to age- or gender-based starts or mass starts).

**sheltered-side breathing**—Breathing away from the waves or elements in open water swimming.

**shoot the gap**—To swim in a narrow gap between two competitors, especially in a pack during a race.

**sighting**—The act of seeing or navigating in the open water, generally toward landmarks, turn buoys, escort boats, or the finish. Lifting the head to look ahead, to the side, or behind to decide the optimal direction in which to swim in an open water race or swim.

**single crossing**—A solo or relay swim in one direction across a channel, lake, river, or other body of water under the traditional rules of marathon swimming. Synonym: *one-way crossing.*

**surface chop**— See *chop.*

**surge**—A sudden increase in speed to break away from competitors.

**three-wide**—Three swimmers swimming side by side during a race. Synonyms: *three abreast, three side-by-side.* The term can be used for any number of swimmers (e.g., *four-wide, five-wide*).

**transponder**—Light, waterproof timing devices with either RFID or GPS capabilities that swimmers wear on their wrists or ankles at major competitions.

**triple crown of open water swimming**—Authenticated completion of three famous marathon swims: the 21-mile (33.8K) English Channel between England and France, the 21-mile (33.8K) Catalina Channel in California, and the 28.5-mile (46K) Manhattan Island Marathon Swim in New York.

**turn buoy**—A distinctively marked or colored float in the water, anchored to mark the course for swimmers. Turn buoys are directional in nature and must be passed on a specific side of the body as race instructions dictate.

**World Swimming Majors**—A database of 30 major marathon swims around the world.

**yellow card**—A yellow penalty card that indicates an official warning to a swimmer as a result of poor sportsmanlike conduct or an infraction of the rules during an open water race.

# REFERENCES

Cypess, Aaron M., M.D., Ph.D., and others. "Identification and Importance of Brown Adipose Tissue in Adult Humans." *New England Journal of Medicine* 360 (2009): 1509-1517. Accessed April 9, 2009, http://www.nejm.org/doi/full/10.1056/NEJMoa0810780.

Johnson, Tim. *The History of Open-Water Marathon Swimming.* Buzzards Bay: Perfect Paperback. 2005.

*Channel Swimming Association Handbook.* 2009. Accessed April 9, 2009, http://www.channelswimmingassociation.com/handbook_2009_63.html.

Critchlow, Julian. *Channel Swim Database.* Accessed 2010, http://home.btconnect.com/critchlow/ChannelSwimDatabase.htm.

Virtanen, Kirsi A., M.D., Ph.D., and others. "Functional Brown Adipose Tissue in Healthy Adults." *New England Journal of Medicine* 360 (2009): 1518-1525. Accessed April 9, 2009, http://www.nejm.org/doi/full/10.1056/NEJMoa0808949.

Popov, Alexandr. http://www.swimpsychology.com/motivational_quotes.php3 (n.p., n.d.).

Munatones, Steven. "Fears of Open Water Swimming." *Daily News of Open Water Swimming.* Accessed January 1, 2010, www.dailynewsofopenwaterswimming.com

Van Marken-Lichtenbelt, Wouter D., Ph.D., and others. "Cold-Activated Brown Adipose Tissue in Healthy Men" *New England Journal of Medicine* 360 (2009): 1500-1508. Accessed April 9, 2009, http://www.nejm.org/doi/full/10.1056/NEJMoa0808718

# INDEX

# ABOUT THE AUTHOR

**Steven Munatones** is a former professional marathon swimmer and a renowned coach. He has served as the national team coach at the 2001, 2003, 2005, and 2007 World Swimming Championships and the 2004 World Open Water Swimming Championships. In addition, he serves as editor in chief of the *Daily News of Open Water Swimming* and created the Open Water Swimming Dictionary.

Munatones manages the International Marathon Swimming Hall of Fame Web site and served as the NBC commentator for the men's and women's 10K marathon swim during the 2008 Beijing Olympics. During the Games he provided his expertise on the sport to a variety of media, including NBC-TV, Universal Sports, *Wall Street Journal*, National Public Radio, *USA Today*, *New York Times*, *National Geographic* magazine, and the Associated Press. His writing has appeared in *Swimming World*, *Australia Swimming,* and *USMS Swimmer.* He annually publishes the World's Top 100 Open Water Swims and America's Top 50 Open Water Swims. He also created the most popular Web sites on open-water swimming, including www. openwatersource.com and www.10Kswim.com.

He is also on the FINA Technical Open Water Swimming Committee that serves as the world's governing body of the sport and provides information and guidance to the Amateur Swimming Union of the Americas, USA Swimming, and U.S. Masters Swimming.

Munatones lives in Huntington Beach, California, with his wife and four children.